CISTERCIAN STUDIES SERIES:
NUMBER TWO HUNDRED THREE

A Hand on My Shoulder
Volume Two
Monk and Bishop

John Willem Gran OCSO

Cistercian Publications
Kalamazoo, Michigan

Originally published as
Terskelen: Av en katolsk biskops erindringer, Bind II, Oslo: Aschehoug, 1995
Det annet Vatikankonsil: Oppbrudd og fornyelse, Oslo: St. Olav Forlag, 2001

Cataloguing in Publication information
is available from the Library of Congress.
ISBN 0 87907 341 1 (vol. 1)
ISBN 0 87907 342 X (vol. 2)
ISBN 0 87907 353 5 (set)

The work of Cistercian Publications
is made possible in part by support from Western Michigan University
to The Institute of Cistercian Studies.

Printed in the United States of America

CISTERCIAN STUDIES SERIES:
NUMBER TWO HUNDRED THREE

A Hand on My Shoulder
Volume Two
Monk and Bishop

TABLE OF CONTENTS

Thirteen

A WORLD APART

To you then my words are now addressed,
who are renouncing your own desires and,
on entering the service of Christ the Lord
our true King, are taking up the strong
and glorious arms of obedience.

The Rule of Saint Benedict[1]

T EXACTLY TWO O'CLOCK at night a monk passes quickly through our two dormitories ringing a handbell.

A few minutes later, joining the monastery brethren, I make my way to the church, where we take our places in the choir. On the stroke of a quarter past two the prior taps a small gavel as a signal, and the night office, the first in the twenty-four-hour round of the canonical hours, is begun. Before us on the sloped desks on either side of the church lie huge illuminated books, each weighing about twenty-five pounds, with large characters readable at a distance of well over a yard. Here too, we are to have everything in common.

Soon the Gregorian alternating recitation has begun. The three nocturns, which together may last about an hour, are followed by half an hour in meditation or silent prayer. We remain at our places, kneeling or standing in the dark. When the half-hour is up, the church bell rings for Lauds, the daybreak office of the seven liturgical hours.[2]

After fully two morning hours in church we proceed in single file, with the prior leading, through the cloister to the scriptorium, or the monks' day room which, since the great fire in 1942, also functions as chapter room. From a lectern in the centre, the monastery's cantor recites several texts: first, a chapter from the Rule of Saint Benedict,[3] and then the day's martyrology from a thick book with accounts of martyrs and other saints commemorated by the Church. Finally he reads death-notices received from other monasteries in the Order (both monks and nuns) with requests for intercession. All in Latin. After this, the prior comments on the day's text from the Rule—now in English, and if necessary also in French (the mother tongue of our older monks)—and turns to various practical matters concerning our daily existence. He rounds off with some news from the Order, from the Church—and perhaps from the world at large. The chapter is brought to a close with the recitation in unison of the *De Profundis* in Latin, after which half an hour is spent on spiritual reading or study at one's desk, here or in the novitiate.

Some choose to work, especially those who find themselves short of time for their allotted work-tasks.

The bell rings again calling the monks to Prime, the next fixed hour of liturgical prayer. Afterwards we go in single file to the refectory, where the first meal of the day is consumed in silence. The spartan breakfast—a good four hours after we have risen—consists of bread and butter together with coffee or tea with milk and sugar. Certainly welcome, but not luxurious, since the blessed Father Benedict insists that the monk must show 'restraint in all things'.

Time permitting, yet another hour is dedicated to spiritual rumination or intellectual pursuits. In any event this is a pleasant time of the day, because the meal—in particular the coffee—has an invigorating effect. Nevertheless, quite a few monks usually have to go straight to their work.

When the time comes, the great bell summons everyone to the solemn Mass of the day, which all except the lay brethren are obliged to attend. The Mass, always sung, is the day's liturgical highpoint and concludes with all present receiving Holy Communion.

Our real working day starts when we hang our habits in the changing-room and put on working clothes.[4] At this point the cellarer in charge of all practical affairs assigns duties to everyone who has not already been given some task. We in the novitiate, without special areas of responsibility, are directed to work such as cleaning, shovelling muck, haymaking, weeding—or whatever else needs to be done. Those of us who are to work outdoors set off in single file in order of seniority, for in monasteries age is irrelevant. Seniority is counted from the day of receiving the habit, although choir monks, who are mostly priests, normally rank before lay brethren. We carry any necessary tools, faithful to Benedict's words: 'The monks shall live by the labour of their hands'.

At the end of the first work-stint the great bell rings as a signal that there is half an hour until the next office. I hurry back to the monastery so as to be ready, after washing and changing, to take my place in the choir for Sext. The Angelus prayer follows, at precisely one o'clock. Then, in a simple procession, we move into the refectory for the main meal of the day.

After the meal we have time for some chosen spiritual or intellectual study in the day room—those of us, that is, who do not need this time for our allotted work-tasks.

At a quarter to three the community assembles in church for None, the last of the day's 'lesser hours', after which the afternoon period of work begins.

Again the great bell calls us in, half an hour before the evening office of Vespers, which should ideally take place at dusk. We remain in church for a quarter of an hour in silent prayer. This is possibly the best moment of the day. Our labours are over and we can enjoy a sense of physical and spiritual peace.

The evening meal, usually the midday meal warmed up, follows. Shortly afterwards the sound of the last bell calls us to the chapter room where we have ten minutes or so of reading aloud in English, most often church history or perhaps a travel journal or an extract from a biography. By now the gathering is light-hearted, so that any unfortunate phrase open to misinterpretation in the text causes a hum of amusement. It even happens that a book has to be exchanged for another after being drowned in laughter.

Compline—the relatively short evening service—rounds off the day in a dark church, always with the people of Caldey reverently in the background. We conclude with a resounding rendering of the moving medieval hymn *Salve Regina* before leaving the chapel in a simple procession. At the door we bow before the prior, who blesses each of us for the night with holy water.

The period reckoned as night is spent in dormitories with no more than a thin plywood partition between the beds and a curtain to screen off the central area. These cubicles are all alike, without deference to rank. In here I have my bed with its straw mattress and chaff-filled pillow. There are two hooks, with almost nothing ever hanging on them except, by turns, the ordinary habit of undyed wool, the black scapular, or my working overalls with their anorak-type hood.

We sleep fully clad, though without footwear. Benedict is both precise and considerate: 'The monks shall sleep fully clad, with a strap or cord around the waist, so as to avoid having their knives [which they habitually wore] with them in bed, with the risk of cutting themselves when asleep.'

Our set bedtime is announced by the ringing of a bell at 7 PM. After that there must be absolute silence—which does not mean that we are obliged to go to bed. Nevertheless, anyone moving about in the dormitory after that time has to carry his shoes with him.

Benedict ordains: 'The monks must always be ready to rise at once when the signal is given. They must quietly encourage one another, because of the excuses of the sleepy.'

This regulated round-the-clock rhythm, with its divisions marked by signals, from small handbells to the great bell's heavy clanging, is very demanding in contrast to everything in my life up to now. Here we have a clearly structured and precisely detailed society where normally the only people you meet or have any contact with are your brethren. You are contented with the thought that in ten years your life may be expected to be just the same as it is today. The course you are committed to concerns first and foremost your relationship to God. At the same time, your relations with your fellow men, both within and outside the community, have been extended and enriched as an integral benefit of this closeness to God.

The Cistercians are known as 'the silent monks', having only sign language for communication. 'The monks shall cultivate silence', says Benedict. 'Even healthy, pious and constructive talk should only occasionally be permitted to the disciple, since as a general rule he ought to maintain a reverential silence. For it is written: "When words are many, transgression is not lacking".'

But if it is quiet you are seeking, this is the hushed centre.

Saint Benedict's pivotal thought is that the monastery shall be a school for lovingkindness. Here I have the chance to observe it in practice, for there is much unobtrusive saintliness to be found at Caldey, especially in the elderly who have followed this precept through most of a long life. Gradually it becomes clear to me that not least *faithfulness* to the vocation is a decisive criterion.

Equally clear is the fact that the Cistercians live a family life. Our venerated prior, the Belgian Dom Albert Derzelle, puts it like this: 'We are always together—twenty-four hours a day. We undertake to live as simply as possible. Simplicity, in fact, could well be said to be the "trademark" of the Cistercians.'

But this family life was not the only one. As in most monasteries, there were also the so-called 'familiars', laymen who had found life difficult in the outside world, but discovered security and peace as members of the monastic family. One such was Mr Parker, the community cobbler, once an infantry captain, but now beset with nervous problems. His English could, without any corrections, have gone on the air in the BBC World Service. Tim, the island's self-appointed comedian, was a simple, helpful, good-hearted and industrious handyman on the farm. Then there was a shabby old man with a fag-end always at the corner of his mouth who had been a Methodist preacher and now helped in the garden. He eventually died on Caldey at a ripe age without ever becoming a Catholic. And there were more such familiars who found a refuge at Caldey over the years; these are just a typical few.

The contemplative life, as I learned to know it, also revealed a marked eschatological, eternity-conscious dimension. To turn your back on the world with its superficial time-is-money mentality and enter into a timelessness of this nature involves you in a way of life almost totally lacking the popular conception of a world in a constant state of evolution with man forever improving on the past. Instead, you become slowly inured to a notion of time not unlike that held by people in earlier epochs: a continuously repeated cycle, not only in harmony with the four seasons, but also with the Christian year and its successive reminders of Christ's birth, growing up, work, suffering, death, resurrection, and return to the Father. All the way to Pentecost with the coming of the Holy Spirit.

But I learned too that there was a price to be paid for all this. The lack of relaxing company, of holidays to look forward to, of newspapers, television, and radio—all these taken singly posed no great problem, but together they resulted in some unexpected reactions because of my untrained physique, ingrained media-habits, and independent lifestyle. I became tense, and after a time as thin as a rake. This was partly my own fault, because in my eagerness to fit into the community I never helped myself to a portion larger than what I could see was considered normal.

Contact with the mainland was maintained by our rather battered boat, which carried supplies as well as passengers.

As his assistant on board, Brother Thomas had young Jerry Cummins 'junior', born on Caldey to the last family having legal rights of domicile there.[5]

The slip was primitive and exposed, and the waves often washed right over it. A small wooden swing-crane with a hand winch was the only means of loading and unloading. Goods usually had to be taken to and from the slip in small carts. All very primitive, but everyone was used to it. Of course, we also had to be able to transport larger objects, for example livestock, in crates. When this happened a tractor was hitched to the hay waggon, with its side-rails removed. The place beside the jetty was too cramped for turning, however, so the tractor-driver (usually Jerry 'senior', young Jerry's uncle) had no option but to reverse, with the freight-crate behind him, along the final hundred yards or so of the winding gravel track to the jetty—both a feat in itself and a test of patience (which I had ample opportunity to try out later).

The tide governed all sea transport. At low tide the boats lay on the sand, constructed as they were for this part of the world with minimum keel. Ebb and flow followed no convenient rules, but were predictable and precisely listed in the meteorological tables for high and low water for each day of the year. Every season had its spring tides which made a difference in height of at least twenty-five feet. This had its uses for certain purposes, but was not without danger in bad weather, when it could mean several days with no transport. Those responsible for a 'department' in the monastery therefore always had to have strategic reserves in hand.

The large, composite farm was the backbone of the whole complex. The buildings were timeless. No one knew when they had been constructed, probably as part of the monks' 'new' layout in the thirteenth century. The former monastery church, dating from the same century, was a landmark, with its curious steeple leaning against the winds from the Atlantic. This steeple, which is intact, *may* have developed its deviation (one metre from the perpendicular) in the course of the centuries—but, if so, long ago, because no increase in the deviation had been recorded within living memory. Low Masses were regularly celebrated there.

The farm activities traditional in the region were managed by the community's former prior, the Belgian Father Jerome, an omnipresent bundle of energy. In his opinion, the surest income was still obtainable from grain crops. But the keeping of livestock was important, too, on account of milk production and the churning of butter. When I arrived on the scene, there were also sheep, but these were replaced by pigs, which unexpectedly proved to be more profitable. Even monks have to keep a wary eye on the vagaries of the market.

Inevitably, the mechanization of our agriculture was under way. Caldey's last horse had long since passed into history. Father Jerome had arranged for the grain harvesting that year to be done by a combine harvester—in the eyes of the local population a monster of a machine—which was a nightmare to bring across from the mainland. Henceforth the corn would be cut and threshed in the field in one and the same operation. At the same time, we acquired a machine on wheels which, hitched behind a tractor, gathered, pressed, and bundled the straw, which could then without further ado be driven directly into storage.

As a consequence of its dependence on the state of the tide, the monastery had become an almost totally self-supporting household. Practically everything we ate came from the farm or the kitchen garden. One monk baked bread for the entire population of the island. Another was the electrician and was in charge of our fuel-driven powerhouse with its rows of interconnected accumulators. All repairs of machinery, tractors, generators, and so on were dealt with by the fifteen or so brethren and their handful of lay helpers. Some monks were cooks, others looked after the garden and sold any products not needed by the community. One father was the house tailor.

Benedict prescribes that the brethren shall work for the common good, and he states that anyone who has a skill from before entering may practise his craft in the monastery, provided the abbot approves. But a brother shall immediately be removed from his work if he begins to think too highly of himself for it.

As far as I was concerned, there was something deeply satisfying about an existence that provided for its own needs in this way.

The arrival of the coalboat was an annual event that intensely affected our life. Coal was very strictly rationed and the authorities considered it simplest to work out the year's ration as a whole for all of Caldey's households together, including the monastery. This amounted to a total of around 105 tons, which always seemed to come with the same old wooden tub whose engine could be heard miles away. Every year careful calculations had to be made as to when the summer spring tide would be at about its highest at dawn, to allow the boat to come in as far as possible over Priory Bay to the long sandbank east of the slip. It would then be left there high and dry after the tide went out. In the interval the crew had to prop up the hull with large wooden struts brought for the purpose.

All the able-bodied men on the island had to work together to empty the boat before the tide came in. It was an annual race against time. Everyone wore the oldest possible clothes, since you were coal-black from the start. The strongest, with a cloth tied over nose and mouth, acted as coal-heavers in the hold. The coal was hoisted up in huge, bulging baskets and emptied into the trailers behind our alternating tractors, which at all costs had to manage to keep on the temporary iron underlay leading up to the road. From there the route continued to the coal store.

So that the unloading could be effected without any pauses, Father Jerome and Brother Thomas had lists showing who would do what and be relieved by whom, as well as when everyone should eat (meaning a picnic on the spot) and in what order. As a rule it was a cheerful sort of day with everybody smiling and joking despite the general grime. Meanwhile, in the monastery church the older monks took care of the liturgy as well as they could, for—as Benedict cautioned—nothing must ever be put before the Work of God, that is to say, the Divine Office.

Most often we were lucky with the weather, but if by chance it rained, the situation was indescribable, for part of the cargo consisted of coarse coaldust, all of which had to be brought ashore. At the end of such a day's work no amount of effort could make you really clean, and it could take weeks to be completely rid of the dust, which had a way of getting into every crevice. The monastery laundry worked overtime, and there, too, everything was in a mess. But, apart from newcomers, everyone knew that on coalboat days it could hardly be otherwise.

The monastery administration was responsible for rationing out the coal to each household. This was no easy task, since all felt entitled to more than they got, and some even complained to the ('otherwise so kind!') prior, usually in vain. It often fell to me to drive round delivering the sacks with the year's rations, and I had to pretend not to notice people's disgruntled expressions. To be fair, I should add that Great Britain was still suffering from postwar scarcity of almost everything, including supplies known to have been long since obtainable on the continent—even in Germany. And the winter on Caldey was often hard. On top of everything else, the houses could not be heated by electricity, for that too was rationed on the island, while wood, apart from driftwood, was nonexistent.

In the novitiate there were five of us of about the same age under the leadership of Father Shanahan, a monk in his mid-thirties on loan from the great southern Irish abbey of Ros-crea. Most of our time was spent in a high-ceilinged room on the first floor above the monks' day room. The windows here face some tall trees in the graveyard, affording beautiful, and sometimes dramatic, glimpses across the sound that separates Caldey from the mainland. The walls were lined with book-shelves, and at long tables arranged in two rows we had our set places facing the novice-master's desk under a crucifix. All the teaching took place here, whether by Father Shanahan, by the subprior, Father Basil, who lectured on monastic history, or by the prior himself, whose speciality was the writings of the Cistercian Fathers.

It was easy to see that our novice-master—whose experience was limited to his Irish monastic existence (after attending the same monastery's own school)—had some difficulty in tackling our increasingly heterogeneous and multinational group, most of whom had wide and varied backgrounds. But to give the father his due, he grew in response to the challenges and developed an increasingly broadminded attitude.

To begin with there were just the five of us up there. Three were English, all very different. Brother Bernard was young, rather rough and ready. Brother Stephen was on the quiet side, always punctual and so self-effacing that it was difficult to make him out at all (nonetheless he became my lifelong friend). Brother Samson was academic, cultivated, full of dignified reserve, self-disciplined. Finally there was the Pole, Brother Thaddeus: a monument of piety and innocence, somewhat naïve perhaps, but not at all slow-witted—a soul wholly devoted to God, who had clearly found the right place for himself in Caldey. For the most part, mature men with long military service in the last war behind them: Brother Stephen had been tail-gunner in a bomber, Brother Samson ground crew in the Royal Air Force, Brother Thaddeus a soldier in General Anders's army, and I myself an intelligence officer. Not a gathering of romantics, but rather men with a realistic set of values, possessing common sense and, not least, a sense of humour. The exception, almost confirming the rule, was Brother Bernard, senior in regard to length of service, but the youngest in age, who one fine day disappeared. As a matter of fact, I had had some doubts about him and thought it right that he gave up.

Amazingly soon our numbers in the novitiate swelled to about a dozen. The additions ranged from a sixteen-year-old English schoolboy to a former police officer who had served in India, both of whom arrived shortly after me. The latter was a priest—a so-called late vocation—who at sixty naturally found it difficult to cope with the drastic change in his existence. He persevered, however, and spent the evening of his life as a monk.

The very young James held out for several months, left, then came back, but eventually vanished for good. After him came his uncle, Gerard, who had tried out Caldey before the war. This time he stayed long enough to become a priest, but left yet again, only to return after some years. Now he lies in safekeeping in the churchyard along with his brethren.

The next was a renowned war pilot, Anthony ffrench-Mullen, a man to whom I must devote a little space. As a flight lieutenant he had flown a bomber and was the only survivor when it was shot down. Interned in Germany in Stalag Luft I in Pomerania, he led a tunnel-digging project that was discovered just before the escape could be effected. After some weeks of tough punishment, he organized the digging of yet another tunnel, which was also discovered, resulting in yet more punishment. He realized that the barracks were bugged, and in fact located a microphone under the roof-ridge. After freeing the cable, he fixed it into the lighting system with the result that the monitoring centre was burnt out. The result: more weeks in a cell deprived of almost everything. He and his fellow officers were then moved to Stalag Luft III where they continued to plan and initiate new attempts to escape— mostly underground getaways. But no one managed to get anywhere—least of all, out. Following the liberation he was promoted, and after all this he decided to become a monk with the Cistercians on Caldey. However, to test his vocation, he first wanted to study to be a priest. He was ordained in Rome and immediately afterwards set off for Wales and Caldey—still with the same motivation.

One day an Irish doctor came to find out more about life at Caldey. He was a colonel in the Royal Army Medical Corps with many years of service, at the time stationed in Port Said. He returned when he reached the age of retirement, became a monk, as well as a doctor for the islanders, and remained on Caldey until his death.

Another type of newcomer arrived in the person of a converted Anglican Franciscan, introvert and unassuming. The next arrival was a young Benedictine monk from the great abbey of Downside in Somerset, where I myself had been at the beginning of my search: the monastery with the large boarding school. He was a likeable chap from Gibraltar with an obviously Spanish background, as was evident from his name: Leonard Gaggero. Like many people from 'The Rock' he spoke distinctly 'elocuted' English. He stayed at Caldey for a long time—but left in the end to marry an ex-nun. Like the stuff of novels.

Different from all the others was young Aelred, who on his mother's side was part Chinese and part Portuguese and on his father's Welsh with the typical name of Williams. He spoke not only several European languages, but also Mandarin, Cantonese, and other Chinese dialects, as well as Japanese learnt during the occupation of Hong Kong. He was dependable, had a happy oriental disposition, and remained faithfully at Caldey until his death.

We also had a number of trial visits from, for example, Dominicans, Franciscans, and even once a Jesuit. This was less successful. It is not unusual for members of other orders to try out life with the Cistercians, but the reverse seldom occurs. Within the ecclesiastical 'hierarchy of orders', if it may be so termed, there is a traditional ranking system based on strictness. To move from a less to a more ascetic order is viewed with favour—but not so, the contrary. By far the majority disappear again, but there are exceptions, and they are to be found in almost all our larger monasteries. Thus the abbot of the impressive Gethsemani abbey in Kentucky was formerly a Redemptorist Father.

Many newcomers and many birds of passage. In our order this is a normal state of affairs. On average one out of ten postulants stays the course through to the final solemn profession.

Something new, most probably due to my being there, was the Dano-Norwegian element. Two young fellow country-men of mine came to test their call. One became a novice, but left after a time—not surprisingly, for his nerves showed more than his powers of resistance. The other went home 'to think things over', but was never heard of again.

However, with time there were also quite a few visits by less 'committed' Norwegians. Some priests I knew came in search of a short spell of spiritual peace. An engineer friend, who had some business in Wales, came on an improvised visit together with a colleague who was not willing to believe what he saw, and absolutely not that a Norwegian could be part of the scene. My old singing teacher who shared so much of my life in Rome, Per Fasting, came and stayed a week. He had returned to Norway and to our hometown Bergen, where he married again and settled for good. I think he wanted to check that I was not the victim of a confidence trick. A Norwegian Dominican, then at Oxford, came on a week's retreat.

The Danish element was perhaps more promising. A young farm labourer whose dream was to be a lay brother arrived to spend a week or two as an observer, but was remarkably crit-ical of almost everything, and vanished from the scene. After that came a romantically inclined young photographer, Per Waagøe, who worked in Oslo where he had heard of Caldey. He visited us, left, then returned and remained for years. That it was not for good was due to circumstances beyond his con-trol, not his own choice. Later a young Danish Benedictine entered the scene. His monastery name was Rembert, and he held out for a long time. His real problem, however, was that he had one foot in the monastery and the other in home and marriage. In the end, not without a struggle, he opted for domestic life. Three more Danes arrived, stayed for a while, and then left for home. Later, in fact, they all married. The community also had an English lay-brother novice, Aelred, who despite his youth sported a full beard and was apparently happy to spend most of his day working on the farm.

★ ★ ★

In the time that followed, some new vocations came to these lay brethren as well. In their brown habits and scapulars they were never numerous on Caldey, therefore we regularly had two or three Belgian brethren on loan from the motherhouse. But we saw little of them, except at mealtimes and at church on Sundays, for they all had work to do which kept them outdoors, often far from the monastery. In addition to Brother Thomas and Brother Aelred there was the very young Brother Louis, also English. Of these, the last two did not stay until the final solemn profession. In my time, even at their most numerous, the lay brethren never numbered more than seven, including those on loan.

In many ways the lay brethren and the choir monks belonged to two very different patterns of life. Let me briefly explain the background for this division, which seems slightly puzzling today. Benedict never mentions this 'lay' type of monk at all. The monastic brethren had been bound by tradition to perform the Divine Office, as is still the case wherever the Rule is observed. During the Middle Ages the canonical services gradually took up more and more of the monks' time, while being dependent on a good education—not least including Latin and the ability to read plainchant. Since no one without such qualifications would seek to enter a monastery, by tradition the monks were recruited from the educated classes. Yet the monasteries somehow had to survive and function, and this was achieved to an increasing degree, even in the Middle Ages, by using hired labour. Then in the tenth century Cluny 'invented' the lay brotherhood which meant that also the illiterate—often those with a background in handcrafts or farming—could enter a monastery. This was possible even at an advanced age, and it was not unusual for widowers to be admitted.

In the later Middle Ages this brotherhood grew in popularity and became an accepted and effective alternative vocation. Although they were never ordained priests, lay brethren were often personages of considerable importance, not least on the administrative side. Traditionally they had full beards and were called *'conversi barbati'*. In my time some of them still had such beards, even if this was no longer obligatory. Some time after my arrival the Cistercian Order initiated a long-term process of amalgamating the two categories of monks, who nowadays wear identical habits (often far from practical since they are generally white), and when possible the non-priest brothers have the opportunity to participate in the liturgical office. The opportunity—but not the duty!

Since the Second Vatican Council (1962–65) authorized the use of mother tongues in the liturgy, a lack of knowledge of Latin is no longer an impediment in the monasteries that have switched to using the vernacular. The lay brethren, who in less enlightened times possibly felt themselves classed as second-rank monks, continue even so to decline in numbers in the well-educated West, while increasing in numbers and importance in the mission countries, where following the gradual amalgamation process they are now, like the choir brethren, known as just monks or brothers. With few exceptions the term 'lay brother' is now obsolete. All follow a formal course of monastic formation, some being selected for ordination to the priesthood, who then usually are sent to university for philosophical and theological studies.

The reason for the remarkable increase in applications to Caldey, a reason Dom Albert naturally had not touched on during our talks, must above all have been his own luminous personality and deep spirituality. This was an authentic man of prayer, both learned and highly intellectual, with a deep inner tranquillity—a monk who (it was not hard to see) had progressed far along the path that must be the aim of every monk. Not least it was a special experience to be present at his lectures on the theology of the early Cistercian Fathers, a subject he knew better than almost anyone. Although unaware of the fact himself, he was obviously a magnet for this new generation seeking the contemplative life.

The novitiate was an entity in itself. In theory we postulants and novices had teaching in the morning, while in the afternoon we took part in whatever work was to be done. But in an existence between the ebb and flow of the tide there are often emergencies which have to be dealt with immediately, and we younger people were useful to turn to when all other hands were already busy: for example, if a boat suddenly had to be put to sea or pulled up on land. Thus the novitiate was also a school in flexibility. You could rarely take anything for granted, with the exception of the Divine Office, for—as Benedict insistently laid down—'nothing must . . . take precedence over the Work of God'.

As for myself, I was above all eager to fit in: to become one of the monks. Life here was so full of timeless tradition that, without any hesitation, I was prepared to let it take me over completely. Moreover, before long I understood that, in a context such as this, there are answers to all relevant questions—which meant that I could expect to be given satisfactory explanations for everything in due course. The two-year novitiate ahead would offer plenty of opportunities in that respect.

I soon discovered, however, that the threshold to be crossed was dangerously high. During my postulant period when I stood, shivering slightly in the monks' choir in my plus fours and tweed jacket, envying the brothers their thick wool habits and cowls, I thought more than once of the sixty or so aspirants to the new foundation here twenty years earlier, all of whom (with one exception) were drawn back to 'the world'.

One day in the course of conversation, Dom Albert told me what he felt had made the needle-eye so particularly narrow for this 'lost' flock of assuredly excellent and idealistic young men. Much of the reason must have lain in the unwillingness of the original Belgian and French monks to conform to a British lifestyle. They wanted to retain the traditions they had brought with them from Scourmont, for they regarded Caldey more as an annex to the motherhouse than as a new establishment moving toward independence. Everything (reading aloud, preaching, the prior's talks and instructions) was in French, while at the same time the monks' customary silence meant that no one felt bound to learn more English than necessary. The upshot of it, therefore, for the majority was *no* English. As Dom Albert commented: 'It's difficult enough to be a Cistercian, but if you need to be French-speaking as well—and more or less almost a Frenchman or a Belgian into the bargain—that could be the last straw.' (Brother Thomas, I remember, had said something similar on my first visit.) 'It's only now that the transition towards becoming an English-language community is gaining speed. With the recruitment we have at present, it looks as if there's a new era ahead. I certainly hope so, for otherwise the outlook is gloomy.'

More and more often I was assigned to work on the farm. The first day that I shovelled muck I was close to fainting from the stench of ammonia and other gases from the underlying layers, but you get used to that sort of thing. In time it felt good to be busy at work on the farm, with simple tasks like cleaning the cattle barns, using the separator, bottle-feeding stray lambs, or weeding. No sense of wasted time—all that was unimportant was eliminated.

I was amazed to find how much work was involved in the ordinary running of the farm. Not least I developed the deepest respect for the efforts that went into our daily bread. In the monastery's 'underworld', our Belgian Father Dominic did all the baking both for us and the rest of the islanders. And it was no mean satisfaction to sit and chew bread baked with flour from the grain you yourself had helped to grow. I often smiled to myself thinking of Benedict's words: 'If local conditions or poverty require them to bring in the crops themselves, let them not be distressed, for then they are truly monks, when they live by the labour of their hands, as did our fathers and the apostles'. Yes, and here we had to take on the whole cycle from harrowing, fertilizing, sowing, spraying, and rolling, to reaping, binding, threshing, transporting, and mechanically drying the crop.

The physical adjustment was certainly demanding, but expected. Indeed it had been unambiguously presented to me, for had I not already on the threshold to the novitiate been warned (in Benedict's words) 'of the hardship and the roughness of the road to God'? Among other things I had to become a vegetarian overnight (apart from one egg a day as a transitional arrangement). To sleep fully dressed felt like a punishment to begin with, though little by little it became a matter of course. Physical labour was an unfamiliar lifestyle; new muscles had to be put into use, often with intense stiffness as a result. The prohibition against talking—especially difficult, I imagine, for someone from gregarious Bergen—produced inner tension, which to begin with was released in waves of internal chatter. The overall simplicity of our way of life—attractive enough in theory—was not so easy to adopt in practice, for nature would not be denied. I was a natural late-riser. Now I had to get up at 4 AM—much later actually than the monks, who normally rose at 2 AM. Added to that there was the unusually severe, damp climate here in the face of the Atlantic, with bitingly cold autumn and winter storms as the norm.

In the Cistercian Order, which with the Carthusians is the Church's most ascetic, such a change of circumstances (in my case at a rather forced pace) is often made at a price. My period as a postulant would normally have lasted a month, the minimum according to the regulations. Despite everything just mentioned, I was eager to don the white habit, to be one of the novices.

Since I had been accepted into the Church in Rome eight years previously on the Feast of the Immaculate Conception (8th December), I felt I should like my admission to the novitiate to take place on that date. Dom Albert, however, sent for me and gave me a mild reprimand. *He* was in no hurry. Since I was just thirty, he first wanted to see whether I had the stamina to master this mentally and physically demanding upheaval in my life. Because he had observed my tendency to show an excess of zeal, the burden of his message was 'Take it easy!' The result was that I had to calm down, but I still felt exhausted, often shaken at the thought of the sixty who had left, yet at the same time reassured by the example of the good Brother Thomas, who was clearly a happy man.

Christmas came like an oasis. The Midnight Mass was sung from beginning to end with the well-known texts decorated by a series of flowing Gregorian melodies. Even the long lessons from the Bible were chanted. Time seemed to have stopped.

After the service came a surprise. We went in procession to the refectory, myself second last. A bright fire was blazing in the shoulder-high fireplace that ordinarily stood there dark and empty. A big table was spread with cakes, chocolate, preserved fruits, and much more: the year's only exception to the rule. Everything sent in by friends of the monastery for the festive season was laid out bearing the donors' cards with good wishes. What was fascinating for a newcomer was that the joyful feast which followed took place without a single word being spoken, for the prohibition against speaking not only applies every day of the year: it is particularly enforced in the refectory. Even the prior, who may speak whenever and wherever he pleases, refrained from speaking here.

I have kept my Christmas mail unopened. Now I take it out, sit down comfortably beside the fire, read the letters and Christmas cards and enjoy a cup of cocoa while the storm howls round the buildings. I envy nobody anything at all.

It is well on in January before the prior calls me in again, this time to be sure that I still wish to be admitted to the novitiate. It is only now that I am judged to be acclimatized to the extent that I may safely cross the actual threshold to the life of the Order. Nonetheless, I could leave the monastery at any time, without needing to ask permission or give a reason for my decision. In other words, I did not have to commit myself to anything beyond obeying the rules and my superiors as long as I wished to remain a novice.

On 2nd February—at Candlemas (Feast of the Purification of the Virgin Mary)—still in my everyday clothes, I kneel on the floor of the chapter room. The entire community is present.

Among the other things Dom Albert says in his speech of welcome is that already at this stage he wishes to express his hope—and will strive to ensure—that Caldey will one day be able to bring the Cistercians back to my homeland, where the Order had performed such beneficent work over the centuries. There is no denying the fact that he opens up horizons I myself have not dared to envisage. Then I am clothed in the novice's warm, white habit.

At long last I have come to harbour.

Fourteen

NOVICE

THE NOVITIATE INSTRUCTION gave us new insight and broadened our understanding. The essential elements in it might be summed up like this: The primal form of Christian holiness was martyrdom. This I recognized as something I had learned and accepted from my earliest schooldays in the phrase, 'the blood of the martyrs was the seed of the Church'. After the persecution of Christians under Roman rule ceased, martyrdom was replaced by asceticism, ideally conceived as a lifelong but nonviolent testimony to identification with Christ. I was no stranger to that thought either.

The Church's original ascetics, called anchorites, withdrew to live in solitude in the Egyptian desert. They practised abstinence, often in extremely harsh forms. They were thus people who endured a self-imposed martyrdom!

Saint Benedict (480–547), already mentioned here several times, was an Italian who had long felt impelled to live as an anchorite—but in his homeland. After a time he reluctantly had to accept having disciples who were eager to learn about, and share in, his solitary form of life. He even felt obliged to organize a small group of like-minded companions in Subiaco, southeast of Rome, where he himself eked out an existence in the mountains. Not far from there, in about the year 530, he founded the monastery of Monte Cassino, which was to become the cradle and focal point of monachism in medieval Europe. Here, the hermit's way of life was radically replaced by *the family lifestyle:* the brethren were to share everything and practise the love of God and of their fellow men (in other words, of their fellow monks) in accordance with the Gospel. Martyrdom had faded still further into the background, or so it might seem.

Benedict has been called the father of Western monasticism, and rightly so, for the entire Latin church in the Middle Ages owed its complex monastic system to his work, *Regula Sancti Benedicti* (the Rule of Saint Benedict).[1] All subsequent Western monastic reforms resulted from endeavours to return to his ideals.

Benedict postulates that God invites and that man responds. His prime concern is the sufferings of Christ, and above all the wish to bear the Cross with him. His priorities are clear: God first, and then man. Somewhat oversimplified, one might say that the modern active form of monastic life seeks God through mankind, while the contemplative life seeks men through God.

Benedict is not very concerned with speculative theology, but rather uses the Bible as a foundation and guideline for the monk's life. He shall strive to follow in Christ's footsteps. Christ chose poverty and humiliation. His suffering and death on the Cross are decisive realities to every monk. But the absolute essential must always be that the monk unreservedly seeks God *(ut revera Deum quaerit)* through obedience to his will.

'The abbot is Christ's deputy in the monastery', Benedict writes in one of his leading phrases. This was not his own doctrine, but traditional teaching, although no one knows for certain (not even in the light of modern research) who first formulated this vital principle so important to the concept of monachism. He defines precisely: 'As soon as a superior has commanded something, it is as if God himself has given the order, and they [the monks] do not hesitate for a moment in executing it. . . . It happens so quickly where piety prevails that the master issues the order and the disciple carries it out almost in the same breath. For the obedience shown to the superior is in reality shown to God.'[2] Benedict, however, takes it a step further: you shall see Christ not only in your abbot but also in your fellow monks; indeed, you shall set them before yourself and be the servant of all by serving Christ in each one of them.

Why were we given such a thorough introduction to Benedict's Rule? Are the Cistercians the same as the Benedictines? Both yes and no.

The old saying that all great movements begin in mystery only to end in administration also applied to medieval monasticism. Yet it was not so simple, for reform movements with new and vigorous elements repeatedly led to the revival of the whole idea of monachism—until, after a time, once again, it lost its original fervour and ascetic idealism.

An epoch-making reform movement was instituted by the abbey at Cluny in France in the tenth and eleventh centuries. For the first time, monasteries following the Rule of Saint Benedict were organized in a proper monastic *order,* which slowly spread throughout the whole of Western Christendom.

A milestone comes in 1098 with the founding of the monastery of Cîteaux in Burgundy, by a handful of monks who some years before have abandoned the once famous Cluny-abbey of Molesmes. From the outset these monks intended to live by the labour of their own hands rather than by the labour of others, as was unfortunately too often the case in monastic life. Thus, while the Cluny expansion is at its peak (although decline is already latent), they struggle to wrench each single tillable patch from the reluctant land, and drain whole marshes to survive.[3] Their aim is to live in absolute poverty and without compromise in accordance with Saint Benedict's Rule for Monks in its original, unadulterated form. But so far, no one has sought to join them, and life has become so fraught with difficulties that they have to consider giving up the attempt.

At this point something strange and momentous takes place in those depths of Burgundy's inaccessible forest. Early one morning there is a knocking on the door, and the English-born abbot, Stephen Harding, looks out in amazement at a mounted assembly of about thirty men, nobles, most of them in the prime of life, who straight away ask to be admitted to the company of the monks. The group of thirty gives the Cîteaux undertaking a new lease on life. And this is the beginning of one of the great medieval monastic sagas: the genesis of the Cistercian Order.

The men are under the leadership of the very young Bernard of Fontaines, later called 'of Clairvaux'. This quiet, unassuming student, for whom no unusual career had been foreseen, is destined to become one of the pioneering spirits of the Middle Ages and a powerful tool in God's hand. That he is a man of prayer is evidenced by all we know about him and can deduce from his prolific writings. He is no less a spiritual renovator and a founder of monasteries on an incredible scale.

Bernard had found not only the long-sought radical poverty, but also an increasing depth of understanding in prayer, not least in the Divine Office, and in the study of Holy Scripture and the Fathers of the Church. The two years or so of instruction that the group had to undergo were also put to excellent use, as later developments would show.

Only one year after the arrival of the group, Cîteaux was able to found its first monastery (La Ferté), and in the following year, yet another (Pontigny, near Auxerre). In 1115 two new pioneer groups could be sent out, one of them to a place that was as barren as Cîteaux, northwest of Langres. They named it *Clairvaux*, French for *Clara Vallis*, the bright valley. Abbot Stephen sent as its founder the young Bernard, accompanied by many of those who had initially arrived with him. It proved to be an inspired choice, for it was as abbot of this monastery that he would come to be famous as Bernard of Clairvaux and set his mark on the rest of the century.

The motherhouse of Cîteaux was the home base for far-reaching expansion. In 1115, as already mentioned, there were four daughter houses. Fifteen years later the number had grown to eighty, and so it continued at a steadily increasing rate. The original intention, however, had not been to institute a new order. The prime aim was to live uncompromisingly according to Benedict's Rule. By 1119, however, so many foundations had been made both by Cîteaux and its daughter houses that Stephen Harding considered it advisable to invite all the abbots concerned to a conference at Cîteaux. They decided to establish an independent order of monks, and to draw up statutes for it. The form of organization accorded to it proved to contain such power of survival that it has endured until the present day.

The constitutions of the Cistercian Order were set down in a document entitled the *Carta Caritatis* (Charter of Charity) with Holy Scripture and love of one's fellow men as the joint fundament for the community of monks. It was laid down that the supreme authority of the Order should be exercised in fellowship by an annual General Chapter consisting of the abbots from all the monasteries, assembled at Cîteaux on the Feast of the Exaltation of the Cross (14th September).

A new feature was that each abbey was to have responsibility for and supervision over any monastery, or monasteries, it founded. This great mass of widely dispersed and often isolated houses was therefore linked together as an organized whole—not horizontally but vertically. Highest in rank was Cîteaux, then the four first daughter houses, including Clairvaux. The abbots of these five monasteries would constitute the Supreme Council, which could meet as required.

Thus the Order was founded, being in all major respects the work of Stephen Harding (and not of Bernard, as is generally supposed).

As time passed it was inevitable that Bernard became involved in contemporary issues. And so, his personality and boundless energy were to predominate in one field after another, with the result that he was called upon to give assistance or counsel further and further away from the monastery, both at royal courts and in papal Rome. Recruitment propaganda for the Second Crusade was one of his many activities.

The Church had long sought to free itself from pressures exerted by the numerous lesser powers, and Bernard felt it his duty to stand up for the Church's right to determine its own affairs. Moreover, for several years he was drawn into the conflict between the pope (Innocent II) and the antipope (Anacletus II). Not only Innocent, but also the emperor (Lothar), found it necessary on several occasions to seek Bernard's aid.

Something that struck me about Bernard was the impression he apparently made every time his duties brought him outside the monastery. He often returned with a flock of young men who wanted to become monks. For example, he came back from Flanders with over thirty candidates from the country's most respected families. In 1140, after he spoke to the students in the Latin Quarter in Paris, two hundred and twenty of them returned with him. In fact, it was said that when Bernard was on the way, women hid their husbands and sons for fear they might go off with him.

At his death in 1153, Bernard had either founded or attached to Clairvaux no fewer than sixty-six monasteries. At the time of the Order's greatest point of expansion around the year 1500, the number of monasteries amounted to seven hundred and thirty-three.

It was only natural that a branch for women had been established at a very early stage, and this, too, duly produced offshoots in the same way. Saint Benedict had confined himself to writing about monastic life for men. His sister Scholastica shared his monastic ideals, but, as far as is known, without founding any community. The desert father Pachomius, Saint Basil the Great, and Cesarius of Arles all had sibling sisters who followed in their footsteps with monastic foundations.

While the Cluny order slipped into a gradual decline before disappearing completely as a consequence of the French Revolution (1789), the Cistercians survived, thanks to their firm principles and austere form of life. There certainly had been tendencies towards backsliding here too, but rescue was close at hand. New thoughts and impulses, so typical for the complex history of monasticism, emanated from the monastery of La Grande Trappe in Normandy. In 1664 the abbot there, Armand de Rancé, effected a thorough reform modelled on the original Cîteaux. A radical process of simplification was introduced. The monks were to follow Benedict's Rule to the letter: rise at 2 AM, refrain from speaking to one another, be vegetarians, live by the labour of their hands, do without servants, and so on. La Trappe was soon the Church's strictest monastery. Yet what happened? It attracted many vocations and could initiate several foundations. The commonly used name 'Trappist' originated here.[4]

In the eighteenth and nineteenth centuries many religious orders in Europe were prohibited and their monasteries dissolved by those in power. It is a long and complicated story. One keyword, apart from the French Revolution, was Austria's so-called Josephinism, which led to the dissolution of monasteries that would not adapt to Emperor Joseph's plans— for example, by establishing schools, children's homes, and hospitals. The members of the monasteries were then simply turned out on to the streets.

In the Cistercian Order's homeland, France, after 1789 all the monasteries were dissolved, except for one: La Trappe. The abbey's reputation for high morals and formidable discipline was so widely known that the ruling powers did not dare to attack it. But they adopted fiendish tactics instead. The monastery was allowed to continue, but not to take in any aspirants. In other words it could die a slow death—in peace. But the monks were not so easily tricked. One night in 1791 they crossed the frontier to Switzerland where they were allowed to settle in a disused Carthusian monastery (Val-Sainte). Here the community experienced a revival and expansion that resulted in new foundations, not only in Europe but in Canada and the USA. After twenty-five years in exile, they succeeded in winning back their confiscated abbey. La Trappe survived excellently and still carries on.

★ ★ ★

In 1950 the monastery acquired a new boat. Only islanders will really be able to understand just what that means. *Lollipop,* or by her proper name *Caldey Island,* was navy blue with red railings, a sort of medium-sized, diesel-driven six-cylinder fishing boat, 'under the command' of Brother Thomas. The price had been three thousand pounds, mainly collected by friends of the monastery—like a gift from heaven.

On the day before the handing-over ceremony, we monks took part in a boating tour round the island—with dispensation from the silence rule! The outing began in calm sunshine, and for most of us the round trip was a first-time experience, as well as the last.

Brother Thomas made his way over to me: 'Do you see that bay there, right below the lighthouse? A Norwegian freighter called *Le Bel Pareil* ran aground there in February 1940. The crew, who thought the coast was uninhabited, stayed below deck until the storm blew itself out. One morning when some of them managed to climb up the steep rocks, they suddenly came face to face with the unexpected sight of tonsured monks in habits, and had no idea where in the world they could be. When things were explained they just stood there and had a good laugh about it all. It took the crew quite a while to repair everything, so we came to know these Norwegians and got along with them very well, helped them with food, water, and so on. After a few weeks a tugboat came from Liverpool and pulled them free—and out to sea again.'

An older father who had been one of the founders of the monastery sat beside me. He seemed completely spellbound. 'I've never seen Caldey like this—from the sea. I'd no idea it was so beautiful!'

Someone called out: 'Look over here!' Close in front we saw a school of porpoises coming toward us, obviously delighted at having found a playmate. They began to race with *Lollipop,* seeming to smile when they sprang high out of the water as near to the bow as possible. We were so absorbed in watching this strange game that no one noticed the sun had vanished. Our outing ended in a cloudburst. Brother Thomas was the only one who had thought of bringing a waterproof.

Towards the end of my first year in the novitiate I was appointed tractor-driver, and spent most of my working hours out on the windswept fields, happy to be learning a new skill—knowing full well that Father Jerome had arranged things so that I should later come into his service for good. Had I been allowed to choose for myself, I should hardly have wanted it otherwise.

The summer of 1951 was a busy season. Teaching in the novitiate had ended and would be resumed in the autumn. Most of the novices were involved in some kind of farm work, mine being mainly on the tractor.

I had developed a health problem, however, which Dom Albert suddenly decided ought to be dealt with. To cut a long story short: ever since I had taken my matriculation in the space of one year before coming to Caldey, I had suffered from recurrent headaches in connection with mental effort, as well as difficulty in sleeping. The prior was not very happy about this, for in the autumn I was supposed to begin studying philosophy. If something was to be done, he thought it had better be done now. I had only one hour's warning to find and unpack my stored lay clothes and grab some food. A Belgian monk on loan to us, Father Robert, had a similar problem, so Dom Albert (who had to go to London in any case) took us both with him.

There was a feeling of unreality about coming back to the noisy, dirty capital, where the two of us were handed over to a doctor of the non-nationalized kind (almost certainly expensive). He was ultra-professional, examined us thoroughly, took notes, and murmured 'Ah, yes' and 'Oh, yes' and a few other words over and over again, but enough that we could notice his educated accent with its distinct Scots undertone. I could give him no account of any illness, only headaches, palpitation, insomnia, and fatigue from reading. In the waiting room where I happened to catch sight of myself in a mirror, I could see I looked the picture of health, especially in comparison with the typical Londoner's pasty face, run-down as people were by too much soot, too much drink, too little food, and (according to them) too high taxes. After the doctor's examination, the result of which would be reported later, Dom Albert took the two of us to a restaurant for a much-needed meal. I gazed longingly at the roast beef, but this time, no: it had to be fish!

We were given beds for the night in Sloane Street by some modern 'nuns' in ordinary dress (actually, members of a Secular Institute, very much a novelty at the time). One of them, Ingrid, who was Swedish, sat winking patriotically at me— as if we shared all the secrets in the world. Next morning we had to go back to the doctor, who had thawed a bit and took time to show me his collection of antique glass, including no fewer than six flawless Nøstetangen carafes, which he well knew were Norwegian. I was examined once again, was given some harmless sleeping pills, with a warning to take things more easily and get nine hours' sleep, and then see how things developed over a couple of months. The 'diagnosis' in Father Robert's case was almost the same, so reassured we could travel back to Wales, Caldey, and our own special brand of normality.

The cure worked as intended, and sleep returned. I learned to treat the headache like an old acquaintance, useful for giving warning signals during periods of study. But then and there, what mattered most was to get up on the tractor again and out into the fields. And I was perfectly contented, now even more overwhelmed than ever by this our life apart—an existence to which I felt more and more convinced the Lord had directed me.

I had one slight secret anxiety: that I might be asked if I could cook, but fortunately this never happened. Soon after I had donned the habit, however, I was questioned as to whether I could play the piano or the organ, perhaps even sightread music. My positive answer in regard to the piano and sightreading led to the monastery organist, the French Father

Edmund, arranging for me to learn to play the harmonium (the organ, like the church, the chapter room, and the library, having gone up in flames during the war).

First of all I was to learn to accompany the different services of the Divine Office. This proved to be an immense task in itself, for the organist has to match his harmonies to all eight church tones used in varying order. Furthermore, I had to transpose from the sheet music to make the pitch suit the liturgy's principal tonality, which with us was A-flat (major or minor). But also the numerous separate items—mostly antiphons—had to be accompanied, with only the first note given in the margin. I was more than a little scared at the thought of the flexibility and powers of invention required of me. When I was at length put to the test of accompanying the service, I would spend part of the night (plus my 'free time') practising and experimenting. To crown it all, at High Mass on the main feastdays there had to be several voluntaries. Father Edmund and I alternated in playing, with my taking it on more often, since as first cantor he preferred to be in the choir. Keyboard, workshop, and farmwork required different skills from one's hands. But bit by bit I came to enjoy this strange rotation of tasks.

Two hands pretending to play an organ in the air soon became the description the brethren used among themselves to denote my person. We all had this type of symbolic signature, often used when someone wanted to know the whereabouts of this or that monk. You stared questioningly into the eyes of an approaching colleague while your hands made the sign for the man you wanted to find. The response could be a complicated series of pointing and sign language—or a shake of the head.

The silence was an incomparable gift. It also had a special side effect. Your sense of hearing became acutely sharp, so that you immediately knew who was close at hand, without having seen him. The sound of footsteps, of breathing, or something else was enough for identification. The most noiseless of all was the prior, but even by such a characteristic, people could be identified.

One day in late autumn Father Jerome came hurrying up the long slope to the farm. He was in quite a state: 'I've got a puncture down at the slip, and now the load is stuck there. Can you repair tractor tubes?' 'The big one or the small one?' (At work we were allowed to exchange essential sentences with whoever was in charge.) 'The big one', he replied curtly. I had more doubts than I cared to show, but I heard myself say: 'I think I can'. Our Fordson tractor had shoulder-high back wheels. How would this go for somebody who had never repaired anything larger than a lorry tyre? I loaded a wheelbarrow with everything that could possibly be needed and wheeled it down the winding road to the slip, without any real belief that the operation would be successful.

First, off with the wheel, with the tractor propped up on blocks; next loosen the tyre on one side; then out with the tube and blow it up in the shallows to check the hole, or holes, underwater. Ice-cold hands. Beat your arms round your body to keep warm. So seal the hole with glue and a patch, and finally go through the whole procedure in reverse, holding your breath so as not to pinch holes in the tube with the heavy crowbars. It worked, and proved to be my unplanned apprenticeship test. I observed Father Jerome's approving gaze as I drove the tractor with assumed nonchalance and took its load into the farm. 'Good work', was all he said, without realizing that I was now lost to him as far as farming was concerned. For Dom Albert, who must have heard about this episode, said a few days later during the assignment of work-tasks: 'You can give me a hand in the garage.' Our prior, in addition to everything else, was also the community's mechanic.

After that, under him, it was my job to see to the upkeep of our growing number of vehicles, for the process of mechanization continued slowly but inexorably, and naturally we had to be self-sufficient in this as in all other fields. In due course, I knew every spare part, and often had to make do with more or less ingenious improvisations when there was no chance—that is to say, no time—to obtain reserve parts from Carmarthen, Swansea, or distant London.

The alpha and omega of monastery life is to be at God's disposal. In himself, a monk is an ordinary human being who nonetheless has been chosen by Our Lord to seek him in every way and by all means. The monk does this by consistently striving to do Our Lord's will, both through a life dedicated to God and in the many details comprising that life.

Benedict advocates that the lives of the brethren be organized carefully towards the goal of ensuring that every single monk may *know* for certain what Our Lord's will is before he can endeavour to *comply* with it. And this the monk practises, as already mentioned, by demonstrating obedience to the person who for him is Christ's deputy, the superior of the monastery—who may perhaps make an error in a decision or a decree, as the monk is permitted to point out, though *he himself* cannot do wrong by thereafter obeying it.

The vocation does not demand that you are perfect, but rather that you wish to follow a path leading towards total devotion, with fewer and fewer reservations, to God's will. However, the way is long, arduous, and full of hazards—and you will often fall. You are a long-term apprentice, who when he stumbles will pick himself up again and stagger on. In keeping with this picture, Benedict views the monastery as a school, and life there as a permanent pedagogic exercise. You are never finished with learning. His comforting message, however, is that the devoted monk will find that his heart is expanding, so that after a time he will hasten along his chosen path; for in his soul the divine love will gradually spread and take over completely.

In the late autumn of 1950 the community had at last begun to realize a long-planned undertaking: the restoration of the burnt-out monastery church whose damaged walls had marred the landscape for almost a decade. The task was particularly complicated because of our insular situation. The church roof had to be laid with beams shipped over by Brother Thomas and Jerry 'junior' on a somewhat inadequate boat, even if *Lollipop* was definitely more robust than our old one, which had been scrapped after many years of service.

We spent months in a state of emergency—not to say confusion—side by side with a workforce from the mainland. Improvisation was the order of the day, not least because the tide meant that we had to go down to the slip at all hours of the day and night to bring the building materials ashore. But it was far from a depressing time, for the church is every monastery's heart, being the sacred setting for regular services, Masses, meditation, and private prayer, as well as for the tabernacle where the Sacrament of the Altar is kept. So we worked with a will towards our goal, longing for the day when we should at last be able to take possession of our spiritual home.

Our joy was somewhat diminished by the fact that the monastery's burnt-out library and chapter room were not allowed to be rebuilt at the same time, because of the post-war shortage of building materials. At the present moment of writing (2003) they are still unrestored. But at all events it seemed a real luxury to have the church back again, now with a free-standing altar in massive concrete, as the centre-piece in a spaciously designed choir, where even the greatest festivals of the Christian year could be celebrated with style and dignity.

Gradually it becomes distressingly clear that involvement in the life of an order such as this means that powers of endurance have to be mustered, whatever the cost. It is said that all beginnings are difficult. Not necessarily, for the solutions to difficulties can evolve spontaneously. Often it is rather the continuation that proves a challenge. You have to learn to grit your teeth and think unflinchingly: if it is God who has called you to this, you are not allowed to fail; and if it is *not* so, your superiors are sure to discover this and will prevent your taking a step that is not backed by the hand of the Lord. Our own Dom Albert once took up the subject: a lack of vocation to the life of the monastery—and to *this* one in particular—would be detected and the consequences inexorably drawn, 'for no one can adhere to this life except by virtue of the grace which is inherent in an authentic vocation'.

As for myself, I quite simply did not dare to think of leaving, for what then? But this was not the whole scope of the question. In an earlier conversation Dom Albert had drawn attention to the underlying problem: 'It is one thing to have a vocation and quite another to interpret the vocation correctly. Everyone who applies to a religious order comes up against this problem.' And, more and more, I had to admit that this was indeed the core of the matter. The vocation had burned in me so steadily that I would find it hard to believe that it was not genuine. For long I had believed that it was in the ordinary priesthood that God would have me, but slowly I had come to the conclusion that it was not so much ordination and pastoral duties that appealed to me, but rather to put myself unconditionally in God's hands. I increasingly felt—and with no small degree of relief—that my vocation was not merely to the Cistercians, but to this very monastery. In fact I thought with little enthusiasm of a hypothetical entry into the houses of some of the other orders I had visited during the previous summer. When I mentioned this to the prior, he nodded: 'Our Lord usually works like that. You go from place to place until suddenly you find the right answer. I remember a young man who came here on his search and would hardly stay to tea, so little did he like it here.'

In the novitiate we still saw much coming and going, with many newcomers and many who went their way again. A Welshman of the more serious West-country type who entered, but broke down due to lack of inner stability, had to be sent away; a young Irishman who came and stayed for some years before he went back to get married; another young

Irishman who had instruction for several months, but who was too immature and had to be sent home; yet another Welsh-man, Joseph, who stayed at his post and was for a long time the monastery's subprior. For quite a while we also had three novices from Ceylon (Sri Lanka), a young man from Trinidad, and one from India—in the end they all left. Others came and went, including a London lawyer (LL.D) of impressive bearing. We were never bored.

What is interesting in this connection is how we reacted to newcomers. After I had been a novice for a time, I found I was on the same wavelength as my brethren when it came to assessing whether a new arrival would fit in with us or not. Unfailingly we would exchange telling looks which meant thumbs up—or down. I cannot now remember a single in-stance when we were mistaken. A selection process that was a mystery, or so it seemed.

With fierce tenacity I determined to cling to my post, be-lieving the Lord would surely one day provide the necessary clarification. In any event the thought of returning 'to the world' seemed ever more meaningless to me.

In the period before I had actually taken the first vows the prior had made a decision that proved to be crucial for my future. As it happens, it is up to the superiors of our Order to judge whether a monk is to study for the priesthood or not. When I was admitted, I myself had in fact no longer any particular views about this, something which Dom Albert considered a good sign. 'Those who want to be admitted here and who constantly have the thought of a priestly vocation in mind are generally those who have not understood their vocation correctly', he had observed. Now he told me, almost out of the blue, that it had been decided that, assuming I took the provisional vows, I was to study theology, because it was considered I had both the educational and the psychological qualifications required; something that would normally lead to ordination.

So in the autumn of 1951 I started to study philosophy under the Belgian Father Robert (from my trip to London),

as well as another teacher, Father Charles Dumont, who was
sent from our Belgian motherhouse. I was fascinated both by
the studies and, not least, by our teachers: two gifted men with
impressive educational backgrounds. It made me understand
why Scourmont had such a distinguished, indeed unique,
standing in our Order, which was otherwise not especially
brilliant in the academic field.

For us students the starting point was Einstein's theory of
relativity and the premises on which it was based. Other interesting themes were to follow, so it was an exciting time.

Mother made the long and complicated journey from Oslo
to Caldey three or four times, probably with more internal
'butterflies' than she dared to admit. Nevertheless, she came
to like staying in the garden house 'Saint Philomena', where
Mrs Shand, who was in charge, immediately took her to her
heart, doing everything that lay within her powers to make
this out-of-the-ordinary mamma—who was not a Catholic—
feel at home.

Mother found Caldey enchantingly beautiful, and she liked
to go for long walks all over the island. Dom Albert made a
great impression on her: 'A man of rare stature—and, as well
as that, a gentleman.'

Not surprisingly, she understood little of our life, which to
her was like a remnant from the Middle Ages. But mothers
know when their children are thriving, and in this case she
could only find confirmation that it was true. It was clear to
me that she had suffered a lot, and was indeed still suffering,
but I could do nothing about that beyond praying and trusting
in the Lord. And in fact, in the end, though admittedly not
for several years, she came to terms with her—and my—fate
with increasing goodwill, for my happiness in this existence
was beyond all doubt.

Father, who was almost an atheist, never came as far as
Caldey. He simply could not bring himself to it. Once, when
he wrote that he was to go to London on a business trip, Dom
Albert told me I could travel to London to meet him halfway,

as it were. I was amazed and said something about how liberal this seemed to me. 'We can never be more broadminded than Our Lord', remarked Dom Albert. Later this sentence was often a help to me.

Father was staying at the Savoy Hotel, where I felt like a fish out of water, though I tried not to show it, for he was so touchingly pleased to have me with him again, even if only for a few days.

On a later visit to England, he managed to come as far as Tenby. We took the opportunity to drive around and look at some of the sights of South Wales, but he pretended all the time not even to see our island out there in the sea.

To comfort my parents I had carefully explained to them how impermanently I now was—and for long would remain —bound by the provisional vows, and how gradual the whole process of integration was. That gave them some hope, which I clearly understood they needed, for both of them feared that I was lost to this world.

The hour of decision approached slowly: to make or not to make the vows which would bind me for a three-year period to sharing the life of the community. The monastery for its part would not be correspondingly bound, for a monk with temporary profession is still on trial and can be sent away if he fails to come up to standard.

Two years after my admission to the novitiate, Dom Albert summoned me, partly to find out where I stood, but also to tell me where his council probably stood in this matter. 'I feel convinced', he said, 'that if I were to lay an application from you before my council, their reaction would be positive. I don't think you need have any worries on that score.' But he hadn't quite finished: 'It may well be that you yourself still don't feel entirely certain. If that's the case, I have the power to extend your novitiate by up to two years. But after that time if you are still undecided, you must leave us.'

I listened patiently to this well-meant explanation, which I had long ago read in the Order's constitutions. 'I have thought the matter over thoroughly, Father Prior', I said, 'and I have no thoughts of returning to the world.'

One day Dom Albert announced that a distinguished visitor was expected. We pricked up our ears, because this was a rare event. Father Aelred Carlyle, the founder of Caldey's original Benedictine monastery, had given notice of his wish to revisit his old haunts.

And a fascinating 'comeback' it was for this seventy-nine-year-old, yet still ramrod-backed, priest. It was especially moving for him to see again those of the islanders who had been there in his time. A festive event was arranged in the village hall, where members of the lay population put their best efforts into an entertainment—to which our community was invited. The programme included recitations, singing and dancing, the playing of several unusual instruments, and the performance of sketches. Perhaps the charm of the event lay mainly in the revelation of unexpected talents, known only to a few others, in several of the performers. And all this in honour of the 'Abbot Extraordinary' who—moved to tears—rounded off with a speech full of recollections and anecdotes from 'the old days'. Afterwards his travels took him to Prinknash where he again entered his old community and, with permission from Rome, renewed his solemn profession. (The ring had come full circle. In 1955, at eighty-two years of age, Aelred Carlyle died, as an abbot emeritus of Prinknash Abbey.)

Hurricane. Shipwreck. After the coastguards have observed three distress signals in the middle of the night, the big lifeboat from the quayside in Tenby is launched down the steep ramp making it independent of the tide. But only wreckage is found. Boats have broken loose from their moorings inside the harbour and are either smashed to pieces or swept out to sea. Our own *Lollipop* has engine damage which we cannot repair ourselves. This means that we have no connection with the mainland for a whole week just before Christmas. Still, with our self-supporting household, neither we nor the rest of the islanders suffer any real need. And the new church-roof has passed the test.

Shortly after the night of the storm, Dom Albert summoned a council meeting, the purpose of which was clear to most.[5] Later he stopped me on my way to the garage to tell me with a smile that I had the goodwill of the community, and was welcome to make profession. I was overjoyed.

I was given eight days' 'holiday' before my profession, which was to take place on 2nd February (1952). Exempted from all duties, even the organ, I divided the time luxuriously at my disposal between prayer, reading, and rumination—and went for as long walks in the open as the topography of the place allowed. For the last time, I could take a good look at what was now ahead of me.

The difficulties along the way had not only been of an outward character. Frequently I had to pull myself together to overcome inevitable feelings of antipathy in regard to some of 'the chosen'—feelings which arose from everybody's constant close proximity to everybody else. That this was the most usual and the hardest test of asceticism was something I had all too often experienced. It is not least this 'intrusive' common life, demanding the constant denial of self-will and egoism, that—if mastered—has a chastening effect, and that slowly but surely leads to inner liberation, spiritual maturity, and peace of mind. The greatest problems had come from inside. Early in my monastic existence I had no reservations about my aim of submerging myself in the community's anonymous brotherhood. The difficulties had not least consisted in managing to keep myself in my place. My inborn desire for action ('busy-ness' some would say), independence, and ambition repeatedly came to the surface. Because I could be fairly hot-tempered, it was a fight with a lot of lost points. More often than not I had wondered whether I was really cut out to be a member of a community. But after a while I realized that this was normal, and that everyone felt (or had felt) the same. It had taken me time and been a test of patience to become a genuine, not just a 'would-be', member of the brotherhood.

But now I no longer doubted that I was doing the right thing—what, in fact, in my inmost self I most wanted. No mulling over the matter was necessary. There were no unforeseen problems left to resolve.

The day before the ceremony I received an unexpected visit. The English priest, Father Peter Lowry, who was chaplain at Saint Olav's church in Oslo and who had been my spiritual adviser when I was about to enter the monastery, appeared on the scene. This was something he wouldn't miss!

Dom Albert has had a good idea: on this occasion the ceremony will take place in the guesthouse, where there is more space than with us and where, moreover, women can be admitted. The large reception room used by guests is turned into an *ad hoc* chapter room with space for both the community and the guests, several of whom were islanders.

The prior in the 'high chair' asks me (in Latin) to come forward and state my errand, whereupon I express my request to be admitted as a choir-monk to the priorate of Sancta Maria de Caldey. Dom Albert gives an address (now in English) with a rich spiritual content, though warm and humorous in tone and without any hint of sentimentality. Following this I read out loud—again in Latin—my monastery vows, add my signature, and kneeling, hand it to him.

In the last part of the ceremony, Dom Albert removes my novice's white scapular and clothes me in the distinguishing dress of the Order: white tunic, black scapular with hood, leather belt, and a loose cowl for use in church and during meetings of the chapter, as well as for protection against the cold—but never for work.

In conclusion we sing the Benedictus, Zacharias's song of praise from the Gospel according to Saint Luke.

Later in the day our cantor, Father Edmund, who is also our barber, performs the obligatory tonsure. I find it hard to resist taking a stolen glance at my 'new look' in the mirror in the washroom. It gives me the same sort of feeling as when I changed into officers' uniform during the war.

Soon I move from the novitiate down to the monks' day room and, almost with a sense of awe, take possession of the place indicated among the seniors. Brother Stephen, Brother Samson, and Brother Thaddeus have been there for quite some time already: as former novices we four are almost a family within the family.

Fifteen

THE HOLD TIGHTENS

> There is a good zeal the monks should practise with the
> most fervent love, so as to be first in showing honour to
> each other.
> Let them bear with infirmities, whether of body or of
> character, with the most tolerant patience.
> Let them vie with one another in showing mutual
> obedience.
> Let no one follow what he thinks is useful to himself, but
> what is of use to another.
> Let them practise fraternal charity with all chastity.
> Let them fear and love God.
> Let them love their abbot with sincere and humble charity.
> Let them put absolutely nothing before Christ,
> and may He bring us all alike to life everlasting.
>
> *The Rule of Saint Benedict*

THE DAILY ROUND of liturgical services is the
solid backbone of the monastic form of life. Benedict says: 'We believe that God is present everywhere . . . but most of all . . . when we are assisting at the
Divine Office.'

Except for half an hour for meditation early in the morning
and a quarter of an hour's silent prayer between Vespers and
the evening meal, the community's existence is interwoven
with the liturgical prayer whose highpoint is the celebration

of the day's Holy Mass. [1] All this takes place in the church choir, where each person has his place in accordance with a descending order of priority from the prior on the right-hand long wall (the subprior having the corresponding place on the opposite wall) down to the most recent arrival—not the youngest. For on the subject of precedence, Benedict decrees: 'All shall have precedence according to the order of their entry; for example, one who came into the monastery at the second hour of the day must know that he is junior to one who came at the first hour, whatever his age or dignity'. [2]

The picture of monks who stand, rise, sit, bow, straighten up, and sit down again is timeless. [3]

One of the first things I learn about in my new insider-existence is the chapter of faults. Once a week the community gathers for a morning meeting in the day room. At a signal from the prior those of the brethren who feel they have offended against the monastery's regulations prostrate themselves on the floor. After a new signal they rise and go forward one after the other to declare their self-reproaches. One may have disobeyed the silence rule, another may have been impatient with a fellow monk, a third has perhaps broken a tool or a cup. Sometimes a monk raises his hand to ask to speak, which means that he wishes to add something to the self-recriminations made by the monk concerned, or he may have a complaint about a brother who has not reproached himself for something. The interpellant is obliged to be concise in the formulation of his criticism, which in any case may only relate to a breach of the regulations. For example: Father NN has ordered a novice to do a job without having cleared this with the novice-master, or Brother X has spoken to Brother Y in the cloister (where all talking is forbidden). The alleged offender is given the opportunity to state his case, but this seldom happens, for Benedict makes it clear that a monk should 'suffer patiently wrongs done'. After the meting out of penance (possibly some extra prayers) to the 'offender', the chapter ends with further Bible verses recited in unison.

From now on my assignment was to attend to the church bells. In the beginning this was not at all easy, for often I was lifted off my feet into the air without a sound coming from the great bell; the small one was easier to handle. Furthermore, to be the bell-ringer seven days of the week was far from simple, for the monks' daily rhythm and division of time are governed by the signals given by the ringing of bells, of which there are many in the course of a day. The ringing must take place precisely, at any rate within the minute. There had to be two bells, as with us: a larger one which could be heard all over Caldey and a smaller one (not so small, either). As well as its liturgical function, the great bell had a more secular use in signalling the end of work, normally half an hour before we were to take our places in church. Before the most important canonical hours, Lauds and Vespers, warning was given first by the great bell, and then—just before the beginning of the service—by the small one. The signal for the lesser canonical hours was given only by the small bell. As well as all this, the bell had to be rung at specified points of the Mass. Indeed, all in all, I was responsible for so much ringing that my subconscious mind was constantly occupied with checking the time and dashing to the belfry (which had fortunately survived the fire). I was kept at the task much longer than was usual, so long, in fact, that punctuality has been part of my nature ever since.

Problems connected with leisure time were nonexistent. On important feastdays, however, many of us could relax, because work assignments were then waived for everybody without some vital function (and naturally there were bound to be some of those in a self-supporting household such as ours). Then we had the chance to read, meditate, write, go for walks, or just lie in the grass and have a short doze, weather permitting.

Some Sunday afternoons those of us who were interested could listen to classical music on the gramophone in the guesthouse chapel. The few records we had we already knew by heart. But after her first visit, Mother left a cheque earmarked 'Records for the Sunday concerts'. Dom Albert consented to the purchase. Father Edmund was to be responsible for the music, and I for the technical side.

We were still in the 78-era, which normally meant frequent record changes and sharpening of needles. These were of hard wood and had to be cut in a special apparatus each time the record was changed. A lot of fiddling, but it meant the records were practically never worn out.

A discreet notice in the cloister announced the first purchase: Beethoven's *Missa Solemnis.* The work did more than enrapture and fascinate us: it made us want more. Our very young English novice, James, had even borrowed from home a dramatic—indeed rather melodramatic—recording of Verdi's *Requiem,* moreover with some of my former opera idols as soloists. And that, too, was given the all-clear for Sundays. Some of the more pious monks could be seen raising their eyebrows during Verdi's full-scale dramatic outbursts—accustomed as they were to the tranquil Gregorian cantilenas.

In a letter to my mother I wrote—for it was not always easy to find a subject that might interest her—that, thanks to her, our concerts had taken on a new lease of life. Since it was certainly not my intention, it was a surprise when another cheque came by return, again earmarked 'For the Sunday concerts'. It came at a very fortunate moment, too, for something new and almost incredible was happening in the gramophone world: the advent of the long-playing record. In England, Decca was to the forefront with this revolutionary system, and for the money in hand we were able to buy a record-player with a reversible needle for use with both 78 and 33 speed records. The very first time we listened to an LP recording we found it hard to grasp that it could play for so long and reproduce sound of such superlative quality—without the slightest distortion. *Tempi passati!*

Friends of the monastery who had either heard our concerts through the wall from the guesthouse—or had heard *of* them—now gave us various additions to our collection, which grew both in scope and in quality. A special patron was my old acquaintance Edwin Scott-Davies, who loved classical music. Particular favourites were the Brandenburg concertos and Handel's *concerti grossi*. Fauré's *Requiem* found more favour than Verdi's 'opera version', and for me was an enriching discovery. For many of us Sunday afternoon thus became a cultural highpoint in the week.

Most of the monks, especially the older ones, had not been away from Caldey for very many years, and apparently had no regrets on that score. But occasionally someone might visit us, normally only a near relative. Then we had time off, to the extent that this was feasible.

The guesthouse, 'Saint Philomena', some distance away, was particularly used for female visitors, and it was there that we could meet our relations. The likeable and cultivated intendant, Josephine Shand, had been an actress, and her whole personality unconsciously conveyed the aura of London's West End theatre world. She was also a full-time nurse, for in their private quarters upstairs she took care of her cancer-stricken husband, both day and night. After his death, it fell to my lot to drive him with the tractor to the churchyard, to a grave I myself had helped to dig. A solemn procession consisting of his widow, children, and grandchildren, together with Brother Thomas and many of Caldey's inhabitants, followed the bier on the trailer—decorated with flowers from Mrs Shand's incomparable garden—past the monastery and up to the beautiful, ancient Saint David's church, where a funeral service was held, immediately followed by the interment. I was glad Mother had not come on this occasion, for it would have affected her deeply—even though in this case the deceased (unlike the monks) lay in a coffin.

Early in the autumn of 1952 I am called in to Dom Albert, which always means something is afoot. I kneel, as is the custom, beside his desk, and am blessed by a slight movement of his hand. I feel a sense of anticipation. 'I shall be making a trip to Scourmont fairly soon,' he says, 'and I should like you to come with me.' He smiles: 'Not of course just for the visit, but because I have decided you will take your final year in philosophy there—then we'll see how things go later.' I feel my heart sinking. Leave Caldey! 'You will naturally spend your summer holiday [or did he say 'holidays'?] here as usual.' He explains why: Our other students are to begin theology, and it would be an unreasonable strain on the minimal teaching staff to have to provide a philosophy class for me on my own. Moreover, in the motherhouse there are two young monks, both of whom have made their temporary profession like me, who will be joining the same course—so it's as simple as that. Dom Albert no doubt notices my lack of enthusiasm, but such matters are never discussed. I realize, too, that in a way it must also be a sacrifice for Caldey to let me go off for an uncertain term like this, for as well as being organist, bell-ringer, and mechanic, I have also been put in charge of the library.

The motherhouse, Notre-Dame de Scourmont, lies in the very south of Belgium, in the region of Hainaut, with the cathedral city of Tournai as the nearest large centre. For practical reasons Dom Albert also brings along our new administrator, Father Anthony ffrench-Mullen. I assume that behind this lies the hope of obtaining further help and personnel for Caldey.

The flat landscape is dominated by the monastery complex with its soaring church and heavy, greyish-brown brick buildings, erected towards the end of the last century. There are about eighty monks, with a fairly even spread of age-groups. The majority are Walloon, the rest are French. Flanders seems remote here, while France is just round the corner.

We three had hardly come into the day room in the guesthouse before a special piece of news exploded. The guestmaster could not contain himself: 'What do you think?' he said, letting the cat out of the bag. 'We're going to found a new monastery—it was announced in chapter this morning.' Dom

Albert looked shaken: 'Where?' 'In the Congo—near Lake Kivu.' 'Is it possible?' Just at that moment the acting superior, Dom Guerric Baudet, came to welcome us. 'So you're going to found a new monastery', remarked Dom Albert, crestfallen. Frowning, Dom Guerric turned to the guest father: 'You've spilled the beans, then?' 'I just thought—well, it's all in the family', came the halting answer. Dom Albert's reaction was understandable, for until now Caldey, as Scourmont's only daughter house, had received all the support it was possible to give. From now on things would be different.

The start of my study-time in the motherhouse there-fore came to mean participation in the large-scale process of preparation for the foundation, right through to the great farewell send-off for the 'swarmers' two years later. Little did Dom Albert know then—when he had to swallow his disappointment—that he would spend many years, including the last part of his life, in this African daughter house (Notre-Dame de Mokoto), for a long period as its abbot. He lived to be a very old man—venerated, revered, and indeed loved more than most.

At the time when we were staying at Scourmont, a young English monk was also a guest there. He was on his way from the abbey of Mount Saint Bernard in England to complete his doctor's thesis in Rome. Like myself, he was far from pleased to be away from his community for so long. And neither this monk, whose name was Ambrose Southey, nor any of us had the slightest idea that he was destined to be the Order's first English abbot general since Saint Stephen Harding in the twelfth century. Still less that, having resigned after fifteen years in that office and returned to his monastery, he would be appointed temporary superior—of Scourmont! We all lived in the present, which was just as well.

That Caldey had not yet the status of an abbey was both rea-sonable and understandable. Why Scourmont was governed by a prior and not by an abbot was more puzzling. The rea-son, however, was this: the monastery's abbot (whose name had once been known far and wide), Dom Anselme Le Bail, had not long before suffered a brain haemorrhage and been reduced to a wheelchair-existence. Rome's decision was that he should continue as abbot in name until further notice (in other words until his death), but in fact be replaced by his prior.

Everything at Scourmont, seen with Caldey eyes, was on a large scale and well organized, almost another form of life. Only the novitiate came off badly by comparison: no novices, let alone postulants, only the two young Belgians with simple vows. The dimensions of the place allowed for a far greater number. The problem of the lack of vocations was probably connected with the fact that Belgium had no less than five large monasteries of our Order. Even though recruitment had not dried up completely, the situation here, too, was affected by the usual circumstance that at best only one in ten made it all the way to final profession.

For my part, it was like beginning all over again. I had to grit my teeth and repeat to myself: 'Keep at it!' And slowly but surely I grew accustomed to this different life. I even began to thrive on it, something I would never have believed when we arrived.

There were, in fact, many good points about Scourmont. The monks were good-humoured and friendly; above all, they were mature men. Their average intellectual and cultural level was high, as was evidenced not least in the weekly lectures given in turn by the fathers on subjects of their own option. Moreover, those with the best education belonged to the teaching staff. I had already had a foretaste of this while studying philosophy at Caldey with the two Scourmont fathers who were now back here.

The hours of instruction became the highlights of my existence. There was no doubt that the lecturers' degrees, or more often doctorates, were in order. Scourmont's reputation as a kind of monastic university seemed to me well deserved. Dom Anselme Le Bail, who had been responsible for the raised standard of teaching, could be seen around, sitting in the wheelchair which he himself was unable to move. Nor could he speak, much less write. Yet, strange to say, he could read, and most of his time went to monastic studies. As soon as he had a new book in his hands, he would turn to the index, running his finger up and down to check the contents. Then, having found some topic of particular interest, he would open the book at the right page and bury himself in the text. What was regrettable was that his ever greater hoard of knowledge could only be of benefit to himself. His smile was always friendly, even if slightly sad, but he seemed to have come to terms with the limitations of his existence. It was a blessing that he was able to remain so—fortified by his life's work and by the devotion of the brethren—until his death.

I had developed a particularly good relationship with one of the monastery's oldest monks, Father Joseph Cannivez, who became my father confessor. The greater part of his life in the monastery had gone to studying, copying, and editing the annual reports and documents of the General Chapters, right from the time of the foundation, and he had produced volume after volume after volume, a whole library.

I have seldom come across anyone who radiated so much spirituality and with such a blithe nature. He was lovingkindness personified. One morning when I came to make my confession, I found him lying in bed, clearly very weak—I knew that he had been ill. But he heard my confession, and we talked for several minutes as usual. He was on the way to the next life, he told me with deep contentment, for all he wanted now was to cross that threshold. Moreover, the manuscript for the last volume in the series lay ready for the printer. When I asked whether he would pray for me on the other side, he replied that he would indeed, more than gladly. A couple of hours later Dom Guerric came into church when we were about to begin the service. 'Father Joseph has just passed away. Peace be with him.' It was a moment when I felt profoundly aware of the privilege of having known this man who had so convincingly lived up to the best in his vocation— and also the privilege of having been among the last who had talked with him. A saintly life, one to emulate.

Someone else I mention with great pleasure is my teacher in cosmology, Father Thomas Litt, whose everyday occupation was as the monastery's chief economic administrator, in itself a totally time-consuming task. But his great interest in life was the medieval—and especially Thomas Aquinas's—vision of the universe, which in no way resembled our own.

The father had two doctorates from the university of Louvain. Unforgettable is the adjective most apt for his descriptions of the medieval concept of the movement of the celestial bodies and their interaction: the earth, the centre of the universe, was certainly round, but immobile; both the sun and the stars were set in transparent spheres that moved in relation to the earth and one another, linked together by an extraordinarily complicated system of connecting rods. As the centuries passed and new stars were discovered with the aid of improved methods, astronomers had to resort to more and more intricate systems of interacting spheres. 'People of that time', Father Thomas would say, 'could watch the night sky in fascination, amazed that these spheres could rotate— all simultaneously—without the slightest creak being audible. The Creator had indeed made all things well.' Over the course of several months I was presented, often in detail, with the implications of this astonishing cosmology, only to move on afterwards to its irrevocable breakdown, thanks to Galileo, Kepler, and Newton. Father Thomas was a happy man with a large measure of charisma—knowledgeable and intelligent, and with no grudge or bitterness about anything or anybody.[4]

One day I was stopped at the door into the library by the same Father Thomas: 'Do you know anyone by the name of Sigurd?' he asked, as if sounding me out. 'Yes, I know a couple of Sigurds', I answered—and strangely enough thought first of Sigurd Leeder, the head of the Jooss school in England. 'Well, a person of that name has died', said Father Thomas in a gentle tone. 'Might it perhaps be a relation?' He consulted a piece of paper in his hand. 'Let me see' I said quickly, guessing the connection. It was a telegram—to me: SIGURD DIED QUIETLY TODAY LOVE MOTHER. We stood there in the doorway looking at each other. How could it happen that one of my teachers went round with a telegram addressed to me, yet already opened? The father looked slightly confused. 'The prior is away,' he explained, 'so I have to take charge of incoming mail. I didn't know the addressee, but on opening it I saw it was from Norway.' I understood at once: WILLEM GRAN was scarcely a name he could know, for as far as the monastery was concerned I was only Brother John. I nodded to show there was no ill-feeling, and went off to write a letter of condolence to Mother who had lost her husband after over fifteen years of marriage. Sigurd's health had been failing slowly but surely over the last year or so. Perhaps it was best like that, for after all, he was eighteen years older than she was.

'When Sigurd died,' wrote Mother in her reply, 'I was sitting with him. So I experienced it all very clearly: He did not die—*he moved on.*' I understood that this experience made a deep impression on Mother, who had never been particularly religious. Life—and death—are often our best teachers.

Like all so-called Trappist monasteries, Scourmont had agriculture in the widest sense of the word as its basic industry. Forty cows provided the milk for the modern dairy where after a long process it became a well-flavoured Port Salut cheese. However, as anyone who has spent any time in Belgium knows, it is beer that people there think of in connection with the Trappists. Sometimes the wind carried with it the noise and odours from our own brewery, for Scourmont, too, had this supplementary industry. It could happen that, as an afternoon job, we students had to keep an eye on the conveyor belts. An enormous machine did almost all the work—washing, rinsing, filling, and corking seven thousand bottles an hour. No contemplative silence here! There were many working shifts of this kind when we were divided beween the beginning and the end of the process. But we were never asked to take part in the actual brewing, which was in the hands of experts, mostly lay employees. The managers, however, were monks who had gone through all stages of the business and knew it as well as anybody. The head of the brewery, Father Theodore, was especially proud of the feastday beer which was pressed up to the nine degrees of alcohol the fermentation process could attain without the addition of spirit. On the principal feastdays it sometimes happened that we were allowed a bottle for dinner—unless it had all been sold, as sometimes happened.

So the monks themselves drank beer? Yes they did, but normally only a low-alcohol brew, of two degrees' strength. The small bottles we were given with dinner were never put on the market. Scourmont's products were indeed among the best, it was claimed, despite the fact that Belgium is the nation with the highest beer consumption per inhabitant in the world, with an overwhelming choice. The brewery sold its production without difficulty—and without advertising. Some of it went to export. Today I even sometimes see Scourmont bottles in supermarkets in distant Corsica.[5]

I was told that the abbey's wide-ranging farming activities were only just managing to survive financially, and this was also the case for the other monasteries, and indeed for agriculture as a whole in Belgium. Without the beer the prospects would be dim, also for the daughter house in Wales.

In Scourmont, unlike Caldey, I had no set area of responsibility, but was allocated various tasks as they arose. That was, until the day when our organist—also here called Father Edmond (although here spelled with an *o*)—took me under his wing. For now I was to have proper organ lessons: pedals, registers, three keyboards. The harmonium, which I had once found so complicated, was nothing compared to this. The father, who was also our teacher in New Testament exegesis, had a passion for exactitude, so there was no question of my playing in church before he was thoroughly satisfied. But at long last the day came—followed by a whole string of corrections. I found, however, that the accompaniment (not only of the Divine Office, but also of Mass itself) gradually, with practice, came more easily to hand—and not least to foot! It was not long before the father and I divided the organ duties between us, and it was obvious that he felt relieved and pleased to be able once again to take part in the choir liturgy.

The high level at Scourmont was not least reflected in the outside lecturers who were now and then invited to address the community. They were often university professors who brought news of the latest advances in fields as dissimilar as nuclear physics and the Qumran parchment scrolls. Close to Christmas we had the fascinating experience of a week's retreat with the well-known French theologian, the Jesuit priest (later cardinal) Jean Daniélou. We hung on his every word as he expounded with vigorous and profound insight and a delivery that was a joy to hear. When I had the chance to have a few words with him one afternoon, it turned out that in Paris he knew several Nordic Catholics, some of whom he corresponded with. He particularly mentioned the Swedish author Gunnel Vallquist, whom I too had met and with whom I later developed a warm friendship that has lasted ever since.[6]

I completed my philosophy examination with a study on Plato's and Aristotle's theories of knowledge. I only wish I could still remember something of the content of that paper.

As usual I spent the summer as a farm labourer on Caldey. When I myself had been the tractor-driver, I had had Louis, our seventeen-year-old English applicant, as assistant. Now he was a lay brother and tractor-driver, and our roles were reversed. I realized that this was healthy from a spiritual point of view, but it wasn't entirely easy to stomach.

In August there was an unexpected hurricane unlike anything anyone could remember having experienced at this time of year. I had to hang on to the steering wheel to avoid being blown off the tractor. But it was even worse at sea. An open boat manned by a father with his four children on a summer outing was wrecked against the cliffs not far from Caldey. The thirteen-year-old eldest boy managed to struggle ashore and contact some farm people. When they reached the scene, they found the bodies of his brother and sister on the rocks, while another brother had been trapped in a cave by the high tide. The father had disappeared—with the undertow.

I have already mentioned that my father never came nearer Caldey than to Tenby. However, in Bergen he had a visit from me, and it happened like this. In 1953 the Norwegian Lutheran Church and the Catholic Church each celebrated the eight-hundredth anniversary of the institution of the Norwegian ecclesiastical province in Nidaros—by the English cardinal Nicholas Brekespear (later Pope Adrian IV)—which meant that Norway had her own archbishop until the Reformation. The celebrations were to take place around Olso (in late July) and a large number of guests were invited. The principal Catholic guest was the archbishop of Westminster, Cardinal Bernard Griffin, appointed papal legate for the occasion. Since the Cistercians had played a considerable rôle in the High Middle Ages in Norway, an invitation was also sent to me, as the only Norwegian in the Order. Dom Albert more or less ordered me to go, although I, myself, had little desire for any further leaves of absence.

On 22nd July in perfect weather I crossed the North Sea to Kristiansand, and continued by train to Oslo where the celebrations were already in full swing—for Pope Pius XII had used the opportunity to re-establish the hierarchy in South Norway, so that Oslo now acquired the status of an independent diocese. At the same time Central Norway's prefecture was raised to the rank of a vicariate apostolic.

In Oslo I met again an old acquaintance from wartime Rome, the Danish bishop Theodor Suhr, who as a Benedictine insisted on having me at hand as a colleague. He had come by car and had taken it upon himself to be 'chauffeur' for Cardinal Griffin, so on several occasions I was a fellow passenger. The cardinal sat in front to have a better view. It was easy to see that the otherwise so energetic prelate was now a marked man. A massive stroke had led to a state of passivity which doubtless was as strange to him, himself, as it must have seemed to his associates.

Not only 'the whole of Catholic Norway' was gathered together for the celebrations. Many guests from abroad, not least German prelates, cast an 'arch-Catholic' grandeur over the festivities, which most likely for that very reason were fully covered in the media.

It is doubtful whether anyone in the city of Trondheim had ever seen anything to match the procession past the ancient Nidaros cathedral and on over Elgeseter Bridge. Several hundred nuns in their different forms of dress; many bishops and prelates in liturgical vestments of various colours; Dominicans in their black and white and Franciscans in their brown habits; all the other orders and congregations in their clerical robes, not to mention schools with banners, emblems, and brass bands, as well as a milling crowd of both Norwegian-based and foreign Catholics. To Norwegian eyes all this amounted to an almost southern-style pageant.

The culmination of the procession was a dark red American cabriolet, on loan locally. In it sat the cardinal smiling and waving, he, too, red—both his robes and his face. In front of the vehicle I strode along in my choir habit, holding the processional cross on high. And above us shone the sun— despite all threatening forecasts.

The ceremonial pontifical Mass, the Cardinal's Mass as it was generally dubbed, could not be celebrated in the cathedral. The submission had been turned down. The Norwegian Technical University in Trondheim, however, had made its grandiose stairway-hall available. A large sanctuary-space had been prepared with an altar and all that was necessary, so that one had the impression of entering a veritable cathedral. The local Protestant bishop sat on the guest-bench, joining in all the singing, standing and sitting with visible gusto. A warm-hearted man of the Church!

The celebrations continued the following day at Stiklestad, the place of Saint Olav's martyrdom, where the excellently restored medieval church was kindly put at the disposal of the Catholics, presumably to make amends for the rebuff from the cathedral. It was my impression that this whole effort, which taxed our small Catholic entities almost to breaking point, had a positive effect on Norwegians of the same persuasion as myself. They let it be known that their Church had here and now come up to their expectations—and that they were proud to belong to it.

Bishop Suhr, his *ad hoc* chauffeur—a young Dane who had never before been out of Denmark—and I drove by Hamar and Oslo to the south of Norway where we made an impromptu visit to Mother's place on the coast. And she was happy, partly at having me back (even if only for two nights) and partly at meeting the charming and cultivated Bishop Suhr, someone who could give such a lively account of the time when he himself was a convert and had reached the same point of life where I now found myself.

Afterwards I visited Father who, hardly believing it was true, treated me like the returned prodigal son, while his housekeeper Marie knew no bounds in contriving wonderful meals to please me.

The boat for England brought me back to Newcastle, after which I returned to my very different monkish world, where there was no mistaking that the age-old slogan *Ora et labora* (pray and work) was still honoured—even if I could occasionally be tempted to say that the Cistercians' motto must be *Labora et labora*. That I was needed both at the harmonium and in the garage, as well as on the farm, was easy to see, and this was a source of tacit pleasure. Here they had use for me, and showed it openly.

We got the harvest in without any great loss, which could often be caused by too much rain. The fine, old buildings were stowed full of wheat, barley, and oats. We threshed, carried sacks, lifted sacks, lowered sacks, and stumbled over sacks from sunrise to sunset. The dubious pleasure of feeding the sheaves into the threshing mill fell to me—dubious, because the grain was mixed with thistles which found their way into your fingers and the palms of your hands, only to stay put there. After this was over came the drying process, which was also generally my job. That year we had installed a machine with an engine-driven drum for producing dry air, attached to a metering device that showed the degree of moisture in each sack. More mechanization in the interest of progress! In its Welsh setting, Caldey Farm was now something of a model estate, even if on a modest scale.

Father Anthony, forever on the lookout for some means to overcome the problem of the tide, was burning to acquire a helicopter, but he was stopped in his tracks by Dom Albert who disapproved of everything that might attract any form of limelight.

At the end of September I was back at Scourmont, but not without problems, for the weather-gods gave full vent to their feelings as so often before. It blew up to yet another disastrous storm. A lightship went down not far from Caldey, though the crew were saved by our own *Lollipop*. However, a few days' delay, what did that matter?

Actually it was the studies at Scourmont that held some promise of progress in my existence. I could now begin my theology course. The monastery had no fewer than eight teachers engaged in instruction, as well as Dom Guerric in church history, and Father Charles Dumont (one of our philosophy teachers, formerly on Caldey) in patristics: a teaching panel and syllabus equal to any. That autumn Caldey sent us three of its theology students (which was a notable sacrifice), all with greater seniority educationwise than I had. The number of students was thus doubled, something which still further served to justify Scourmont's considerable academic investment.

On Sundays we 'Caldeyans' were allowed to arrange tea parties in the guesthouse—a quite exceptional variation in our otherwise strict pattern of life. It was a sort of safety valve perhaps. The fact is that being forced to get through our curriculum in French was an advantage intellectually and as far as language was concerned, but at the same time a considerable extra burden. At any event we had a good time then, sipping tea 'made the English way' and commenting on our teachers' foibles with the lack of respect typical in students.

One problem begins to loom: I am in danger of settling in at Scourmont. My relations with my brethren are developing all the time and continue to enrich me. The spiritual and intellectual level is as captivating as it is challenging. To study theology here feels like a gift. The Belgian students are in general considerably younger and without any complicating background experience. In comparison to our local fellow students, we 'Caldeyans' are in a way more advanced. But the community has invested its best talents in this study course, and they seem to regard us relatively mature students from the daughter house as a stimulus. Everyone gives his best.

What is impressive about the instruction is the teaching staff's store of knowledge. That the father who lectures us on Old Testament exegesis has a fluent command of Hebrew—with and without vowel signs—is simply taken for granted here. At least I understood much better than before what an advantage it is to have a teacher capable of putting across knowledge in his own personal way.

The study of philosophy, which I had behind me, with its emphasis on pure knowledge, on the history and influence of speculative thought, and on psychology, had demanded clarity and intellectual stringency, but not only that: the study had shown itself to be the prerequisite for gaining deeper insight into the revealed mysteries, even if these will always retain their essential character of being inexpressible. In fact I was struck by a telling definition of a mystery: *Something that is clear in itself, but not to us.* You attempt to get to the heart of the matter, knowing all the time that because of your total dependence on your senses you can only succeed to a limited extent. Of course you can understand, clearly and with conviction, *that* something exists and *that* it must have certain particular qualities—for example, that if God exists, he must be everlasting and almighty—but without being able to understand *how.* Even the greatest minds have had to admit defeat in front of a door they could not open, let alone enter. Thomas Aquinas's way of systematizing Aristotle's philosophy, in order to throw as much light as humanly possible on the theological implications, took me into new territory with enlarging horizons.

The study of theology was obviously more complex, with the approaches to what we call revelation correspondingly signposted with question marks. In the course of disciplines such as, for example, Bible studies, dogmatic theology, and ethics, it became clear that no one by his own endeavours could come much closer to the perennial truths than the great Greek philosophers had managed to do. When studying philosophy, how boundlessly had I not admired the strength and universality in the thought processes of an Aristotle and a Plato! On the other hand, it was strange to note how the *religious* universe of these giants was riddled with extraordinary legends—of gods, goddesses, and other creatures beset by human faults and frailties of far from noble character. Antiquity had certainly made gods for itself, but in its own image.

Christian theology on the contrary starts out from truths about which we for our part can know nothing certain. I was increasingly fascinated by the degree to which *revelation* now was a central concept—and must be so. For even if we ourselves may have recognized the inherent necessity of the existence of one being above all others, perhaps even of an almighty Creator and Preserver of the universe, our mental limitations make it impossible for us to envisage this being other than with the help of images which we immediately have to reject as totally inadequate. The eternal cannot be perceived.

More important still, perhaps, is to recognize that we ourselves cannot know for what purpose the universe has been created, much less the meaning of our own existence. Has this Being—call it God—communicated anything about these things to us humans? If so, in what way? History brims over with 'answers'—answers often full of superstition, quaint

fetishism, and muddled mythologies that may often call forth
a smile.

The history of religion was a fascinating study which gave
me insight into man's timeless need to believe—to believe in
something, almost anything, at all events in something greater
than himself. For people have an inborn instinct which fum-
blingly, often yearningly, searches for The Absolute in one
form or another. There is no lack of 'answers', whether free
or for sale, often 'do-it-yourself' answers making no attempt
to provide evidence or logical backing. Occult sects have always flourished in abundance—today, strangely enough, more
than ever.

I learned that you had to separate the wheat from the chaff
in this multiplicity, that you had to steer clear of artificial-
ity, and take a closer look at the great religions of the world
and any claim they made to being messengers from the lord
of the universe. In keeping with this I could cut out a fair
number. Even Buddhism, for Buddha—pure philosopher as
he was—never himself made any claim to being a prophet. In
the final tally three great religions remain, all of them claiming
to be mouthpieces for the creator of the universe: Judaism,
Christianity, and Islam. The fascinating thing is how they are
linked together, for all three regard Abraham as their 'progeni-
tor': Jews and Christians through Isaac, and Muslims through
Ishmael who was Abraham's illegitimate son by the slave-
woman Hagar. Moses, too, is their common property. The
Jews' Yahweh, the Christians' God, and the Muslims' Allah
are recognized by all three religions as being the same god-
head: the everlasting Creator and Preserver of the universe.

Through the theological studies, I acquired growing insight
into how Judaism in the Old Testament and Christianity in
the New hang closely together—the latter as an inherent consequence of the former. Both have their core in one being:
The Messiah, the saviour promised by Yahweh. While the Jews
are obdurate in the belief that he is yet to come, the Christians
firmly contend that he did so two thousand years ago.

It was exciting to have the sense of looking through a mag-
nifying glass at the step-by-step process of revelation throughout four thousand years of the history of religion, beginning
with Yahweh's commands to Abr(ah)am, who believed all
that was made known to him and who willingly did all he
was ordered to do.

Two thousand years of a pedagogic process steered by the
divine will seemed to me to be crystallized in the historic
course of events leading up to God's ultimate intervention
in history, as it is recounted by the evangelists Matthew and
Luke and which culminates in God letting himself be born
into the world as man. Matthew, who time after time recalls
the Old Testament, maintains that the longed-for Messiah
was of much greater consequence than a prophet on a level
with Moses, Isaiah, or Jeremiah. The New Testament shows
us how the limits of Judaism were transcended 'in the fullness
of time'. Here one sees how revelation, which until now had
been reserved for a particular people, is opened to *all* mankind.
And here, too, one finds the answers to the questions: Who
is the Creator, and what is the intention behind his works?
Above all, one understands that Christianity is a *person*—Jesus
Christ being the only person we come across in the whole
of history who not only claims to be the Word of God, but
himself to be God.

Lengthy and intensive study on the person of Jesus, on his
pronouncements, his life, work, and miracles, together with
the account of his passion, death, and resurrection, throws
light on the underlying links that serve to confirm that Christ
was—and is—what he claims to be. And it is not least against
this background that a serious study of Mohammed's claim
to be Allah's ultimate prophet must even pale in comparison,
for Mohammed never claimed to be anything other or more
than precisely that.

It goes without saying that Christianity stands or falls with
the identity of Jesus of Nazareth. During my study-time,
what I had from the start and long afterwards experienced
as something existentially moving, became a lesson in logical

development, a source of insight into the supernatural, and a sacred abundance that not only spoke to the heart, but also satisfied the understanding. Once again I was confirmed in my belief that the arrow had found its true mark the day I sought admission into the Catholic Church.

The study that claimed most of my interest was Holy Scripture. But now I was subjected to a process of 'demystification' which was not easy to take. For here science came first: the results of research. My horizon had to be widened in several fields simultaneously. At times I had to struggle not to let secondary considerations invade my somewhat rudimentary relationship to God. The less important aspects kept trying to get the upper hand. Heart and head could be so at odds that it was sometimes hard to know which was winning, though things tended, all in all, to even out in the long run. I was consoled by the thought that I did not intend to be a career theologian. Nor a teacher. The latter was more suited to my three university-educated colleagues. Or so I thought.

I was grateful to Dom Albert for having given us this chance of intellectual and spiritual nourishment, for Caldey was still far from being able to offer anything similar. Meanwhile, having the four of us absent for so long was in itself a sacrifice of a tangible nature, so also the community in Wales deserved our gratitude.

Both my parents visited me during this Belgian period of my existence. Mother, alone now after many years of busy married life, had spent some weeks on the Canary Islands. She arranged to come to us on her return journey, but without knowing anything about either southern Belgium's raw climate or the inhabitants' peasant toughness (or frugality). She was taken to a damp, cold, and unattractive guest house for ladies, without warm water (not uncommon in the region), and developed bronchitis overnight. She therefore made a swift departure and booked herself into a hotel in the nearest small town, Chimay. So I took the tram to join her there— instead of the other way round. (Belgium has an unusual system: the trams run not only in the cities, but also on an extensive rural network connecting smaller towns.)

After a few days she felt restored enough to pay a visit to the monastery, but I hardly imagine she was thrilled by what she found. Dreary brick buildings from before the turn of the century were not what she had expected. I had no doubt forgotten to tell her that the abbey did not, as she had imagined, date from the Middle Ages. She was able to assure herself, however, that her son, the monk, thrived here too and was in excellent shape.

Father came as well, and true to form would not set foot in the monastery, refusing even to come within range. So I had to visit him, too—in Mother's former hotel in Chimay, no less. He brightened up and thought I had never looked better—thus his visit was a relief for both of us. Both my parents seemed to be beginning to accept the apparently inevitable: that as far as my life was concerned the die had finally been cast.

In February 1954 we students were witness to the event that had so long been prepared for: Scourmont's send-off for those who were to found the African daughter house.

What was interesting in this connection was the new tendency within the Order to establish monasteries in the so-called Third World. Previously this had not been the case, quite the opposite. New foundations were generally made in areas where the Catholic faith was traditionally strong, the reason being that suitable local vocations could then be counted on. An attempt in the last century to establish a monastery in black Africa had resulted in its rapidly becoming a mission post which had to be separated fom the Order, later flourishing and expanding as an independent mission institute (the Marianhill Missionaries). Since the last war, however, our General Chapters had begun to pay serious heed to the many requests coming in from mission bishops who wished to have a contemplative monastery in their neighbourhood, not least as a centre of prayer for the spread of Christianity in the country.

The guidelines later issued by the Order laid down that our abbots were welcome to make foundations in mission areas provided that binding agreements were made with the local hierarchy to the effect that the members were not to be drawn into the active apostolate, nor to an excessive degree into the ordinary spiritual counselling. Without exception the aim must always be to maintain the contemplative character of the monasteries. The result was that in the space of a short time many foundations were made—both for monks and for nuns—in areas that lacked the traditional prerequisites. At present, apart from its many abbeys in Europe and North America, the Order (that is, the Order of the Strict Observance) has monasteries for monks in Argentina, Chile, Mexico, Venezuela, Brazil, the Dominican Republic, New Caledonia, Algeria, Cameroon, Kenya, Madagascar, Zaïre (Mokoto!), Angola, Benin, Nigeria, Morocco, Lebanon, Australia, New Zealand, the Philippines, Japan, Hong Kong, Taiwan, and Indonesia—and on the Danish island of Bornholm.

As a rule, it may be said that the initiatives come from the bishops, and seldom from the monasteries themselves. The fact that the Cistercian Order is especially qualified for this type of expansion has its basis in the almost thousand-year-old practice which ensures the founder's permanent responsibility for the daughter house, including, for example, willingness to follow up both the economic and recruitment aspects on a long-term basis.

Scourmont had thus agreed to be responsible for a foundation near Goma on the shores of Lake Kivu. The place lay in the Belgian Congo (the Democratic Republic of Congo) not far from the frontier with Burundi. For a long time the monastery had been buzzing with strange names, names which in recent years have been much in the news and with tragic connotations: Bujumbura, Burundi, Goma, Kivu, Rwanda. And now the day of leave-taking had arrived.

The large room in the guesthouse was transformed into a festive setting for the occasion. Dom Guerric and the six 'swarming' monks were placed at the high table. There were speeches, music, four-part singing, and the presentation of gifts. With dispensation from the silence rule, the celebration held few reminders of monastery life, except the black-and-white habits. Yet there was a hint of sadness, for Lake Kivu was very far away and no one knew what the distant (or even the near) future would bring. For now Belgium was in the process of decolonizing to let the Congo become an independent state. With hindsight it could be said that if the superiors of Scourmont had been able to foresee even a fraction of what was to come, they would not have dared to launch this venture.

The leave-taking must have been agonizing for those who set off, for each of them had once upon a time bound himself to Scourmont for life and was now—despite all the muster of free will—being inwardly almost torn to shreds. To leave like this for good was more than just dying a little. In my mind's eye I can still see the bus with the waving pioneers roll slowly out of the gate. Most of them never came back.

After all that has happened since, I feel I must add that the new monastery, Our Lady of Mokoto, lying 1,750 metres above sea level at a remote lake where even a hen snatched by a leopard was big news for days, has survived many terrible situations arising from the conflicts in Rwanda. In May 1996 the complex was attacked by the Hutus because some Tutsis were said to be hiding there. The monks were warned and managed to escape in time. But no mercy was shown to between 100 and 150 people who had fled to the church or other buildings for shelter and refused to leave.

The handful of monks who later succeeded in returning under police protection found the destruction and desecration of the monastery far less painful than the fact that also people from the surrounding district had taken part in the plundering—people whom for years the monks had helped in all possible ways.

Today, after having for long lived a divided existence in other African monasteries, most of the community is reunited on a property close to the Congolese border with Goma, still hoping to return and rebuild their destroyed monastery.

The thought of requesting to be transferred to Scourmont for good smouldered away inside me, for I felt I had become part of the life there. It came to nothing, however, because suddenly there was a new and desperate need for us younger ones on Caldey, to which we had returned after passing our exam.

Summer went by, to all appearances normally, with more than enough work for us mentally exhausted theology students. But was there not a sense of something oppressive in the air? Dom Albert looked tired and anxious. It was not until the beginning of September that we younger monks understood that something out of the ordinary was brewing. Under pressure from the previous General Chapter,[7] the abbot general, Dom Gabriel Sortais, had sent us a Visitor, the Irish Dom Columban, abbot of a newly established monastery in Scotland. Each of us separately was called in to a private talk with him, and the abbot had many questions. As time passed the atmosphere seemed to be more and more charged. Dom Albert, now looking even paler and worse than before, suddenly ceased to attend Divine Office, where otherwise, like an example to all, he was always present.

Towards the end of the visitation the whole story came out: With tears in his eyes Dom Columban told us that, in accordance with the authority placed in him by the General Chapter (but which we others now heard about for the first time) he had sent our prior back to Scourmont, allegedly for a recuperative stay—for an indefinite period. Dom Albert was said to have himself chosen to leave without any farewell, which in the event would have been deeply painful for all parties. Dom Columban added his personal opinion that Dom Albert ought not to return to Caldey, where the climate was clearly too much for him—as well as other circumstances. We guessed at inner conflicts in addition to health problems (Dom Albert's perpetual Anglicizing measures?). To talk about this, however, was impossible, for sign language was inadequate in such situations. As a consequence, we of the younger generation tried independently to sort out our thoughts about the mysterious 'dispatch'. It was not a good time. Fortunately we were needed so much at our various posts that the priorities were clear. Life had to go on.

I myself had my hands full, after overnight having to take on responsibility for all the machines, the garage, and the repairs.

The former abbot of Cîteaux, Dom Godefroid Belorgey, had voluntarily retired owing to illness, and now, at the end of a long period of convalescence, was staying with us. In reality he should have gone back before the visitation, but had been requested to remain.

To say that Dom Godefroid was a legend within the Order is no exaggeration. As a high-ranking French cavalry officer—moreover an atheist—he had had a dramatic conversion experience which had caused him to dismount from his horse, throw off his uniform, and knock on the monastery door. Of course it was a long time since this had taken place, but his reputation as one of the Order's great and remarkable personalities was no less. He would tell the story of his conversion over and over again, as if it had only just happened. Now, in a way, he became an angel of rescue, because before Dom Columban left he managed to arrange that Dom Godefroid—then seventy-five years of age—should act as the monastery's temporary superior. That he neither spoke nor understood English was naturally a handicap, and that he daily gave long spiritual discourses to monks, most of whom failed to grasp a single word of them, was another. Nonetheless, this rock-solid Abbot Emeritus with his humanity and his quaint, humorous expression became a reassuring factor and a rallying point. None of the young, not even those who were entitled to do so, deserted Caldey during this difficult and insecure period. (Brother Stephen chose to postpone his final vows one year, but that was all.) The insecurity stemmed mainly from the fact that no one could envisage what the future would bring.

During the General Chapter at Cîteaux in mid-September —in which both Dom Albert and Dom Godefroid, as well as the Visitor, Dom Columban, participated—it was decided that our prior would not return to Caldey. To us younger ones this seemed especially hard, but individually we just had to steel ourselves to look forward—and upward.

One name was more and more often mentioned as a possible new prior: Father Eugene Boylan from the southern Irish abbey of Roscrea, the monastery that had helped Caldey by lending us both the novice master Father Shanahan and various other monks, some of whom were still actively engaged at Caldey.

Father Boylan was far from being a nobody. After studying music in Vienna and turning his back on a career as a concert pianist, he had been an assistant professor in nuclear physics at University College, Dublin. Now, long since established as a choir monk with spiritual counselling as his speciality, he had published several books on the spiritual life, some of which looked like becoming classics in the field.[8] He often gave retreats, and during my time in the novitiate, he certainly made a strong impression. Now he seemed to be the only realistic candidate, for there was one thing everyone was agreed upon: the Anglicizing must continue; here there was no way back. But it was certainly a welcome point in his favour that Eugene Boylan also proved to have French at his command.

One day we learned from Dom Godefroid during chapter that Father Boylan—who just now was in Australia finding a suitable site for a foundation of the continent's first Cistercian monastery (planned by Roscrea)—had agreed to act as Caldey's new superior until circumstances permitted a normal election. The news was met with delight and a surge of optimism, for everybody had been greatly taken by Father Eugene's inspiring lectures and mature personality. With him at the tiller we should no doubt get on an even keel again.

The weather-gods are once more up to mischief and produce a night of horrendous rain. Very early in the morning a monk who intends to go up to the farm wants to open the door from the cloister to the fire-damaged library—his customary shortcut. The door is wrenched out of his hand by the mass of water, and soaked to the skin, he has to seek shelter. Everyone possible turns out to help rechannel the water out of another door before too much of it finds its way to the scriptorium, the refectory, and the sacristy.

As far as I was concerned, it was high time to be able to look to the future with a reasonable degree of certainty, for in February 1955 I should normally either have to make my solemn profession, binding myself for life, or else pack my bag (there would be little to put in it). The tempting idea of a possible transfer to Scourmont came up again. A long talk with Dom Godefroid, however, made me agree to postponing the matter until after Father Boylan had taken over. Dom Godefroid disliked the thought of sharing in the responsibility for such an important decision during his temporary regime.

The weather-gods at it again. Full storm! Naturally we are used to the wind blowing so it howls in midwinter, but not like this . . . It is not only howling. There are ominous cracking sounds, and heavy thuds can be heard during the night office. In the grey light of dawn we go out on individual tours of inspection. Trees down all over the place. Later Brother Joachim, who is in charge of this 'department', counts fifty-two large trees, some broken and others uprooted. Added to that, there are damaged roofs, and various minor installations have been swept away.

Christmas is getting nearer, and we struggle to remedy the storm damage. Our Sunday afternoon concerts are especially welcome under the circumstances. We listen to Bach's B-minor Mass directed by Herbert von Karajan—surreptitiously, for it is actually a Christmas present from Mother, who has once again sent an earmarked cheque. There is enough left over for a new recording of Handel's *Messiah*. We always looked forward with silent joy to these Sunday hours filled with music in the guesthouse chapel.

The message finally comes in mid-February: our new prior is due to arrive. I am sent to collect him. But his advent is rather prosaic. Since Dom Eugene's post is temporary, it entails no formal ceremonies. The big bell is rung, however, and as far as possible the monks turn out to greet him and then introduce themselves. Dom Godefroid immediately leaves for Belgium and his new post as convent chaplain to a community of Cistercian nuns in Chimay.

Dom Eugene, who has never been a superior—let alone a prior—and who is also new to this island situation, has a lot to familiarize himself with. His spiritual talks during the early morning chapter meetings are often masterly in form, giving much food for heart and mind in the course of the day. Strange to say, even so, Dom Eugene never becomes a really venerated prior, mainly because Dom Albert is so much in our minds and greatly missed. As well as that, Dom Eugene's Irish temperament can sometimes get out of hand. Yet, like his predecessor, he is a man with wide horizons, and during his time the monastery finally gets the economic upswing it badly needs.

We even begin to produce scent. It happens like this: Stanislaus, our Flemish lay brother, has for years, greatly to the admiration of visitors, cultivated lavender both in his tucked-away herb garden and on the grass in front of the post office, the so-called Village Common, and many small muslin bags containing his dried flowers are sold in our two souvenir shops. Lavender grows readily on Caldey; nevertheless, the brother has to use more and more of his time simply trying to keep up with the increased demand. Father Anthony, still our administrator, now persuades him to go in for the production of lavender water, which is said to be more profitable. The acquisition of a suitable formula leads to a further expansion of the enterprise, which also includes other fragrant herbs. A Polish expert is invited over, and lives on Caldey at regular intervals in order to compound new products and to supervise production. Dom Eugene supports the scheme wholeheartedly.

Father Anthony keeps at it until a small but authentic scent industry is successfully established. And one day the community is informed that 'we' have actually opened our own shop in the West End of London. Although Brother Stanislaus cultivates several new scented plants, raw materials in the form of essences from distant, exotic places are used more and more. 'Caldey Number One' is the name of the perfume which will come to be a market hit—and which still today has a loyal clientele. The much-needed lifeline for Caldey's economy seems to have been found.

I felt uneasy at the thought of possibly being involved in this venture, for it was impossible not to notice which brethren worked in the branch. When they came into choir, they smelled like—yes, prostitutes (not that my experience in that field was more than hypothetical). And the poor monks themselves had no effective countermeasures, for the fumes from the essences permeated their clothes, skin, and hair. Naturally I kept my thoughts to myself, since anything else would have shown a lack of tact. For my own part I preferred thistles in my hands and the reek of engine oil.

Towards the end of the three-year period I had to face the choice between taking the solemn vows (well knowing that these would apply until my dying day) or requesting a postponement—or else leaving. If an application to take the perpetual vows is put forward, the prior must call together all the solemnly professed monks to a closed chapter meeting where, after having expressed his own opinion on the matter, he proclaims a secret ballot. If the monk is approved, a church ceremony for the solemn profession follows—usually on the third anniversary of the first profession. From then on I would be bound to the community, as it would be to me. I could neither leave nor be sent away. It says a good deal that a monk's primary tie is to the monastery, not to the Order—of which, indeed, he is only a member by virtue of belonging to the monastery.

Since things were uncertain, I had not informed my family of my decision to make solemn profession. Mother had got wind of it, however, from a mutual friend who was Catholic. This hurt her feelings and occasioned a depressed letter. To crown it all, at precisely this point of time she 'had' to read Monica Baldwin's autobiography *I Leap over the Wall,* which another well-meaning friend had thrust upon her. In any case, everyone was talking about this nun who had managed to free herself from 'the yoke of the cloister'. Mother and I had an intense correspondence on the subject, ending with her announcing her intention of coming to Caldey in connection with the step I was about to take.

The date set was 25th April, the feastday of Mark the Evangelist. I developed influenza and felt terrible, but was determined not to be confined to bed. When I had been about to take my first vows three years previously, I had not been in doubt about doing, and wanting to do, the right thing. Now I felt strangely terrified at the thought of the irrevocable nature of what I was about to undertake. The temptation, if not indeed the Tempter, whispered inside me: 'Do you really believe God is demanding this of you—never again to be your own master?' For indeed, the Evil One himself seemed to me to be at work here, clearly an expert on how the strategy should be planned. I had been warned about exactly this, yet even so I went through tortures of the soul. Such a total, lifelong promise suddenly seemed to me to be utterly frightening. Alternately shivering with cold and burning with fever, I passed this last night without the slightest chance of sleep. Mother was unhappy. She could see that I was afraid, moreover she knew very well that I was then and there free to turn back to a normal (in her eyes) existence. What kept me from doing so?

In the depths of my being I had no real grounds for doubt. Five years had strengthened me in a vocation which not least manifested itself in this: that I sensed the steering hand on my shoulder. The anxiety which now welled up from inside me was something which I had not felt before and for which there were no logical grounds, therefore I did not dare do otherwise than continue on to the end of the road. I prayed for help with all my might and main, but did not feel I was granted more than the barest minimum required to get me through the eye of the needle. But it was enough.

Solemn profession takes place halfway through the solemn Mass in the monastery church. After the Gospel the liturgy is interrupted, and I am summoned to the altar where Dom Eugene puts to me in Latin the prescribed questions concerning the integrity of my purpose and my desire to give myself to God for ever—in accordance with the Rule of Saint Benedict and the Constitutions of the Cistercian Order. After my *yes*, now given with restored deep conviction and pronounced kneeling before Dom Eugene, the prior gives a moving address, words to which I know Mother is listening with deep attention—and a bleeding heart. Finally I sign the vows, written in Latin on parchment. Rolled up and sealed, the document is then put into my hands so that I shall myself place it on the altar, where—mysteriously admonishing—it remains lying during the rest of the ceremony. In my heart I know there is now no way back. But an indescribable relief and a profound sense of peace take over—even if I also feel (as the saying goes) like a wet rag.

Sixteen

CONSECRATED ANCHORAGE

I N THE SUMMER OF 1955 Caldey received a visit we had been looking forward to with anticipation. The abbot general of the Order, Dom Gabriel Sortais, came on an official visitation. Some years before he had waited in vain for the chance to cross over from Tenby, but was forced to continue to Ireland in order to fulfil his tight schedule. This time things went better.

Almost everything about Dom Gabriel seemed to exceed normal limits. He was large in himself, but with a body completely filled by an integrated personality of considerable charm. His enthusiasm was infectious, whether through spiritual discourses or accounts of his rounds of visitations to the monasteries that took up most of his time. Unfortunately he spoke only his mother tongue, so everything had to be translated, with the interpreter's down-to-earth English often falling short in comparison with Dom Gabriel's poetic and well-phrased French. When he addressed the community it was fascinating for those of us who could follow the original to watch his expression, for while the interpreter translated, Dom Gabriel used the time to think out the next paragraph which was already reflected in his naturally expressive face.

It seemed obvious that this man had been cut out to be propelled upward—from ordinary monk to abbot for a large monastery (Bellefontaine), then to the position of deputy for the abbot general until finally to be elected himself to our highest office. It would be difficult for the Order to muster many of his calibre.

When I was given the opportunity to talk to him alone, he showed an apparently lively interest in Norway and was well aware that the Nordic countries had a significant Cistercian past. I understood that he also knew of the hopes Dom Albert had expressed when I received the habit, and I got the impression that the Order was slowly making strides towards our northern shores.

Otherwise, what I remember best from the visit was that in the course of his farewell address Dom Gabriel unexpectedly gave us permission to swim. A couple of times during the crossing from Tenby he had involuntarily been in contact with the wet and salty element. It would be reassuring, he thought, if everybody in the community could swim. The jubilation this unleashed among the younger guard was unmistakable, even if suitably subdued.

Little did I guess how much I should later have to do with Dom Gabriel Sortais, even to administering to him, when he was unexpectedly dying in Rome, the Sacrament of the Sick, also called Extreme Unction.

The theological studies still seemed to me enriching and enlightening, although I missed the challenging academic level of Scourmont. The clarity and stringency of the French authors attracted me particularly. I had never been Francophile, but now saw that this was what I was beginning to be, in the field of theology. Moreover, I noticed that the English specialists in theology often drew (that is to say, had to draw) extensively on their French colleagues.

And still I was especially captivated by everything connected with biblical research and exegesis. That Holy Scripture was not only the words of human authors, but also the Word of God, was more than enough to arouse and hold my interest. For someone who came from a Lutheran part of the world it also gave pause for thought to realize how much Catholic research on the Scriptures owed to the work of Protestants. The exegete von Harnack, long seen as 'the root of all evil', was now to be regarded as both a pioneer and a liberator.[1]

In 1943 Pope Pius XII had issued a papal encyclical, *Divino afflante Spiritu,* an epoch-making approach to the incumbent updating of research on the Bible. It laid down guidelines which it is no exaggeration to state represented a watershed in Catholic biblical thinking. For one thing, he made it clear that the Bible does not attempt to give an account of history as such, but of *religious* history. A continual process of research using all available scientific disciplines is not only permissible but absolutely necessary for gaining insight into the deeper content and meaning of revelation. He advocated the careful analysis of the most ancient texts in order to come as near as possible to their origins, but also encouraged researchers to employ all known scientific methods for the optimal identification of the literary genres used by the authors of the Bible. At the same time, he delineated certain limits to prevent any abuse. An exciting time for biblical studies and exegesis! The best-known Catholic researchers of the day merely observed that the pope had approved principles and methods they had long employed.

I was so carried away by this development that I went in for learning Greek, despite the fact that I should have to teach myself and in my free time. Nonetheless I slowly got to the point of enjoying being able to read the New Testament in the original language, and did so every day as spiritual reading.

I found it rewarding, indeed thrilling, to delve deeply into writings that in a mysterious way had been inspired by God— aware that it was not possible to come any closer to the revealed truths. What struck me as especially fascinating was the Catholic understanding of the biblical concept of inspiration: at one and the same time, both the Lord and the people who had actually written down the texts were the authors of the Scriptures in both the Old and the New Testament. For a long time I mulled over the comparison which might be put like this: just as Christ is wholly God and wholly man, so each single Bible text is wholly the work both of God and of the human author.

But what was the key to understanding the texts of the Bible? Here Catholic exegesis was perfectly clear: the meaning intended by the Lord is the one the author of the text (for example Saint Paul) deliberately lays in his words. That the authors seldom—if ever—were aware that they were writing under influence from above was a doctrine as full of insight as it was liberating. The subject of my first lecture to the assembled community was, naturally enough, biblical inspiration.

There was no lack of challenges, but I felt all was going well and was happy that the perpetual vows were behind me, not glimpsing any shadows on my present horizon.

Father wrote from Bergen that he was dismayed by my brother Jens, who had for a long time worked as a junior partner in the family shipbroking firm. He had suddenly sold his house and set off for Peru without any explanation regarding his further plans. Jens had visited that country the previous year, on what was supposed to be a summer holiday. But now he let it be known that he intended to settle there. For Father, this meant it was now only a question of time before the firm of I. Gran & Co. would be out of the family's hands. A little later, this time from Mother, I received the additional information that Jens intended to open a paper factory—with the rather grand name of Dominador (the Dominator)—and would also be an agent for a Norwegian manufacturing firm whose winches were on all the markets. Mother felt sad about this too, for now both her sons had moved out of her life, or so it seemed to her.

At Whitsun that year there was something unusual and in-teresting to see in our otherwise so modest cloister: a local palaeontological exhibition. The person behind it was a lay brother on loan from Scourmont, Brother James (Jacques), who for a long time now, like some archaeological hound, had been on the trail of Caldey's past, bringing to light many things of interest. Not to say that he was the first; far from it, for even before the turn of the century researchers had found proof of fauna having been here for at least twelve thousand years—from the time when Caldey was still part of the mainland. They had discovered the remains of hyena, reindeer, lion, wolf, Irish elk, bison, wild ox, mammoth, hippopotamus, and rhinoceros bones. The oldest inhabitant, however, was the wildcat, which had also lasted longest, only having disappeared within man's memory.

Similarly there was evidence to show that Caldey had been populated by cave-dwellers since the beginning of our era. And it was in such a hollow, Nana's Cave, that Brother James had dug down through the detritus of two millennia. The finds had been examined by experts, classified and marked with red labels, and were now on exhibition for us monks to peer at. Later, to make it possible for others to view these interesting items, the showpieces were transferred to the guest-house and finally to the Caldey Post Office museum.

My former spiritual adviser, Father Peter Lowry, in the end had found out that Oslo was no longer for him. He had held out for several years as a support for his sister, who was a member of the community of the Sisters of Saint Joseph in Oslo. Now she had been transferred to India, and Father Lowry found himself restless and rather lonely. It was clear that he had been very taken by Caldey on his previous visit, and now the desire to share in our life had become a persistent longing, to the extent of being almost an obsession. Did I think he had a chance? I reminded him of something he said when I had told him of my forthcoming entry into Caldey: 'Giving it a try is the only way to find out.' He agreed of course, but was clearly anxious about taking such a big step at the age of forty-three. I understood how he felt, and I too had my doubts, though of a different nature. Could this man, who in my opinion was a 'born' secular priest and spiritual adviser with every indication of being at home in his vocation, adapt to our way of life? (A typical example was that I had never seen him without his roman collar, and when I once asked him whether he did not own a shirt and tie, he had answered in the negative.) Personally, I found it difficult to believe that the Lord would suddenly call this natural shepherd to such a total change of rôle.

Nevertheless, Father Lowry took the step, left Norway, and came to join us. We had ample opportunity to feel sorry for him in the time that followed, for he proved little suited to our tough existence. Brave and generous as he was, he struggled perseveringly against all the odds. The intense family life—communal existence wherever you looked or turned— gradually got on his nerves. But also the more practical tasks, our constant daily challenges, were beyond him. After only a few months the answer came to him: he was not cut out for this life. From the prior downwards, I think we were all aware that what was involved was a midlife crisis—something most people experience, and which can be extremely trying. I assume that he and the prior must have reached a decision together: the cure of souls, pure and simple, was undoubtedly Father Peter's real vocation in life.

He departed, but without any sign of bitterness. One thing was certain. He was cured of his nagging unrest, and soon recovered his balance and former energy. He spent the rest of his life as a cherished parish priest in the centre of London, but regularly found his way back to us for spiritual renewal.

Another parish priest, John Mostyn, was a Welshman and the nephew of a former Catholic archbishop of Cardiff. He had doctorates in both philosophy and theology, and a re-spected name as well. That summer he rented—together with two Irish housekeepers who were blood sisters—the disused lighthouse-keeper's dwelling at Caldey's highest point. It was rumoured that he was a well-to-do man, as his summer res-idence seemed to indicate. He was greatly devoted to our monastery, however, and often attended services with his pious companions. It was clear that he would not be a parish priest for much longer, so this house, if necessary, could also be his home in winter.

Dr Mostyn, as he preferred to be called, liked to invite people to tea, and it happened that I—since I had to attend to his motorized water-pump, installed because the house lay too high for the water supply to reach it—sometimes had to take on the rôle of a guest, something which Dom Eugene tolerated out of considerations of politeness. On one such occasion Mostyn confided that in the not too distant future he was going to be appointed a canon at Saint Peter's in Rome. 'In that case', I said, 'I know one of your future colleagues, Bishop Johannes Olav Smit, who used to be the vicar apostolic of Norway.' It turned out later that they were to live on the same floor in the canons' grand *palazzo*, where they became good friends.[2]

I thought I could detect a certain loneliness, even bitterness, in this ageing priest. Perhaps he had aimed higher than was reasonable under the circumstances and saw the Vatican as a last resort.

The farm had become more and more dependent on its growing number of machines. After the service of None my first set walk every day was up to the workshop, or 'the garage' as we called it. There we had an ingenious hoisting system consisting of long steel chains with various pulleys and hooks that allowed us to hold machines for repair hanging from a beam centred over a steel workbench. Whenever anything needed to be replaced, the replacement part had to be made as far as possible on the spot, so we had a battery of special devices and tools for the purpose.

In 1955, with summer and harvest time just round the corner, one after the other, all three tractors were sent in for a complete check-up. As if that were not enough, Father Anthony had sent up for thorough overhauling the six-cylinder engine belonging to our reserve boat. Dom Eugene was an interested party here. Having a mind of his own, he liked to use our nameless auxiliary boat, which he manoeuvred himself, to cross to and from the mainland, independent both of *Lollipop* and—to a certain extent—of our problem, the tide. Father Anthony was now wisely keeping quiet about his old arguments in favour of acquiring a helicopter.

As sporadic helpers in the garage, I mostly had novices little acquainted with machines. What counted for most was the extra muscle power. One exception was a young English fighter pilot fresh from the Suez Canal battlefront. He knew a lot about aircraft engines, but here he could naturally take stock of his situation, which he piously did. In my innermost thoughts I had already appointed him my successor (eventually, of course), but this time it was no. After a year had passed, he too had gone. I had foreseen this, however, for when novices began to waver, it was usually detectable well ahead from their growing insecurity and shifty glances.

Still vivid in my memory are several 'scenes' where I am at work in the garage when suddenly the door-opening is overshadowed by inquisitive 'trippers', for whom this was a fascinating sight. Caldey's self-sufficiency had become something of a local legend.

The summer seems tropical. We theology students have long since put aside our books. Now I am working with my machines, mornings as well as afternoons—more when necessary. The heat makes the work shifts exhausting. One day in good time before Vespers I see a chance to put aside my tools and hurry over the wide enclosure to the inmost beach in Bullum's Bay, where it is possible to bathe. I start off, happily swimming out, for there is no undertow here. All of a sudden a large round head bobs up right in front of me and I am gazing straight into a pair of very dark brown, gentle, and inquisitive eyes. A seal! It dives, only to come into view again a little further out. My presence no longer seems to be of any interest. I have the feeling the animal belongs here. Does it? Yes, indeed, I am told at the first opportunity—which of course means by Brother Thomas—Atlantic seals have come since time immemorial to the caves under Caldey's ocean-

facing cliffs in order to calve there. They are there now. My
new acquaintance and I greet one another on several occasions
afterwards, until bathing is stopped because the growing numbers of novices allow their interest in the sea to take the upper
hand. They could swim when they came—for that matter so
could we all; now the abbot general's green light is switched
to red again. But before that happens, the seal has gone off to
the open sea a number of times and always returned again.

Richard, a young English convert who has previously been
a Benedictine in the abbey of Prinknash, has taken his temporary vows with us. In his former monastery he worked as
a potter and is now asked if he would be prepared to set up
a one-man pottery to make monastic objects for sale in our
two souvenir shops (for we also have one in Tenby, now the
apple of Brother Thomas's eye). Yes, he would indeed.

A 'lightning-course' teacher is summoned for the purpose
from the famous Potteries in Staffordshire, bringing his traditional potter's wheel. He demonstrates his skills with breath-
taking precision for the brother and some of the rest of us. In
answer to my (probably naïve) question he tells us that he is
descended from a family of potters that has kept the tradition
alive from father to son since the fourteenth century. 'No one
dares to break it', he adds with an unscrutable smile.

Now we have our own pottery, which soon does so well
that Anthony, who is also in charge of this side of things, can
divulge that it alone shows a larger surplus than the whole of
Father Jerome's farming activities. But about that my mouth
is even more tightly shut than usual, for I have to deal with
Father Jerome's Walloon temperament every day.

One of the greatest events in the history of the community
became imminent: the ordination of not just one, but three
monks. My immediate seniors Thaddeus, Stephen, and Samson were now ready for ordination in accordance with ecclasiastical requirements. The last two had been ordained as
deacons in Scourmont, and beginning next autumn were to

continue their further education in Rome. As will have been understood, these ordinations were the first of their kind on Caldey. The many that in theory could have taken place had all been quashed at their inception. On the same occasion I myself was to be ordained as a subdeacon, at that time still the first sacramental step on the way to the priesthood.[3] There was, however, an obstacle. Because my parents were non-Catholics, canon law demanded that dispensation be sought from the Holy See. Although the request had been sent in good time, no reply had been received. The day before the ceremony—after the bishop[4] had moved into the monastery's guestrooms (including the bedroom of the former English abbot)—a telegram arrived from the Congregation of Religious: DISPENSATION GRANTED. Thus it happened that I had the honour of being first man out during the ceremony, which was as solemn as it was elaborate. Formally this threshold entailed certain consequences, in that the person who had been ordained was henceforth barred from contracting a legal marriage.

Bishop John Petit, a man in his fifties, was always welcome on Caldey, perhaps less on account of his high office than for his winning personality. He was uncomplicated, humorous, friendly, and (something that counted for a lot in this country) a gentleman of the old school. He and I later came to be good friends, but just now I was if anything simply a troublesome extension of a ceremony that was already sufficiently protracted (and which the Vatican Council would come to curtail considerably). Brother Thomas told me how once a comic note was struck when the bishop, sitting on his 'throne', was to have the mitre placed on his head by a nervous assistant. Mitres have two long bands of embroidered material which hang down side by side from the back of the neck. The assistant made the mistake of placing the mitre back to front which meant these bands suddenly hung over the bishop's face, so that he turned red with anger—in full view of everybody. Instead of reversing the mitre himself, he sat politely waiting for someone else to do it. To make matters worse, the assistant grasped the two bands by their ends and lifted them hopefully over the top of the mitre, from where they immediately slid down again. The bishop, now a brilliant hue, then removed the headgear himself and placed it back correctly. An amusing episode—not least for Brother Thomas who could add another story to his popular collection of anecdotes.

At one fell swoop our monastery had three new *patres,* a relief for the rest, who would now have much longer intervals between their weekly liturgical duty. My task as a subdeacon was to participate at the altar during the solemn Mass, when the celebrant had on his right hand a deacon, who among other things chanted the Gospel, and on his left myself who chanted the Lesson—also called the Epistle—and otherwise assisted in the service.

In May Father came again on a visit—still only to Tenby. My old acquaintance, I could well say my friend, Edwin Scott-Davies, whose affection for Caldey in the course of time took many forms, had acquired a small beach house on the mainland a few miles west of Manorbier castle.[5] Edwin could appear unexpectedly anywhere, but always discreetly. One day he called on the two of us at the hotel. The weather was perfect, and since I had to spend the next day at the monastery, he volunteered to drive my father on a day's outing round southwest Wales. They had had tea on Edwin's terrace, from which one looked across to Caldey, though with his usual tact he had not even once drawn attention to the fact—which must certainly have been an effort for him. Father was delighted, only really now for the first time discovering that Wales was a different and very 'un-English' country.

For us on Caldey it was good news that the whole coastline from Tenby, past Manorbier and to the Irish sea, had recently been declared a nature conservation area, for this meant that we need have no fear of an architectural degradation of this magnificent coastal region. Edwin was particularly pleased, since nothing was to be demolished!

★ ★ ★

In October came the long-expected message from Scourmont: Dom Anselme Le Bail was dead, after having been
abbot for over forty years. Who was to be his successor was
naturally an important question, important not least for the
abbey's Welsh daughter house. As already mentioned, after
Dom Anselme's brain haemorrhage, Guerric Baudet had been
appointed by Rome to be acting superior. Now there was to
be a free ballot, and it could lead to an unexpected result.
Some of us nourished a silent hope that the choice would fall
on our former prior, Dom Albert Derzelle. We should have
liked him to make a comeback and to have him as our new
'father immediate'. The tension was relieved in November:
Dom Guerric had been elected. I suppose most people were
contented. One knew what one had.

On 27th October 1955 I was ordained as deacon in a ceremony very like the one already described. I received the diag-
onal stole, and was liturgically legitimized to read the Gospel
during Mass. At that time my English colleagues Stephen and
Samson were already in Rome in our generalate, which included the Order's only student hostel. At that time it was not
permissible to pursue higher studies elsewhere, for monastic
obligations always had to be given priority.

The increasing numbers of applicants—there were constantly about twelve in the novitiate—meant that the monastery's capacity had reached its limit. In particular, the two
dormitories were packed, so that a couple of rooms in the
guesthouse had to be commandeered. I myself was relegated
to the closed library annex (in monastery parlance referred to
as 'the library hell') in which were stored books considered
unsuitable for general consumption, in other words books on
the *Index*—either by name or because of their contents.[6] The
small room always had to be kept locked, although it was
almost never used. The rules must be followed. It had the
smell of a second-hand bookshop, to which I soon became
accustomed. I could certainly have taken my pick of bedtime

reading, although I never got round to it. I always came late to bed and needed to sleep. Nevertheless, I enjoyed the luxury of now having my own table and chair, almost a monastery cell. As long as it lasted.

One day an unusual person was placed under my wing. Pietro, our new farmhand, was from the village of Ravello in the Bay of Naples. From there by some extraordinary means he had made contact with Caldey. And now he was to help us in various ways. Pietro possessed only two language variants— Neapolitan and 'ordinary' Italian, the latter with a strong local accent. I was told to be his contact—and interpreter, if necessary. He was probably in his mid-twenties, short, blithe, and talkative. Moreover, he knew nothing outside his own home circumstances. He arrived with a small suitcase, which he immediately opened. It was full of gifts of fruit from the farm he came from. Father Anthony, who spoke very tolerable Italian after his years in Rome, was to choose first, then Father Jerome, next the prior, and lastly I myself. By then the case was empty except for a change of clothes. Who practised poverty here?

Pietro's work mostly came to consist of cabbage cultivation —from planting to shipping. Our prior had got the notion that cabbage was now the thing. Twenty thousand plants were set out—with all of us on the job. Later there were endless problems connected with the transport. Pietro did his best, but what our gradually less blithe Neapolitan found hard to accept was that on Caldey there was not one single bar, no matter how small, not even a cafeteria where a tired workman could spend his free time in relaxed contact with his colleagues. The winter evenings in his room, with the radio turned down low because of the neighbours, were not his idea of leisure. He made a half-hearted attempt to learn English from a Belgian lay brother he worked with, but whose language skills were at the most basic level. Pietro's 'English' was the source of some merriment in which he goodhumouredly shared, clearly without quite grasping the point. At any rate, he did not stay a day more than the contract stated, and disappeared to the mainland where he had somehow or other managed to track down other Italians, which brought him a new job and perhaps, with luck, some cafeteria life again. As far as I remember, the cabbage-growing was dropped soon afterwards when it became clear that it could never be a profitable business.

Christmas came with the traditional bad weather. Storms howled round the roof and tower. But autumn had been abnormally dry, and we were faced with a problem that was unusual at this season: a shortage of water, with all the consequences. Drinking water had to be transported from the mainland, where the situation was somewhat better.

My parents had sent boxes and boxes with fruit, sweets, nuts, and so on. Indeed, the two of them gave as much as all the rest put together. I felt slightly embarrassed. Who on earth would the others think I was? And my Christmas mail actually grew larger every year. My efforts to keep a low profile seemed useless. Letters even arrived from distant Hong Kong. And Terry, my old friend from Dartington, could joyfully announce that he had become a father for the third time— after two boys, a girl.

When given the chance, I am working seriously on yet another internal lecture, this time about a theory which is now being developed in biblical theology. *Sensus plenior* was the hypothesis that certain sections, paragraphs, or phrases in the Bible can have an inherent meaning in addition to the one establishable by ordinary exegesis: in other words, over and above the author's intention. All my leisure time (such as it is) goes to the study of publications on the subject, and to preparing the first of two conferences. And ahead of me I still have my examination in dogmatics which will decide whether or not I qualify for ordination. For my part I feel I am more than sufficiently occupied when, out of the blue, I am asked to translate Robert Louis Stevenson's famous essay on the Belgian missionary Joseph Damien, who in the last century cared for lepers on Hawaii until he himself died of leprosy. (Father Damien was beatified by Pope John Paul II in Malines in spring 1995.) The bizarre side of the assignment is that the translation is to be from French to the essay's original English. For one reason or another the original cannot be found here on Caldey, and it is needed in a hurry. I was never told the reason.

I notice more and more that the concept of *time* is becoming meaningless, not so much from the philosophic angle as in reality. The built-in 'circularity' of monastery life is slowly becoming a challenge.

As a young monk you stride forward—and upward—in an existence bearing the inviting stamp of step-by-step progress, all the time with new goals to be mastered: the postulant period, the novitiate, the temporary vows, the perpetual vows, the study of theology with its many stages and ordinations. You have experienced and mastered a series of challenges—culminating in ordination as a priest. But what then? I had observed some of my brethren later drifting slowly into a midlife crisis. Nothing left to look forward to. Was that all there was to it? Although it will be many years before this turns into a pressing problem for me, it is important to be prepared.

As for myself, I had to admit that my unabashed ego was still active and eager to express itself on its own terms. I constantly had to strive—all the time praying for mercy—to rise above a stream of such urges.

And I had to recognize that also frustrated ambition can undermine one's existence if it is not detected and dealt with. For example, the dream of being one of the superiors—sitting at the abbot's table, or even taking his place—can threaten to fill your heart, though you yourself are perhaps no more than vaguely aware of it. Not to be chosen for the top position, when in your own eyes you seem to be the most suitable candidate, is one thing, but another, just as serious, is the bitterness that can take over in someone who 'for one reason

or another' has not been reappointed. The intense disappointment at not having an ambitious dream realized can be deeply
felt, and some people never recover from it. 'Know thyself',
said the Delphic oracle. But in fact how little we do!

Even if a monk has not consciously excluded a fellow monk
from his goodwill, it may happen that he senses smouldering
within himself a constant feeling of frustration, very likely on
account of the other man's supposedly 'out of turn' promotion, which seems hurtful and an unfair passing over, possibly
even as an 'act of revenge'. If he gives in to such ideas, he will
slowly but surely sink into a 'chip-on-the-shoulder' condition, and once in this attitude of having been ill used, he is in
a bad way, and may stay stuck there for years.

For those who have made progress, a different sort of bogey
lies in wait: routine, the perpetual challenge of monastery life.
Saint Benedict gives explicit warnings on this score. I had to
recognize the fact that the endeavour to retain a zealous spirit
and unbowed heart, and to have a fresh and vital relationship
to the many monastic duties—none of them with any of the
charm of improvisation—had become my main occupation.
Everyone who preached to us felt it necessary to hammer
this home, because if you are the slave of routine, this too
is a treacherous swamp. Not, of course, that you sink and
disappear, but the longer routine is allowed to become part
of your nature the harder it is to pull yourself out of it.

Nevertheless, as I have already mentioned, the area which
evil itself seemed to regard as its particular field of action—
lying in wait round the clock—was the relationship to your
brethren. Time after time I had to check in myself the tendency to 'cultivate' my apparently incorrigible dislikes which
forever struggled for their place deep inside me. It helped, as
a warning, to be able to note, not without dismay, that one or
the other brother had clearly lost such a battle, for bitterness
is the emotion that is impossible to conceal in a society such
as ours. And I realized it was a pitfall I must avoid at almost
any cost.

Yet also one's likings can be a problem. The affective ego has a natural inclination to select: all friendship is founded on that. The ideal, however, is to be the same towards everybody. Not easy!

All this is very human. Such challenges, however, make themselves even more felt in monastic life than in other forms of existence, not least because escapism—the speciality of our times—is well-nigh impossible here. True enough, you can pursue some special interest to the extent of being carried away by it. Some monks do this and possibly remain less affected by their problems than those who slowly let themselves become encapsulated, who go round in a circle and end up beating their heads against the wall.

On Caldey it was hardly possible to let a personal interest be all-absorbing. For that our hands were too full. Brother James had the chance, of course, to busy himself with his palaeontology, since he could 'go off and dig' without this interfering with his task in hand. But our existence largely went round in a never-ending ring, as I have described. Heart and mind had to be anchored in God's incomprehensible will which always manifested itself otherwise than you had imagined— and generally through your superiors.

It was more or less the idea that my ordination could take place before the summer of 1956, examination results permitting. Bishop Petit of Menevia was to be invited to Caldey as usual, and feelers were out. It had been mooted that sometime after 20th May would be convenient for us.

My old acquaintance, Bishop Suhr of Copenhagen, wrote unexpectedly that he was thinking of coming to England at that time to contact some Benedictine monasteries about a possible foundation in Denmark. Could he attend my ordination? Dom Eugene was immediately fired by the thought: 'I shall ask Bishop Petit if he would not just as soon let Bishop Suhr do the ordination. After all, he is both a monk and a Scandinavian, and you yourself are the Order's only Northerner.'

Bishop Petit was heartily in agreement—probably because for all bishops May is the busiest month of the year, with all the confirmations and so on.

Bishop Suhr said he was glad he would be able to undertake the ordination. 'Not least', he wrote, 'because it happens so rarely.' And now there were signs that more and more people were going to come.

Mother announced that she would be there, pleased that it was a bishop she knew—and moreover had liked so well—who would officiate. Enquiries about attending (and a bed) came from Father Peter Lowry, still active as a parish priest in London, and from the chief editor of an English theological magazine *The Month*, the Jesuit Father Philip Caraman, whom I knew only from hearsay (he had his own motives for the visit). My old friend and colleague from wartime London, Lord Ventry, sent a brief but definite notice of arrival. And of course Edwin Scott-Davies. The guesthouse was going to have more than enough to do. Mrs Shand for her part said she was glad she would again have my mother under her wing.

I myself would have preferred less fuss, because the ordination first and foremost requires inner calm, time for meditation and prayer, as well as concentration both on what has to be done during the ceremony and—not least—on the complicated rubrics of the celebration of Mass. Fortunately I was given a week's retreat—though it was repeatedly interrupted by questions about the preparations and about who was coming. Our guestmaster, the former police officer from India, went into a spin when he heard it was to fall to his lot to quarter a real, live lord. Vanity can be more than skin deep, even in a monk.

Mother arrived first, bringing with her a rare and unusually beautiful altar chalice she had tracked down in London: an exact copy of the famous Tassillo chalice from the year 777. It was a gift from her and Father together. We had exchanged some letters about this, but I was deeply touched, even moved, when I understood the chalice was from both of them.

You may ask how it can be possible for a monk, who has made a vow of poverty, to accept such a valuable gift. The answer is that the gift, in the final instance, is to the monastery. However, since the priest celebrates Mass daily, by tradition a chalice given to him at his ordination may follow him throughout his monastic life. (At the time of writing this chalice is safely back in the Caldey 'treasury'.)

On 20th May all was in place. Unfortunately Mother became ill immediately after her arrival and had to stay in bed. She was able to be present at the ceremony, however, well aided by the other guests and by her guardian angel, Josephine Shand.

Bishop Suhr, with his incomparable calm and natural dignity, celebrated the ordination Mass. The entire community took part actively, with the guests and the locals packed into the gallery and up the staircase.

In the Catholic Church ordination is a sacrament, focused on some audible words and a simple, visible act, which taken together have a supernatural effect. Because it concerns an effect with lifelong consequences, the sacrament can never be repeated—as is also the case for baptism and confirmation. Once a priest, always a priest. I was myself intensely moved by both the solemnity and the irrevocability of this step.

After the ordination itself, which took place halfway through the solemn Mass, I was able for the first time to participate actively in the celebration of the Eucharist. Together with and at the same time as Bishop Suhr I pronounced the words—Our Lord's own words—by virtue of which the bread on the altar becomes his body, and the wine in the chalice becomes his blood. Who can ever forget such a moment?

The next day was equally rewarding: the celebration of my first Mass. The guesthouse chapel had been chosen because it was the only one which could be heated, and Mother had insisted on being present, even if she could hardly have understood much of the deeper, and by that I mean the *mystical,* meaning of the Mass.

The chapel was full to overflowing. Throughout the Mass I was flanked by Father Lowry and an older father who had been diligently teaching me the rubrics. Bishop Suhr was placed by himself with his own *prie-dieu*. Only the low-voiced Latin dialogue between myself and two of the priests broke the silence. The eucharistic prayer—the heart of the Mass, indeed its alpha and omega—had then to be said so quietly that the celebrant could scarcely hear himself.

The silent attention of the gathering was very moving. Some of those present commented later that they would not have believed it possible for such a large assembly of people to remain so silent.

When, at the very end, I turned round to make the sign of the cross over those present, I found—unexpectedly—Mother kneeling alone on the altar steps, in order to receive there her newly ordained son's first blessing.

Seventeen

NEW TASKS, NEW HORIZONS

I THOUGHT IT SPLENDID that Mother and Bishop
Suhr got on so well, talked a lot together, and were
clearly on the same wavelength.

Among the visitors, the English Jesuit Philip Caraman
had a name I had seen on books in our library, mostly biogra-
phies of the Catholic priests martyred in the wake of Henry
VIII's Reformation. He was also editor of *The Month*. Why
should he undertake the tiring journey and use precious days
on my ordination? To be sure, he said he had some plans for
producing a number about Norway, but no more than that.
The father was rather short in stature, dark and un-British in
appearance, but spoke polished and elegant English.

While Mother still kept to her bed during the days after
the ceremony, she began rather cautiously to ask me questions about Christianity and about Catholicism. 'I'm being
torn to pieces!' she admitted, uncomprehending and full of
emotion. It was especially my first Mass (which I had said for
her), the silence that accompanied it, and the blessing at the
end that had made such a deep impression, as she mentioned
again several times. And I had replied as well as lay within my
power to questions that sometimes astonished me by showing
her ability to go straight to the essentials. It was obvious that
something profoundly important was happening in the depths
of her being.

The group of guests had broken up and gone their separate ways. Mother felt slightly better and wanted to go straight home. Dom Eugene more or less ordered me to go with her as far as London. But first she experienced the changeable moods of an island existence. Just boarding *Lollipop* was a nightmare for her, because the wind had veered and freshened so that the choppy waves went in all directions. The crossing filled her with alarm at the thought of what might meet us on the Tenby side, for it was explained that the tide was ebbing so that the jetty could no longer be used. The boat was brought as near as possible to the sandy beach, and Mother had to submit to being lifted over the rail and carried ashore by a tough seaman whose beard covered her face. Next it was my turn, and then the luggage. After that we had to somehow drag ourselves up over the wet sand to the road, Mother in totally unsuitable shoes. She hardly spoke and seemed more dead than alive when we reached the boatman's house overlooking the jetty. 'I must lie down', she moaned, and was helped onto a sofa where she lay motionless until it was time to take the long coastroad drive to Swansea. On the train to London she lay full length in the compartment, almost unable to speak. It was painfully clear to me that her experiences, all in all, had been too much for her, and into the bargain it had not been possible to diagnose her illness on Caldey, where there was no doctor. Her will power was clearly stronger than the state of her health. My only comfort was that it was she herself who had insisted on being present at my ordination. And she was paying the price now. Fortunately she recovered to such an extent in London that she was soon able to return to Oslo. Back at Grav, and more or less restored to health, she made an unexpected gesture. She gave a dinner for Bishop Mangers and my two old friends from Rome, the priests Ivar Hansteen Knudsen and Lars Messel, both of whom had posts in the bishop's administration, the former as his secretary and editor of the periodical *Sankt Olav* and the latter as chaplain for the parish. Messel, who was the younger and full of zeal, proposed that my mother should consider giving the Grav estate to the Cistercians, so that I could come back with a flock of monks and found a monastery there. Mother was almost flabbergasted at the thought, but was too polite to comment on the proposal there and then.

In her next letter, written with a certain bemused sarcasm, she regaled me with an account of the young priest's forwardness. I could only reply that this was just Messel's nature, impulsive and free-spoken. She could, however, forget it, because I myself had no such thoughts. Grav lay much too near the still expanding Greater Oslo for us to be able (even under such hypothetical circumstances) to have a monastery there. In accordance with centuries of tradition in our Order, we had to be 'far from the haunts of men'. This somewhat calmed Mother, who might not have liked the idea that her son should go round with his mouth watering at the thought of taking over her home.

One day a surprising piece of news reached our ears: the BBC wanted to do a full-length television programme on Caldey and its monastic community, and it was said that the prior had agreed! Not long after, when I was busy at work in the garage, I had an unexpected visit from Dom Eugene and Father Anthony in company with two men whom I easily identified as media people. As indeed they were: a programme director from the Welsh BBC with his second-in-command out on a reconnaissance. I was introduced to them as the first Norwegian Cistercian since the Reformation, which seemed to arouse their interest. Later the same day the prior said I was free to answer any questions they asked me—which I did on several occasions, until there was almost no peace to be had. Obviously some part of the programme was going to focus on this rare Nordic bird.

The TV team (without a single Catholic, and therefore constantly needing to have things explained that were commonplace for us) was thorough in its work. Cables were stretched in all directions, generators and equipment were brought over. Our little harbour reached bursting point. The group, comprising both men and women, grumbled a bit about a special clause which implied 'men only' inside the monastery enclosure. But on that point there was no weakening.

As for me, I had to give a personal account, such as it was, of my background, conversion, and entry into the monastery. When finally on the air, I felt as though I were acting the part of myself. It was plain that jovial Brother Thomas with the humorous look in his eyes had made a lively contribution. The concluding part was in the church where we sang the Marian hymn, the always appealing *Salve Regina,* which according to tradition has been sung in our monasteries since the time of Saint Bernard.

The programme was sent out 'live' and must have had a certain impact, because those of us who were involved suddenly received 'fan mail'. A repeat programme was shown too, but since we had no television, we were none the wiser. Later it must have been on the network in the USA, judging by our mail. And in the autumn we had an extra influx of 'trippers' who had seen the programme. I was even summoned to the guesthouse to greet a lady from the small Norwegian town of Drammen, now married in Cardiff, who absolutely had to express her feelings. So Norway was on the map, and in an unexpected way! It seemed to me that there were almost too many invasions from the world I had left. Fortunately I was ignorant of what was to come.

The next arrival was a young Norwegian, Jakob Dahl, who came straight from higher studies at the Sorbonne. He was a serious-minded convert who felt he had a vocation to the contemplative life. Some days later the annual coalboat also arrived. The monastery changed character and everything was subordinate to coal. Young Dahl, who felt himself loyally 'called' to join in the shovel-work, was soon as black as the rest of us. This quiet, refined intellectual quickly understood what I myself had realized from the start: neither Caldey nor the Cistercian Order were meant for him, nor perhaps vice versa. After a week, at his request, we two had a talk about his vocation. He felt little inclined to join the Benedictines, because it seemed to him they were constantly drawn in two different directions—the contemplative and the apostolic, often with more emphasis on the latter. I asked him if he had ever thought of the Carthusians, for there I could see a natural and far from unlikely solution for him. 'It would be wonderful to have a vocation to that Order', he replied 'but it's on too high a level for me.' 'Have you tried?' 'No, it would be aiming too high' he insisted, perhaps with slightly less conviction. 'You ought to', I told him, 'then you would soon enough find out—like here—whether you had a vocation there or not.' This was the main content of our conversation. Shortly afterwards he moved off to reconnoitre the situation. How well I recognized my own beginnings!

The story ended like this: young Jak, who knew of the Carthusian monastery of Selignac in the south of France, arranged to stay there for a retreat, felt himself drawn to the place, and asked to be admitted. All this happened almost forty years ago. Jak, or Father Filip by his monastic name, became history's first (and, up to now as far as is known, only) Norwegian Carthusian. I felt we had been instruments in the hand of the Lord.

Dom Guerric arrived on his first visitation as abbot. At the same time, my colleagues Samson and Stephen returned from Rome after having taken their degrees. Samson had hardly stepped on to the jetty when Dom Eugene laid his hand on his shoulder and told him that he was to be guestmaster, effective immediately. The result was that we who had been together at Scourmont were invited to a 'student tea' in the guest wing, with the new abbot of the motherhouse as guest of honour. The occasion also served as a 'welcome home' for our two travellers from Rome. A cheerful party ensued, where a good deal of amusement was caused by comments on what went on (and those involved) at Scourmont. People under vows of silence easily make up for that deprivation when they get the chance.

As far as I can remember, the happy celebration was not much to Dom Eugene's taste; as long as the visitation lasted, however, he had to play second fiddle. Soon afterwards he left to give retreats in several of our American monasteries. Many of these houses, in the wake of Thomas Merton's autobiography,[1] had expanded at an American tempo—not always without problems. Everything seemed to indicate that Caldey had entered an important and expansive period of its existence. But how long was the arrangement with an appointed and temporary head to last? When would we ourselves be allowed to choose our own superior? There was an underlying sense of unrest among us, perhaps because we sensed that Dom Eugene's regime was possibly no longer the one most suited to the situation. He was often away, seeming to prefer to give retreats and spiritual talks elsewhere, while on top of that he sometimes flared up in typically Irish outbursts of feeling.

Mother writes from summery, sunny Norway telling me that she is increasingly preoccupied with thoughts of Christianity and the Catholic Church. Could I come to Grav for a time in the autumn? 'There is so much to talk about and straighten out.' I feel I must wait for Dom Eugene's return to make such an unusual request—a request with little chance of a positive response. And I myself am not inclined to ask for yet another period of absence.

When Dom Eugene gets back, he finds me in the library sorting out books. After the usual greetings, I take the chance to put forward Mother's plea. With a generous gesture he replies: 'Yes, I actually had it in mind to let you make a trip to Norway after your ordination, so take two or three weeks whenever it would suit your parents.' Perhaps it is because he himself has just returned from a long journey that he can so easily let me go off like this. My parents are overjoyed, unlike Father Anthony, who is not at all pleased that I am to be away 'on holiday'. A mechanic's place is in the workshop. I understand his point of view—and even agree with him.

On the farm Father Jerome greatly needed another tractor, but it was beyond our means. And there was a heavy crop that year. What was to be done?

In a corner of the barn crammed with all sorts of odds and ends we had an engine which had once been part of the combine harvester I mentioned. This complicated mobile machine had proved so unsuited to Caldey's steep terrain that we had reverted to using our indoor threshing mill which, however, was dependent on the David Brown tractor: that is, the very tractor needed at the same time for bringing in the harvest. How could we escape from this vicious circle? Father Anthony had the idea that it ought to be possible to use the immobilized engine as an independent source of power. And this would have to be done before my departure. I was allowed to take over two farm-workers and to rope in two young—and enthusiastic—holidaymaking nephews of one of the lay brothers. For twelve days we worked at full steam— I myself free from all other duties—and finally we had 'the wonder' ready. It looked like no other machine on earth. Nevertheless, the 'power-truck' functioned as intended and effectively threshed the year's harvest of wheat and rye. Later it was used for all kinds of jobs—for, as its name indicates, it was mounted on wheels and could thus be put to use any-where.

On 14th August I was able to fly to Oslo. Mother met me at the airport. In the car she told me that my brother Jens had just appeared quite unexpectedly from Lima. She had plenty of room, so the double visit was no problem in that respect. Jens was not in top form, but was full of plans, and there were masses of papers everywhere, which I felt in duty bound to help him sort out, for Mother hated disorder.

The whole visit seemed to me to have an air of unreality about it. Mother had again invited Bishop Mangers and my old friends Hansteen Knudsen and Messel to dinner. The reiterated question was: When are the Cistercians coming

back to Norway? I answered that if we were offered a large
farm far out in the country, that might be a start.

My first ever High Mass was in Saint Olav's pro-cathedral.
That too had a sense of unreality about it, not least because
there I had always been among the congregation. At the most
I had assisted a little during Mass. Bishop Mangers began from
the choir with some generous words about me and about the
Cistercian Order.

During my visit, journalists came and went. A Norwegian Cistercian seemed to be newsworthy material. A young
Danish baker's apprentice, a convert as far as I can remember,
found his way to Grav. He wanted to be a monk, Caldey must
be the place, mustn't it? We talked for a long time, he would
soon come there. I never heard from him again.

The Grav estate was a beautiful sight, with all the most
perfect autumn colours and the garden still in full flower. To
look after it, Mother was in league with a green-fingered
policeman who lodged at the farm. He had night duty, but
needed little sleep and loved to work with flowers. Indoors,
Mother had had the house put in order and redecorated. She
had someone to help with housework a couple of times a
week, but otherwise she managed everything herself: not bad,
I thought.

We often talked together about faith and religion. She had
little good to say about the State church (as she insisted on
calling it). 'I simply can't stand the thought of those endless
sermons and long hymns', she would say, while I myself had
a rather more ecumenical attitude. I advised her to talk to a
priest, and mentioned one or two names over and above those
she already knew. But I didn't really believe she would try to
make any such contact, which in her eyes would certainly
be self-committal. It was more like her to take any questions
like this up with me, as and when they occurred to her. And
what interested her now was the Mass. On Caldey she had
begun to understand how important this liturgical act was
for us. A divine service without a sermon! What was the
Mass?

The question was welcome, too, because in the period before my ordination I had thoroughly gone into the subject
of the Sacrament of the Altar. 'The Mass is a liturgical act of
sacrifice', I explained to her. 'It makes real and present for
us Jesus' suffering and death on Calvary when the words of
consecration—"This is my Body" and "This is my Blood"—
are uttered over the bread and wine on the altar.' What did I
mean by that—could Christ suffer and die again? So I had to
do my best to explain this mystery.

Christ was God's son, yes, was indeed himself God—God
who had allowed himself to be born into the world to save
mankind from the consequences of their own sin, evil, and
misdeeds throughout time. We do not know why he chose to
do this by taking upon himself such an agonizing death. We
must simply accept that this was in accordance with the will
of the Father, a will which Jesus consistently adopted as his
own. When Christ, just before his death, cried out the words
'It is finished', he knew that he had succeeded in reuniting
mankind with the Father. Until that moment disobedience
and sin had made it impossible for us to gain admittance to
everlasting communion with God, a state that had originally
been intended for all.

Jesus' freely accepted suffering and death on the cross were
in essence both an act of thanksgiving and an act of sacrifice,
but an act which could only be undertaken by a person who
fully enjoyed the Father's love and trust, and who had retained
intact in himself the original man—as he was created in God's
image. Only Christ, because he united God and man in one
and the same person, could in the name of mankind make
good all the evil that the world's countless generations had
brought about, and still bring about. It is this liberating act of
redemption on Calvary which is again made real and present
every time the words that instituted the act are uttered over
the bread and wine—on behalf of Christ—by an ordained and
consecrated priest. Through the power of the Holy Spirit the
bread and wine become the resurrected Christ, so that the
people can receive him at Holy Communion.

But that is not all: as a guarantee of permanent salvation, Christ has desired to remain among us until the end of time. One reason why we in our churches keep the Sacrament of the Altar (even if only in the form of the bread) is so that it may be brought out to the sick or others unable to be present. The other reason is because in that way we always have the resurrected Christ present as an object for our worship.

I noticed that Mother followed all this with the keenest interest, as if some deepfelt need were being fulfilled. She had a great many questions, and it impressed her that there were apparently answers to all of them—even if a supernatural mystery like transubstantiation during the Mass could not be explained in concrete terms. But that a mystery is something that is clear in itself, without being so for us, was strangely enough something she could accept. And she rounded off our talks by saying she was glad I had been able to impart this insight. Now too, she could better understand why the Catholic churches are kept open, while those in our Nordic countries are in fact normally open only on Sunday morning. The worship, of course!

One morning Mother was upset: 'King Haakon is dead!' We probably felt the same as the whole country. Our national symbol was no more, after a reign of over fifty virtually faultless years. We went about as usual but instictively lowered our voices when we spoke.

At home in Bergen I was welcomed like the prodigal son, in other words with a great fuss. Father was in excellent form and full of news, wanting to update me on everything and everybody. I was up at daybreak to cover a self-chosen round of daily Masses in our sister institutions—and, of course, in Saint Paul's parish church.

The rector, Father Gorissen from the Netherlands, caught up with me: 'Tomorrow the school is to have a service of mourning for King Haakon, with Benediction, at which you must officiate—after all, you are Norwegian, so that will be more suitable.' I had never officiated at a Benediction before and hesitated, but to no avail. Gorissen was a determined man. I did my best, with the gathering of pupils from Saint Paul's school audibly restless before me. As the service continued, however, they quietened down so that my memorial address was listened to with attention. Afterwards I had to go out into the school courtyard and greet the children, who crowded round me with surprising enthusiasm. I felt flattered until I discovered the reason: it was the first time they had understood what the preacher said. The parish priest received this news with somewhat strained composure.

The sisters in Bergen, or the nuns as many preferred to call them, belonged to something so original as a totally Norwegian congregation, founded in 1901 by our Luxembourg bishop, J.-B. Fallize. They had received many vocations up to the Second World War, fewer since. The mother general for more than thirty years, Mother Beate, was a lively source of pious energy. From the beginning she had insisted that all members of the congregation, which was mainly recruited from the Netherlands and Germany, must apply for Norwegian citizenship, and moreover learn good Norwegian—and speak it to each other, even if they came from the same home village. When I visited the sisters they began by singing the Norwegian national anthem, which was touching, even if slightly outlandish. I could sense an undercurrent of anxiety about the future, however. As a Norwegian foundation, they had no order outside the country to fall back on. And their responsibilities were piling up. Apart from all their institutions in Bergen, they ran four more hospitals round the country, as well as a convent with a novitiate near Drammen and a postulant house in the Netherlands. And the statistical indications were now the same for them as for our other sister institutions: the number of members was dropping, the average age was increasing.

Father and I paid a visit to his Aunt Sofie, my godmother, on her eighty-fifth birthday. She was an original character of typical Bergen stock. She had never used spectacles, and she still liked to go out somewhere every evening, and was a member of four different weekly bridge clubs. Her house-keeper complained to Father: 'Can't you do something, Mr Gran? There's no stopping her!' But he did nothing, and when I visited Great-aunt Sofie nine years later, the situation was exactly the same.

But there was now a note of sadness in the air. Her only child, Aksel, unmarried and a doctor like his father, had died not long before. I had to take over his elegant crocodile wallet. To say that I was not able to accept or own anything at all was pointless. Was I not her godson?

Also Father was downcast, for he and 'Cousin Aksel' had been inseparable, although in a strangely unemotional way, probably because both were so reserved by nature. For many years they had lunched together once a week, and it was this he now missed. I sensed the underlying problem: Father had, more or less deliberately, stopped making new friends. The loss of this cousin seemed to me to signal the first stage in a step-by-step process of isolation.

On my return trip I took the opportunity in London to contact my friend Terry, who lived with his family in a roomy flat not far from Westminster Cathedral. His desired career as a scenographer (in London, needless to say) had temporarily come to a halt after the failure of his first independent West End production. As a matter of fact the scenography got good reviews, but none of the rest of it. So now he was working in the film studios as a stage-setter until another chance came his way. (It never did. Perhaps Terry wasn't pushy enough.) The three children were enchanting, and his wife Philippa had her hands full at home as well as having a job as a 'reader', which entailed assessing manuscripts for BBC Drama. Because they lacked the funds to send their boys to boarding school, they had had the good idea of enrolling them at the French school, with the result that the youngsters already spoke the language fluently.

Edwin Scott-Davies took me to a concert in the new Queen Elizabeth Hall where Yehudi Menuhin managed the feat of playing unaccompanied compositions by Bach for two hours—to a sold-out house. Thinking back, I felt this would have been highly unlikely before the war. London's music life must have been in a constant state of maturing.

I was hardly back on Caldey before Asian flu, a tough variant of influenza, broke out. There were probably some who suspected it had come with the baggage from Norway, though I could assure them that it had not yet reached our shores.

Father Thaddeus was the first to succumb, which meant that, without warning, I had to take over the electrical power plant. Whatever functions might ever be halted, the generator and the accumulator system were definitely not among them. I tramped ceaselessly back and forth between the garage, where masses of work had piled up, and the powerhouse. Luckily the Asian flu missed me, and it felt good to be back in place—and of some use.

Then one day I got our 'Great Dane', Brother Lawrence, who was unable to sing a single note in tune, as a pupil for singing lessons. Father Edmund, who knew I had studied voice production, saw me as the last hope for getting any acceptable sounds out of our hulk of a brother who because of his zeal for the liturgy had become an acoustical problem. We worked hard at it for days and achieved, I seem to remember, tolerable results. At any rate good enough for me to be allocated another pupil, Brother David, who was musical and had a good voice, but who was chronically hoarse due to pitching his voice in the wrong way. Also that went reasonably well. These two, however, made up the sum total of my pupils.

From Mother I learned with more than a little astonishment that not only *she* was beginning to incline towards the Catholic Church, but also my brother Jens—he who for so many years had been a confirmed atheist. During a convalescent stay in Oslo he had announced that he was in the course of converting. I could hardly believe what I read. And the next thing was that Jens suddenly wrote himself (something he had hardly ever done before) telling me that he was about to be received into the Church.

Our new prior knew little about economics and was probably not much wiser about long-term planning. He tended to start off projects without beforehand doing sufficient market-research or making realistic calculations of outgoings against income. Dom Guerric, during his visitation, had fired an unexpected 'warning shot' in the form of an ultimatum, which not least affected Father Anthony as procurator. The abbot gave Caldey five years to get its affairs into economic balance, otherwise the doors would be slammed shut. And this was no empty threat, because it was Scourmont which, over all these years, had covered our deficit. Moreoever Dom Guerric could be expected to receive the support of the Order's annual General Chapter, should it prove necessary.

To make agriculture a paying proposition in Wales at that time was a real feat in itself. To make it profitable in our insular situation was well nigh impossible. There were other islands off the coast of Pembrokeshire. In the course of the past two hundred years there was, however, only one report of agriculture having been maintained on any of them for more than a decade.

Father Anthony, who had long since realized that it was up to him to think up a strategy which could lead to economic balance, began with our surest card: the 'trippers'. Where they were concerned, the transport arrangements could be described as at best chaotic. Absolutely anybody could land day-trippers on Caldey, and as fish prices dropped and fishing diminished, there were many who preferred to use their boats for that purpose.

Anthony now took the stage by calling in the boat-owners of Tenby to a meeting where he put forward his project: they should establish an organized formal Pool in which our own boat would be included; the Pool would operate in accordance with an agreed plan; the owners would undertake to keep their boats in tip-top condition; no outsiders would be entitled to land visitors on Caldey; the boats must not take passengers in excess of a number stipulated in advance, based on the vessel's capacity; and, with the exception of our *Lollipop,* no boat must leave Tenby before its quota was full. In addition, the visitors should not only pay for the crossing but also for landing, and for each ticket sold, the monastery would calculate a certain amount for itself. Tickets would have to be bought in Tenby—something the Pool itself must organize.

Uproar! The assembled crowd left no doubt that this was unthinkable. There were far too many possible stumbling blocks for it ever to work! A challenging silence ensued. At this point Father Anthony rose, went to the door and announced before disappearing: 'From tomorrow Caldey is closed to visitors'.

To say that he had loosed a cat among the pigeons is to put it mildly. However, after a few days a signal was received from the boat-owners who had had to organize themselves to be able to discuss the subject. The problems could now be regarded as sufficiently clarified for Father Anthony's 'suggestions' to be taken up for discussion. In reality there was no obstacle of any significance. Now it was the turn of the excluded boat-owners in the surrounding district to raise an uproar, for the trippers also came from the nearby coastal areas—often only one couple in a fishing smack.

As time passed the Pool was to become a local concept, just as much as 'the trippers'.

But Father Anthony had more plans for these day-visitors, whose numbers increased from year to year. A new Tea Garden was temptingly situated where there was plenty of space and room for expansion, as well as shelter in case of rain. And Caldey's women volunteered as one to provide the necessary staff, with the formidable Mrs Stanton as 'queen bee'. She was a widow who lived with her not-so-young unmarried daughter in one of the houses in the Village. They considered themselves members of the monastery and could always be counted on for support. The surplus farm produce was

now sent down here, which meant less transport and better profit. A milk bar 'straight from the cow' became very
popular.

I have mentioned our progressive potter, Father Richard,
whose products were sold 'hot from the oven'. With all this it
might be thought that Father Anthony could hope to achieve
economic balance within the five-year deadline. Nonetheless,
he still wanted to have another string to his bow, since the
tourist traffic could fail to bring in returns, dependent as we
were on wind and weather. And the future of the perfumery
still had to be considered uncertain.

The next initiative was broiler production, but not just of
any kind. The father had got wind of an inventor who had
succeeded in constructing a poultry-plucking machine which
for the first time could do the whole job properly, thus cutting
out the need for after-plucking. A demonstration convinced
him that this was so, after the newly slaughtered hen which
he had brought with him came out of the machine without
a single feather. The British broiler market was admittedly
undergoing expansion, but still at a modest tempo by comparison with what was to come.

Anthony clinched the deal on the spot and ordered two of
the new marvels. Even before they were in place we had built
up a broiler farm on a line with the most advanced methods
used in the industry. The poultry were kept permanently indoors, in red light which was said to be healthy for them—and
with tranquillizing baroque music by loudspeaker (an exper-
iment with more modern music only led to fighting). In the
monks' choir the smell of countless broilers was added to the
scent of perfume essences. Eventually young Father Leonard
and I were also drawn into the broiler venture—though only
peripherally. Most of the slaughtered fowl went to a wholesale
firm, which itself dealt with that side of the business. But we
made more profit from sales to the restaurants and hotels in
Tenby and the surrounding district. The monastery's car was
swapped for a pick-up, and we two alternated in making the
deliveries—in time even as far away as Swansea, which could

be effected relatively promptly, for in those days there was no speed limit on country roads in Britain.

Father Anthony was now even more eager to beat our arch-enemy, the tide, since it was of prime importance that the broilers should be delivered 'fresher than fresh'. But here, too, he suddenly felt he had hit on the answer at last, and he let me into his highly original plan. Did I remember the big American amphibian used during the war? Yes, indeed I did. Known by the letters DUKW, it was commonly referred to as a 'duck'.[2] During World War II it was an indispensable means of transport for landing troops. The DUKWs were a regular sight on their way to the front with soldiers, following the liberation of Rome. 'I have had my ear to the ground', he said, 'and one of these amphibians is for sale at a military surplus store in North Wales. The price is manageable. I'll buy the monster if I can count on you to manoeuvre it and service it.' I nodded, but was a bit overwhelmed, for this was something on a scale I could hardly imagine Caldey's dimensions could cope with, either psychologically or structurally. I mentioned the latter, but Anthony was a jump ahead of me here too: 'We'll widen the road from the slip to the workshop, and strengthen it with concrete. And my idea is that it should be given its own garage [!] inside the enclosure with a long floor-pit and large workbench, because there'll be a lot of special jobs to be done for which we need to be prepared.'

The challenge gave me a prickle of excitement. Such an elegant solution to the problem of the tide was certainly worth trying out. For days my head buzzed with thoughts, not least at the gruesome picture of how it would be to make the crossing in bad weather with a high sea in a vessel that in principle was no more than an outsized lorry.

One day, when I was in the workshop, I heard a loud drone like an aircraft engine, but the sound came from just round the corner. Suddenly a camouflaged DUKW swung slowly, almost majestically, into the space between the workshop and the old monastery church. I was dumbfounded, for it was even larger than I had remembered. Father Anthony himself sat at the wheel. 'Well, here she is!' he called down to me, as though it were some ordinary delivery. Beside him sat a man I did not know, who had come along to introduce us to the amphibian's many, often complicated, functions. It was a memorable lightning course!

This marvel naturally had both wheels and a propeller—a large number of the former in fact, and no fewer than sixteen gears, of which four were for reversing alone. Its load capacity was correspondingly generous, allowing for 'twenty fully armed men'. But most impressive of all was that on asphalt the 'duck' could be coaxed up to fifty miles an hour. Among the problems which the constructor, General Motors, had needed to solve was the tricky question of how to drive on sand (the ideal landing base) where the tyre pressure ought not to be much over ten lbs, since otherwise the wheels would spin, against which asphalt requires thirty. The solution was a system capable of inflating or deflating the tyres as necessary *while* you drove. An ingenious membrane arrangement, which was coupled to the centres of the wheels and fitted with tough rubber tubes to a compressor, could be regulated from the driving seat where the pressure—always the same in all the wheels—could be read off at any time. The service manual handed to me was as big as a Bible, for there was plenty to keep an eye on. And in advance! For in the choppy waters between Caldey and the mainland it would be too late to start checking this and that.

'I've got an OK from Dom Eugene that only you and I are allowed to drive the mastadon', said Father Anthony with an undertone of complicity. 'I think he has a hankering to drive it himself, but would that be wise?' I understood what he meant, for it was unlikely the prior would have patience enough to learn the many complex routines that were involved. For example, the 'duck' had a large number of bottom valve plugs, which had to be opened as soon as it reached dry land, but which above all had to be closed before you set out to sea.

To board the 'duck' we had to use a ladder. We began
to transport products and other cargo, at long last without
regard to the state of the tide. Of course many people, both
from Caldey and from the mainland, wanted to come with
us. We had to organize a stop near the post office for those
who were cleared for the crossing. But no day-visitors were
ever brought along; for that the situation vis-à-vis the Pool
was too delicate.

A unique opportunity to use the 'duck' arose when Jerry
'junior' got married in our parish church, Saint David's. The
groom's family, who lived in Tenby, were hosting the celebrations. After the wedding I ferried the newly married couple
and the guests in full finery, all singing in typical Welsh style,
across the roughish strait. Halfway over the engine suddenly
stopped, and in my mind's eye I could see us, at the mercy of
wind and weather, being rescued by the Tenby lifeboat which
always lay ready for action at the top of its long slipway, also
able to master the tide. However, after a short interval, a firm
push on the starter brought the engine back to life. I breathed
easily again and observed with relief that the singing wedding
party had noticed nothing.

We had to restrict ourselves in the use of our treasure,
however, for the 'duck' cost a lot to run. From Caldey we
took the shortest course across the strait, crawled up at the
westernmost end of the long sandy shore and drove along the
edge of the sea to Tenby—quicker and cheaper than crossing
diagonally, because it was at sea that the 'duck' used most
fuel. But it had one incomparable advantage: we only needed
to load and unload once. And our excitement was great the
first time we could transport several tons of corn direct from
the farm to the container waggon in Tenby—an operation
which normally entailed several reloadings with cranes at both
sides.

The knowledgeable Father Anthony was of course well
aware that it was impossible for me—with all my other duties, none of which had been reduced—to master our complicated amphibian overnight. One day he gave me a surprising

message. 'I've come to an arrangement with the Amphibious Warfare Department. You are welcome to take a DUKW course in their training establishment at Westward Ho! It begins in a week.' This meant taking a Showboat-style paddle-steamer across the Bristol channel and a bus west along the coast through Barnstaple to Westward Ho!, where I booked in to a modest hotel before going to find the amphibious section's commanding officer, who doubtless thought he had got a very odd fellow in for training; reserved, with cropped hair, and blue eyes full of questions.

The staff, who knew where I had come from and that I was both a monk and a priest, showed a degree of consideration which I could observe was not meted out in the same way to the other trainees. It was here all the British DUKW-operators cut their teeth—and in record time I had become one of them. I felt the course went far better than I had dared to hope. We were out all the time, also in quite heavy seas, to practise manoeuvring this hybrid whose behaviour was different from any other known means of transport. On a flat stretch of road I could get up to 80 kms, so the manual was correct. By the time I left, most of the company felt like comrades, and my head was full of information which would prove useful later, since Father Anthony's blood was up: more 'ducks'!

It turned out, more or less as expected, that the one we had bought (on trial, according to Anthony) would not in the long run hold out against salt water and our harsh climate. The problem was that the DUKWs were constructed during and for the last war—without the idea of any life thereafter. And no new production was under way. I was sent on a tour of inspection to the surplus store in the north. Father Anthony, who subscribed to their sales lists, had noted two 'ducks' on offer. The man in charge up there scratched his head over the young monk who, with a professional air, examined the amphibians in and out, tested them for rust, tried their valve plugs, and so on. As soon as it was evident which one would last longest, I cleared the purchase over the telephone with Anthony.

If I thought I could now return to the normal life of a monk, I was mistaken. For Father Anthony realized that if we were to have any lasting benefit from this means of transport, we must beat yet another enemy: rust.

I was asked to go to Amphibious Warfare's main works, run by Henley's comprehensive organization at Weston-super-Mare at the inner end of the Bristol Channel. A fascinating experience! The enterprise was privately owned, but under contract to the War Department. Barbed-wire fences and police with dogs. Here I had a talk with the person responsible for the rehabilitation of the Forces' run-down DUKWs, which were clearly becoming more and more of a problem. I mentioned our procurator's pet idea: sandblasting inside and out, followed by zinc spraying, the fitting and fixing of fibreglass, and finally impregnation with water-resistant resin. He almost keeled over at the thought of such a programme, but after a moment's thought said with interest: 'Yes, if you can manage that, you might well be on the way to solving the problem. But unfortunately *we* have neither the time nor the means to go in for a project which would entail a total stripping down of the ducks. However, should you succeed, please let me know.'

Now Father Anthony was all set to go into action, fired by what I could report. As soon as the new 'duck' was registered, we drove it to a steelworks in Port Talbot. A large machine workshop which was to be modernized was put at our disposal without charge for up to six weeks. The foreman's deserted office was included in the agreement, and there Father Anthony and I spent the nights on mattresses, his on the floor and mine on a broad shelf. At first I was afraid I might fall off it, but in fact I slept deeply without stirring, and soon got used to my strange bed.

It took us almost two weeks to strip down our colossus, constantly having to deal with new challenges—often in the form of rust in difficult places. Nonetheless, we managed to keep up a steady delivery stream of parts for sandblasting and zinc spraying—until the first stage was completed as scheduled. Then the process was carried out in reverse until the 'duck' stood there again in new, shining glory. The third stage was very time-consuming: the main body and loading platform were brushed with fixative over which we stretched pieces of fibreglass 'tailor-made' by ourselves. As soon as the fixative was dry, the whole thing was given two coats of ochre-coloured resin. For well over a month, our time was taken up with this 'duck-saving' project, which was intended to guarantee us a rust-free amphibian for many years. Our 'duck' did in fact have a long and useful life. But in addition, in a tiresome way, it repeatedly attracted the interest of the media.

On Caldey they were relieved to have us back, although the relief was certainly just as great on our side. For my own part I had begun to wonder if I should ever again be allowed to experience a normal monastic existence.

In the late summer of 1958, Dom Eugene took me aside one day: 'Father Robert has been recalled to Scourmont to help out with the accounts, so we need a teacher in dogmatic theology for the autumn-term students. I'd like you to take over.' Those were more or less his words. I must have blenched, but the prior just stood there waiting, looking at me. After a moment or two he said he thought I could manage the job and added that there was a further perspective. Next autumn he would send me to Rome for a degree in theology, and for that a year's teaching such as this would be a useful preparatory step. I nodded, not knowing what to say. The idea of becoming a teacher had never crossed my mind. A new challenge—and new horizons.

Luckily Father Anthony, for whom signals of this kind were far from welcome, managed in time to track down a fellow officer from the war days. Tom Plant, who ran a car-repair works in Hampshire and whose wife had recently left him, readily agreed to work as a mechanic with us until he got his life sorted out again. This assistance was much appreciated, for I would need time to draw up the syllabus for the autumn course. My new colleague showed himself to be a likeable enough character who knew his stuff inside out, and naturally much better than someone largely self-taught like myself. We worked together very smoothly, and a short while afterwards I succeeded in having Tom appointed to the post of reserve duck-driver, which clearly created a certain amount of envy in some of those who felt cut-out for the job.

I was soon aware of how useful my new 'vocation' was. Admittedly working on theology at the academic level was demanding, but it was also rewarding. Autumn brought me four students, young brothers with whom I had scarcely exchanged a word. I only wished I could spare more time for them. Now as before, it happened that time reserved for one purpose had to be used instead for some *ad hoc* priority. Far too often, when the others went to church at two o'clock at night, I had to repair to the music room to write my lecture for the morning. Oddly enough, the lessons I had prepared during the night were those that were easiest to write and deliver. At an early stage I decided to type the course—I felt safest like that—and I should then have the material available for future use. For once I had the licentiate in dogma I would have to be prepared for similar assignments later—an assumption that proved to be correct.

One day Father Caraman, the editor of *The Month*, wrote to say that he had for some time been collecting material for a special number on Catholicism in Norway, and had been promised contributions by two Dominican fathers and other specialists. In addition, the important English monastic historian David Knowles was going to supply a paper. Father Caraman had heard that in London in mid-June I had given a talk entitled 'Norwegian Monasticism'.[3] He lacked an article on medieval monasticism in Norway which—he understood— had been remarkably rich. Could I send him my manuscript for possible future use in his periodical? Dom Eugene was in favour and encouraged me to agree. For my part, I realized the text would have to undergo a thorough revision because a talk is subject to fewer criteria than an article in a serious publication. The challenge was exciting, and I made several

revisions before I felt I could send it in. The publication—
wholly devoted to Norway—came out in spring 1959, and
to my silent delight was read by all my brethren in turn. Later
Father Caraman could tell us that the issue was sold out—a
rare occurrence.

Pope Pius XII died at the beginning of October. During his
long illness, concern had been expressed both within and
outside the Church regarding the choice of a successor. Who
could ever replace this refined, intelligent, and energetic—
even if rather autocratic—character? For a long time now the
number of cardinals had been falling, and no one who was to
participate in the conclave seemed to be a clear winner. The
respected and much-admired Cardinal Archbishop of Vienna,
Franz König, was an obvious choice. But a non-Italian? It was
'a well-known secret' that the Italian cardinals, who were still
in the majority in conclaves, had the habit of agreeing beforehand on how they would vote. And so it was this time, too.
The choice fell on the Patriarch of Venice, whom few had
judged to be a likely candidate. A poor compromise, some
thought. In any event he would have to be seen as a 'bridg-
ing pope', for the seventy-eight-year-old Giuseppe Roncalli
from Bergamo had done scarcely anything that could now
be recalled and blown up to worthwhile proportions. In the
main he had been a papal diplomat and had been appointed
to a couple of nunciatures, the last in Paris.[4] But before long,
the pious and good-humoured old man on the chair of Saint
Peter had won the world's sympathy, although in a manner
totally different from his predecessor.

The Holy See seemed to be as human under John XXIII
as it had seemed remote under Pius XII.

Eighteen

CALDEY BECOMES
INDEPENDENT

T HE NEW POPE surprised both the Church and the world. In January 1959, after only three months at the helm, he announced to a large gathering of cardinals that he intended—among other things—to summon an ecumenical council, the first for almost a hundred years.

And it was soon known that he did this following a retreat at Castel Gandolfo—after hours and days of lonely meditation.[1] His own curia was thunderstruck, for the decision was taken apparently without consultations of any kind. The pope was doubtless aware that *it* would have advised against the idea in no uncertain terms. But now the matter was common knowledge—and there was no way back. At the same time it was clear in itself that, with a leader so far on in years, the preparations would have to be intense and that they would have to begin without delay. A wind of optimism at long last blew through Mother Church.

I apportion my time as well as possible between teaching theology, organ-playing, the garage, and the 'duck'. And in addition, the authentic contemplative life, which was what I had come for.

In all the bustle of activity, I found more and more spiritual support in the liturgy, in particular in the Psalms of David with their incomparable treasure of praise and thanksgiving, the kernel of monastic life. But during the lengthy spells in the choir it was important to give the task one's full attention. My efforts to make the psalmist's words my own were only crowned with success to the extent that I could keep distracting thoughts at bay. Far too often fatigue gained the upper hand, and routine took over. It often happened that I had to remind myself consciously of Benedict's words about how we stand to sing the psalms 'that our mind may be in harmony with our voice'.

Almost as a surprise in the early summer of 1959 a report arrived stating that Caldey's situation in regard to finances and recruitment was considered to be so promising that our priory would be upgraded to an abbey—which meant the election of an abbot. The community now totalled forty-five members, of whom thirty-nine were Caldey's own and the remainder on loan. Reasonably enough, we were elated about this upgrading that so clearly indicated that our efforts had borne fruit.

The immediate interest concerned the man to be elected. Dom Guerric arrived from Scourmont to preside, as was both his right and duty. Any discussion between us monks was impossible, since this was not a situation for which the prohibition against speaking could be lifted. Dom Eugene was the only obvious candidate, and he had in no way let it be known that he would object to being elected.

The procedure was that each monk with the right to vote was issued with a list of those members of the community who were directly eligible, as well as of those who could be postulated: that is to say, who could in fact be voted for, but who required clearance from the Holy See on account of some impediment under canon law. An example of such an impediment was that the postulated candidate lacked sufficient seniority, which was five years since solemn profession.

Only priests were eligible. I should also mention that such an election may also include monks belonging to other monasteries of the Order. It is often the case that a monk from the motherhouse is chosen. In any event all must be asked whether they will accept.

I myself was pleased that my own candidate came out on top (although not in the first round): James (in the monastery Samson) Wicksteed, thirty-eight years old, a former fellow novice—cultivated and with considerable monastic knowledge. He was, however, among those who had to be postulated on account of having too short a record, which meant that it was not possible to announce the result of the election before approval, if forthcoming, had been received from Rome. Those without voting rights were informed that it had been a postulation, which at any rate disclosed that our prior was not the man.

The same Dom Eugene had a formidable eighty-one-year-old mother of independent means whom I had already come to know a short time before when I was his chauffeur in Ireland. Mrs Boylan, for many years a widow, lived in a large seaside villa surrounded by a garden in one of the grander parts of Dublin. She made a living—apparently with success—by teaching singing and music, as well as directing several choirs. Even her son was outshone in her presence. Immediately after the election, being curious about the result, she tried to telephone him. Dom Eugene, apparently unable to bring himself to admitting his defeat, gave orders to say that he could not be found. The telephone continued to ring, while the prior was still 'not to be found'. Later, when he had recovered from his disappointment, he said with a smile that his mother had taken the news rather hard, for she had already gone so far as to buy an expensive hat for the consecration ceremony.

In the following week or so, the brethren who had not taken part in the election went around wondering who would soon be their new superior. The announcement of the result, made by Dom Guerric in an extraordinary chapter-meeting, to which also the novices were admitted, was a fine end to all the waiting. Rome had approved the election of Father Samson as Our Lady of Caldey's first Cistercian abbot.

I both respected and admired this man. His spoken English was of the noblest variety, but he could be so reserved that it was almost frightening. During our period of study at Scourmont, he had let me into something which might have been the cause of this. Though we seldom questioned anybody, when I had asked him about his background (which I assumed was from some university, with his father possibly an Oxford don), he answered: 'My father was an actor and my mother an opera singer. As for me, I can't stand theatrical people.' I heard later from others that his father was in fact a well-known Shakespearean actor, appearing regularly at the festival in Stratford-on-Avon. He also told me that he had served as ground crew in the Royal Air Force during the war, and immediately after the liberation was in a team which had to clear up the horrors in the Bergen-Belsen concentration camp. After his release he had been admitted to the Benedictines in Prinknash (Abbot Carlyle's former community), without finding what he was seeking—which he afterwards found in full measure on Caldey.

One of the first things Dom Samson told me following his election was that the plan for my tour of study in Rome was not only still on the schedule, but that a ruling about to come into force even made it necessary. The Holy See had emphasized to all monastic orders that a rule which had fallen into abeyance would now again be applied. This stipulated that anyone teaching future priests, whether in philosophy, theology, or any other subject, must—as a minimum qualification—have a licentiate degree in the corresponding discipline.

I was astonished that we, who were charged with so many different duties, suddenly could be dispensed with, but so it was. Others took over and life continued along its usual path—or along its usual crooked path, as Father Anthony put it when someone who was important for him was sent off elsewhere. Rome's enforcement of the ruling on teaching qualifications was to have immediate consequences for our Order. During the annual General Chapter the abbots, who naturally took the directive seriously, prepared a document of commitment, *Ratio studiorum* (plan of studies), which required the approval of the Holy See. The abbot general wished to maintain the tradition that Cistercians selected to take academic degrees had to live in the study-residence at the generalate in Rome. But had this been applied, it would at this time have been impossible owing to lack of space, since in future one would have to reckon on at least one hundred applications. In the student quarters of the Aventine generalate there was only space for thirty, which up to now had been more than enough. Dom Gabriel had his plan ready: 'We'll sell our Aventine premises and build a new place on the outskirts of Rome'. A similar solution had already been adopted on a previous occasion when a similar problem had arisen. Consequently our Order already owned two fairly large buildings in the centre of Rome.

The Order's medieval abbey of Tre Fontane between Rome and the ocean was persuaded to hand over a beautiful wooded hilltop on the edge of its property. A complicated procedure was promptly set in motion and pushed through against all odds. In almost record time (not impossible in Italy, if you meet certain 'conditions') a new building of impressive dimensions was now constructed here. In the centre was a chapel about as spacious as a good-sized parish church. Outside each of its long sides lay a complete monastery building: a smaller one for the generalate and a much larger one for the students, scaled to accommodate about 125 people. A generous, light refectory and a chapter room, both located in the student complex, had enough space for both groups at the same time.

Our new complex was called 'Monte Cistello'—a name derived (rather clumsily I felt) from *Cistercium*.

A short time afterwards, Dom Samson was blessed and installed as abbot, and during the ceremony a cross was hung round his neck and a ring put on his finger by Dom Guerric as a sign of his new rank. But by then I was already in place in Rome and had to content myself with following this event from a distance.

Immediately after the installation, Dom Eugene returned to Roscrea, where a few years later he was elected abbot—to both his and no doubt his mother's satisfaction. We assumed that her hat could still serve its purpose.

My directions for Rome had been: 'Take a taxi straight from the station to Monte Cistello!' Here I found a sort of 'southern chaos', the disorder often considered typical of the Mediterranean region—for in the student section nothing was properly finished. Small, bronzed Italians worked for all they were worth both inside and outside. We had to sleep on mattresses thrown down wherever possible.

Who were 'we'? Well, 101 young and not-so-young priests —all belonging to our Order, from the five continents, the majority being from Europe and North America. Most were destined to teach in their own monasteries, while a few took courses in spiritual or liturgical studies unrelated to any plan for teaching. A handful had been transferred from the old student residence (the house on the Aventine had already become the generalate for another order), while by far the majority were newcomers who knew neither the general curia, each other, nor Rome.

A new development was the appointment of a master of studies who also had an assistant; both were former theologians from 'the old house'. The study-master, Father Basil, was an English monk with a sense of humour who had to make an effort to be authoritarian.

We were divided into 'deaneries', each preferably under a student who had already spent at least a year in Rome. These so-called deans were supposed to be obeyed, as was more or less the case. I was under the most pleasant one, an American father who became a good friend and proved an easy-going 'superior'.

We students were given a great deal to do at the beginning since nothing was ready. On the other side of the chapel-church the work on the interior had progressed much further, with the general administration functioning almost normally.

Dom Gabriel supervised the general fitting up and set his personal stamp on things where possible. Whatever the task in hand, he was always the one in charge, not only by reason of his position, but also because of his personality and the keen interest he took in it all. He was the head of the Order for life, and for me a high-ranking and distant personage, even though I remembered him well from his visitation. What was stranger was that he also remembered me.

It was great for me to be back in Rome, and for a whole year, although not without complications. This was the city I knew and venerated. I would go so far as to say it was the city I loved. Of all the residents in Monte Cistello, I was the only one with a Roman past. But very few knew about that.

I was soon 'unmasked', however, because I was among the few who spoke Italian, which in fact led to my being persuaded to give a course in the language. To begin with I had quite a number of listeners, which dwindled as time went on and it became clear that Italian was more difficult than many had supposed—perhaps also because my ability as a teacher left something to be desired. Dom Gabriel's secretary, Father Clément, held out longest. His 'boss' could never understand that anyone could learn to master another language, but he certainly wanted his secretary to make the effort. In the end, the course died a natural death—to my satisfaction, because the studies themselves proved to be enough of a challenge.

I was enrolled in the licentiate course in theology at the Dominicans' renowned study centre (later upgraded to university), Angelicum, which dominated on the Quirinal, one of Rome's seven hills. A large group of us from Monte Cistello drove there five days a week in a hired bus that later collected us again. Our lifestyle felt strange—not least because the Order's prohibition against speaking could not be enforced here. It was interesting to observe that, despite this, our customary discretion prevailed; there were few, if any, who talked about their earlier life. We talked about things close at hand, not those far away.

The teaching was in Latin, and we were informed that also our examinations, both written and oral, would be in Cicero's tongue. So we had something to look forward to. The teachers were all Dominicans, mainly Spanish or French in origin, although the staff also included an Irishman, a Canadian, and a Dutchman.

The course comprised dogmatic theology, patristics, morals, the history of philosophy, exegesis (both Testaments), Hebrew, and Christian archaeology. I blessed Scourmont's thoroughness and that it had demanded so much of us. But all in all it looked like being an exhausting year.

The switch from the level of activity at the monastery to the sedentary life in a study was problematical at the start for almost all of us, but grudgingly one's physique adjusted itself. Some students experienced the pressure to succeed like the sword of Damocles, and so had trouble with their nerves. For me, what was most important was that my head should hold out. The Christmas examination went tolerably well, but I was full of sympathy for those who after a depressing result thought they now faced a hopeless future. This applied particularly to the group of Americans, some of whom lacked the adequate grounding in Latin. A few left discreetly to go 'home for Christmas', already at this stage. We never saw them again.

The short holiday between Christmas and New Year was spent at Monte Cistello, for most of us were far from our monasteries. On New Year's Eve we put on a sort of cabaret in which everyone had to take part—preferably by singing something. And here the Americans shone. Jazz, with life and high spirits and no inhibitions. Altogether, they provided a freshly different element with their 'New World style', even after several years' of Cistercian monastic discipline.

By way of a letter from Bishop Suhr I learned that Rome had decided to send an apostolic delegate to the five Nordic countries jointly, who would be the nuncio in Finland, the only one of these countries having diplomatic relations with the Holy See. He added that the intention was for the prelate in question to be posted in Stockholm.

Apart from an Italian student from the neighbouring abbey of Tre Fontane, I was the only one at Monte Cistello who knew ordinary people in Rome. My old friend and maestro Fasting, who had stayed on at Monte Mario, paid occasional visits, and through him I could follow what was going on in the Norwegian colony. Otherwise I made two or three Sunday afternoon visits to those I had known longest. 'Aunt' Ciss (Rieber-Mohn) had survived, together with her *pensione* (it would have been a *faux pas* to say 'boarding house'), and there everything was as before, apart from the fact that she now only provided breakfast, which however was of the generous, Scandinavian kind.

Cucù, Fasting's and my Romanian friend, had become a Catholic. She had married an Italian, and now worked on the switchboard at the Excelsior Hotel. Nandor, our Hungarian poet-friend, who had also converted, had died in an Allied camp for displaced persons. Why he ended up there no one knew.

Old 'Father' Knudsen had passed away, while Zita lived on in the large apartment, where nothing was to be altered. She was always out and about helping people in need, tending neglected graves—and Knudsen's memorial.

Naturally there were several newcomers to the Norwegian community, not least due to the fact that the University of Oslo was now in the course of setting up an archaeological institute in Rome.

Going out on visits of a private nature was discouraged and was only permitted as an exception—which I well understood —and moreover I thereby escaped having a bad conscience about having failed to pay my respects. It was good that our existence should have a monastic character: early rising, the full liturgical hours, the celebration of private Masses and conventual High Mass on feastdays. We also had our (vegetarian) meals with reading aloud (alternately in English and French). If we had some errand outside, we had to have permission from Father Basil, whose usual ruling was that we must be at least two together—although this was not always possible, for example in the case of research connected with the obligatory thesis.

My own thesis entailed many long visits to the library in the Papal Bible Institute. I had chosen a subject that turned out (to my growing apprehension) to be rather more complex than I had supposed, so that I had to request several postponements from the Irish Father Kearns, our lecturer on the New Testament. From 'Biblicum', as the place was popularly called, it was not possible to borrow books to take home, thus I had to write large parts of my paper there, often only semi-legible afterwards. Once again I was worried about my head, which from time to time gave signals in the form of unbearable pressure inside my forehead. Luckily Latin was not a requirement for the thesis, since four or five living languages were recognized—in my case English—ending with a fair enough result beyond my expectations. Father Kearns declared himself more than pleased: indeed, he said that he would like to see the thesis published. It never was.[2]

I came under a certain amount of pressure from Vatican quarters. Dr Mostyn, the Welsh priest who rented the lighthouse-keeper's dwelling on Caldey, had acquired the title of Apostolic Protonotary and lived in the canons' *palazzo*, a stone's throw from Saint Peter's. Now he invited me to tea in his newly furnished apartment. Father Basil thought I should accept. The venue was at any rate respectable enough. Here, too, Mostyn's household was run by the two Irish sisters, who produced a memorable spread for tea. Monsignor Mostyn had treated my two former colleagues from Caldey in like manner, so I was mentally prepared. My digestive system, however, was not, so that it went on strike for the next twenty-four hours. My impression was that our ageing friend was still a lonely man. He had not, so he led me to understand, been assigned the expected tasks belonging to his position—if it could be called a position.

My contact with Caldey is rather sporadic, but I assume that Dom Samson is proceeding to reintroduce order and sort things out after his predecessor's more improvised regime. In mid-January I receive both mail and newspaper cuttings: Caldey has again become a focus of interest for the media. And the centre of it all is our new DUKW. For a long period the weather has been appalling (nothing new at this time of year). A Scottish ship is in difficulty and is lying weather-bound and without provisions in an inaccessible position not far away. Radio contact is all they have. Dom Samson and Father Anthony load crates of food and canisters of drinking water on board the 'duck'. In terrible weather, they come to the aid of the endangered crew. The operation has to be repeated twice. In imagination I experience it as if I too have taken part, as would certainly have been the case had I been there. I feel a strong tug of homesickness.

Sometime in March, Father appeared on the scene. With him came his sister, Mass Beer, a widow of long standing who had readily agreed to be his travelling companion. This was her first visit to Rome, and having been married to an architect, she appreciated it to the full. Aunt Mass was a quiet person of few words, perhaps slightly naïve, with an air of belonging to an earlier age, upright and sincere in everything. In silent horror she gazed at the over-sized liberation monument in marble that dominates the most central of all the Roman squares, the Piazza Venezia. I had to explain to her how something so hideous could have come to be erected—and so close to the beautiful Capitoline hill. When Italy became united as one nation towards the end of the last century (Garibaldi and Mazzini are the key names), there was a wish on the part of the nation to raise a worthy monument in the country's new capital—unfortunately on a site as central as possible. Every Italian municipality was required to contribute its share, which resulted in the then incredible sum of eighty million lire. The area of the Piazza Venezia facing the Capitoline heights was studded with ancient palaces. These were now demolished. The marble mastodon blocked out the view of large parts of the hill itself. At the same time, with its pseudo-classical columns, statues, and bronze four-horse chariots driven by angels, it could not be a more bizarre contrast to its antique surroundings. Aunt Mass mulled over my explanation for a moment or two before remarking in her typical quiet way: 'Is that so? Well, I think they ought to have a new collection for its demolition—everybody would contribute.' But the eternal city will no doubt have to keep its pompous monument which houses in its vast interior both historical archives and a museum glorifying *Il Risorgimento*, the late-nineteenth-century national rising for liberation.

A fellow student, however, reported overhearing another point of view. While he was waiting for the bus in the Piazza Venezia, an American couple passed by on their way from the Forum Romanum. Clearly relieved at the sight of the liberation monument, the lady exclaimed: 'Look! The only thing around here not in ruins.' So that was another way of seeing it—and saying it!

One rainy day I witnessed a strange sight here. Dwight Eisenhower (in brown belted raincoat), commander-in-chief of the Allied forces in World War II and now president of the USA on a state visit, laid a dripping wet wreath on the Unknown Soldier's grave, which is more or less a focal point below the conqueror-like equestrian statue of King Victor Emmanuel II, first monarch of independent Italy. The contrast caught my fancy.

Father introduced Aunt Mass to Rome's other unbelievable monument, the Fountain of Trevi, that sculptural orgy with its gurgling cascades of water gushing down over baroque extravaganzas that cover a whole palace façade. Here she was left seated at a pavement café, while her brother went off shopping. When he returned he found his sister in a state of uncharacteristic elation. Had she been drinking? Yes, but only coffee. Father had ordered an espresso for her. It tasted excellent—but was so very small. She had immediately ordered another, and another after that. Now she was on her fourth cup and almost ready to take off, at any rate judging by the excited way she was flapping her arms about.

As expected, Mother too announced she would be arriving, and the reason was clear. In April I would be forty. She booked into the Pensione Norden. Ciss, who could have a rather negative attitude to other women, took Mother to her heart, drowning her in recommendations as to what she must see and do, and where she should eat what. Mother, who knew Ciss (much better than vice versa) from my letters over many years, took it all in her stride, simply relieved and grateful for being so warmly received.

Some of Ciss's 'pensione-people' were distinguished by the fact that they belonged to the cultural elite who regularly visited Rome and were as eternal as the city itself. In her eyes these were special people whom she addressed in the familiar '*du*' form—which was not at all taken for granted in those days. I was allowed to visit Mother, and even to eat some meals with her at restaurants (indicated by Ciss). For my 'big' day, Mother wanted to give me a wristwatch, because I had problems with the time. The gift had been approved in the right quarters at Monte Cistello. Close to the Pensione Norden there was a shop selling Swiss watches. I had heard of a model which sounded too good to be true. It was self-winding simply from one's arm movements—and kept time even if it lay still all night. That the one I used was unreliable was mostly because I forgot to wind it. (This was before the era of the quartz variety.) We examined and discussed the different types—from the dearest to the most modest. I chose a *Seamaster*, partly because the name seemed to suit Caldey.

The climax of the student year came with examinations. The bogey was the written paper. There was a list with twenty-five subjects divided into four main sections, all of which might be on the set paper for us to answer—as mentioned, in Latin. We would not be dealt out a selection of four of the twenty-five subjects, one of which had to be treated *in extenso*, until actually sitting at the examination table. I had reasoned it out, although it was only a supposition, that one particular one of the four main fields would be represented, and accordingly concentrated my final preparations on that. It turned out to be right. I breathed with relief and settled down to writing my answers with a light heart. Others were less fortunate. Some even left the examination room without handing in anything at all; they had backed the wrong hunches, as I might just as easily have done. Before returning to Monte Cistello I celebrated the occasion by taking the law into my own hands. I went into a bar and had a double cappuccino. Father Basil, to whom I admitted my misdemeanour, nodded with understanding: he had heard of worse, and perhaps even done the same himself as a student.

Tired, but relieved, I boarded the train heading north. In those days the travelling plans for young monks had to be carefully worked out. As a general rule there were two points: if possible to be several together, and to stay at night in a monastery, preferably one belonging to the Order. Our first overnight stop was in our motherhouse, Cîteaux, in Burgundy, to which in the year 1112 Bernard of Clairvaux and his thirty companions had been admitted. There were eighty monks here, and here too was our abbot general, Dom Gabriel. Over the years I had more and more come to respect this man and his unusual personality, culture, and natural good manners. In the evening he came to wish me a good journey, asked me to take his greetings to Caldey, and gave me his blessing on the way. A whim of the moment led me to say: 'If you ever had any use for me, Father General, I should be glad to be of service to you'. Words can come true!

The next stopover naturally was at Scourmont, to which I had lost a little of my heart and where for over a week I was spoiled far more than was reasonable. Yet an impatient phrase tugged at me: 'Home to Caldey!'

In the monastery things had changed, that much was obvious. Our young abbot had definitely tightened things up. A couple of brothers were sent back to the monasteries that had generously lent them to us, because Dom Samson had found them too undisciplined—or perhaps too talkative at work.

One or two novices and/or monks with temporary vows had been told to leave on the grounds that they were unsuited to our life. Among these was our Danish Brother Lawrence to whom I want to devote a few words: Brother Lawrence, alias Per Waagøe, learned that he had indeed an authentic vocation, but not to the contemplative life. Deeply unhappy, he went back home, but later applied to join the American Oblate Fathers, who had settled in Denmark and who were happy enough to receive him. He completed his education in the USA and for many years afterwards was a parish priest in Denmark—and finally in the Faroe Islands, where he died.

The abbot's goal was clearly to raise standards all round, although at quite a cost. Even his own (perhaps slightly theatrical) mother was reprimanded for too much and too loud conversation in the guesthouse. Dom Samson was a model of regularity, who never spared himself—in this, an example to the rest of us. As far as I can remember, he never went away anywhere except on business for the monastery, as a rule to the annual General Chapter, or if Bishop Petit asked for his help. However, the Caldey abbot's reputation as a specialist in monastic history had spread and led to assignments which were difficult for him to refuse.

As for me, I was asked to resume all the duties in the garage. The good Tom was still active there, but the sight that met me showed that a sense of order was not his strongest card.

It is only now that the restoration of the monastery church is finally finished. The last bricks fall into place when the specially constructed organ is added. It is a heady experience to be able to accompany the liturgy with the tones of a real organ—and with all the pedals. Towards the end of July the church is consecrated by Bishop Petit in excellent form, and with the islanders in their best clothes. Everyone feels he or she has a stake in the enterprise, which is virtually so. It feels as if we monks represent a community within the community.

Dom Guerric has come for the occasion from Scourmont, and takes the opportunity to carry out his annual visitation, for after all, it is a long journey with many changes of transport *en route*. Dom Samson wishes to give some help with the latter and orders me to drive Dom Guerric to the nightboat for Calais. First our DUKW, next the monastery's car—from Tenby to Dover at one stretch. We just make it. It's a good thing there is still no speed limit on open country roads.

Otherwise my summer belonged to the 'duck'. I was prepared for that. The maintenance had left a good deal to be desired. Father Anthony and I agreed to have another try at Henley's in Weston-super-Mare in order to gain more expertise, but mostly to get certain reserve parts which were impossible to obtain through our usual 'cannibalizing dealer'. I went in for contact at the highest level, wrote and received a friendly reply—with a specified date and time for an appointment.

The director received me in his office. I got the impression that he saw the combination of the contemplative life of the monastery together with the world's largest amphibian as astonishing, or at any rate very out of the ordinary. He wanted to know more about our zinc operation, of which he had heard something. Afterwards I was shown into the enormous works where I counted seven 'ducks' at different stages of stripping down or reconstruction. Servicing for the whole of Great Britain was carried out here. *Our* biggest problem, I told him, was the vulnerable inflation-deflation system for the wheels. Sometimes we had to cut it out entirely and make do with a uniform air pressure—that is, 12–15 lb, which was only just feasible on sand, but heavy as lead on land. When I left the place, it was with quite a feeling of relief—knowing that under my jacket I had precisely the super-sophisticated instrument needed for solving the problem. (I was admonished not to let anyone see it.) And solve the problem it did!

The switch from Rome to Caldey is a test for the physique, but intensely welcome all the same. I thrive on the challenges and what I imagine to be my indispensability. Yet I am also prepared for further challenges, for have I not been in Rome and got a diploma?

Dom Samson calls me in: 'This autumn we are going to start a course in philosophy for our beginners. You must take that on.' Why I have taken a degree in theology when I am to teach philosophy seems a riddle—one of many. 'Yes, certainly', I answer in correct monastic style. I am allowed a generous amount of time to prepare the course, which is to cover two years. In the late summer I have the study plan ready and present it to the abbot who finds it a shade too demanding. 'The most important thing is to be able to keep it going', he says thoughtfully. 'Rather cut down on some of the items to make it manageable.' For my part I would have liked to include everything in the syllabus, even if that would normally require a whole staff of teachers.

I have a clearly set-out curriculum and once again four students. It starts well. As was the case with my theology teaching, I am the one who learns most—again grateful for the corrective balance to all the flurry of other tasks. What is more: the students ask questions, and I always have to be prepared for unexpected challenges, or at least know where the answers are to be found.

I have been given my own room—admittedly in the guest-house, owing to lack of space. During a brief siesta I hear footsteps on the stairs, followed by a knock on the door. Drowsily I tap out my 'Come in!' on the side of the bed. Dom Samson, with a sheet of paper in his hand and a rather up-set expression, uncharacteristically starts talking as he crosses the threshold. 'The General asks whether you will come as cellarer to Monte Cistello. He writes with a sort of despera-tion. Brother Aimable [the cellarer at the generalate] has been recalled to his monastery to take over after the administrator who has died. Dom Gabriel has held a council meeting and writes that everyone agreed with his proposal for a successor. He wants me to ask you. It is not an order; you must say yourself whether you would be willing to do it.' It is clear that Dom Samson expects an answer on the spot. And in my mind I can see Dom Gabriel's problem. That Monte Cistello needs a cellarer—one who speaks, reads, and writes Italian—goes without saying. Above all, however, it is the farewell exchange between the abbot general and myself when I stayed overnight at Cîteaux which is most vivid to me. Why did I say, with no forethought, that I was at his service if he ever had use for me? I regretted these words now, while being flattered that Dom Gabriel remembered them.

Now at last back in my monastic existence, all I want to do is to acquire a deeper understanding of the contemplative life and perform my duties within this framework. At the same time I am so accustomed to being at the disposal of my superiors that I have almost lost the ability to make an independent choice outside the areas allotted to me. Dom Samson notices my irresolution. So what about my 'indispensability' as a teacher of philosophy? I phrase my question in more careful terms. 'At all events we shall have to manage', he assures me. Yet again I marvel at the community's ability to deal with problems caused by the disappearance of a monk, simply by spreading and rearranging duties. I put the ball back in the prior's court. 'What do you think yourself?' He is probably aware that I do not dare to take the decision. 'I shall ring and say that you have my permission to work at the generalate temporarily for one year, and that you will leave here in a few days. Dom Gabriel says it's urgent.' I nod with relief, although still confused. His last words are: 'Now the most important thing for you is to regain the horizontal.' There was little likelihood of sleep.

Nineteen

ROME IN A NEW WAY

A N URGENT MESSAGE was sent to Scourmont requesting that arrangements be made for clothes and other things I would need in Rome, for on Caldey the cupboard was virtually bare. When I arrived, the wardrobe father was just giving the final touches to his work. It was like a complete bridal trousseau.

When I got off the train in Rome, Dom Gabriel and Father Clément were standing on the platform. An unbelievable honour! When we were in the car they brought me up to date. Over a hundred students—many of whom I would know—had either arrived or were expected shortly, at the very moment that Brother Aimable was on his way out. The abbot general himself was soon to make a visitation to our American monasteries and would be away for six months. The master of studies, Father Basil, had given him some information which may have decided the matter: namely, that I not only had a driving licence, I also had practice in driving in Rome's traffic chaos. 'So I remembered the last words you said to me at Cîteaux', said Dom Gabriel and quoted them word for word. 'When I laid the proposal before my advisers, it was gladly accepted.' Although my heart was still in Caldey, I felt a new sense of challenge mounting in me.

In the car, continuing to fill in the picture, Dom Gabriel explained that the reason why he specially wanted me to come at such short notice was that Pope John XXIII was going to visit Monte Cistello in a few days, and that was an event I must be allowed to share in. (Such thoughtfulness was one of the abbot general's many qualities.) But not a word! The pope himself had expressed a wish to visit our new generalate, but nothing was to leak out to the press. Even the students who were already installed at Monte Cistello knew nothing. The pope, said Dom Gabriel, did not want the media there.

My return now was very different from my arrival as a student the previous year. True to his name, Brother Aimable, who was about fifty-five years old with a greying beard, was kindness itself. Systematically, I was introduced to all aspects of the running and maintenance of both sections of the establishment. A great deal had to be absorbed in record time because of the numbers of students about to arrive just when Brother Aimable and the abbot general himself were about to leave. In addition there were many outsiders I needed to get to know, about whose idiosyncrasies the brother gave me plenty of tips. And so I ended up with a whole sheaf of notes.

I was given a newly furnished, pleasantly cool office on the lower ground floor, with a bed in its curtained-off alcove. Here I was to work—and sleep. Two telephones, one to the house and one to the outside world. My staff consisted of a small group of lay brethren recruited from various willing monasteries.

But first the pope. He wished to pay us a visit—a wish none of his predecessors had ever expressed, so this was surely a pope with a big heart! After Pius XII's noble but exalted personage, the contrast was refreshing. There were few, if any, stories circulating about Pius, yet about John there were already quite a number. One of them went like this: A priest somewhere in Italy had been informed by the Vatican that he had been appointed bishop and that this would be made public at such and such a time. He was terrified, because the bishop he was to replace had been a towering personality. The priest managed to obtain a brief private audience with John XXIII who patiently heard his pleas to be excused, and especially to escape following this famous prelate. After a while the pope cut him short in kindly tones: 'Everything will be just fine. Just do as I do: Don't try to copy your predecessor.'

It was only during lunch on the very day the visit was to take place that the students were told about it. It was not April Fools' Day—and many of them found it hard to go on eating without saying a word. Only their eyes spoke.

Shortly afterwards John XXIII was there, wandering around, nodding blithely to all. There was a solemn session in our chapel with everybody present, including the students in their white cowls. The pope, who seemed to be in very good humour, made a longish speech (more like a sermon) in French. The ceremony was rounded off when, sitting at the altar, he personally greeted all the members of the curia and the staff— myself last. When he heard that I came from Norway, he said, pretending to shiver: 'Ah, cold, cold!' I wasted the chance to say that the winter in Italy can seem much colder—indoors.

The visit had a little tail-piece. A week later our church-like chapel was consecrated by a curia cardinal. During the festive dinner a letter from the pope, expressing his thanks for a memorable reception, was read aloud. With it was a large photograph of the occasion with John XXIII's signature in his own handwriting. The cardinal shook his head in amazement: 'I don't know what's got into Papa Giovanni! Usually he never does anything like that.'

Rome is full of large buildings which can be difficult to identify. Many of them are in gardens behind wrought-iron grills. If you fly low enough, you see hundreds of patches of green, some as spacious as parks. Several are precisely that, but not all, for Rome more than anywhere else is the city of institutions. And the authorities have ruled that all green areas shall be preserved intact. No visible change is tolerated. Embassies, institutes, hospitals, prisons, boarding schools, museums, palaces, luxury hotels, and so on, make every effort to be surrounded by their own park. The older the establishment is, the larger this green area tends to be. And the Church owns about half of these 'lungs' (as one might well call them). The religious orders—at any rate those of any size—have their central administration in Rome. That in itself consists of many entities—and a great deal of green. The thousand or so sister communities, too, are normally surrounded by greenery. Monte Cistello was no exception, but with an important difference: our nearest neighbour, the abbey of Tre Fontane, was engaged in agriculture, like all our houses. Our modest park area, with its tall eucalyptus trees, bordered on farmland, with country-style buildings on one side and animal husbandry with cattle and sheep on the other.

In time I learned to know some of the other generalates and could see for myself that all of them, like ourselves, were dependent on the goodwill of remote monasteries, in regard to both finances and personnel. Few, if any, had their own communities. All who worked there were on loan, except for possibly some civilian employees, though that was always considered a makeshift solution.

Three of our small staff of lay brethren belonged to different monasteries in Spain, one was from an Irish community, two came from Thomas Merton's Gethsemani in Kentucky, and one from the abbey of Spencer in Massachusetts. One quiet little lay brother was the exception: he belonged to the monastery of Fratocchie between Rome and Frascati. Our only lay employee also came from Fratocchie—a young general handyman, Eliseo, who had grown up as a carpentry apprentice in that monastery and felt a member of the family. And he still does, although he married long ago and has both children and grandchildren.

As is customary in monasteries, our lay brethren had two superiors: one spiritual, who here was one of the definitors (the abbot general's advisory council), and one for their work—in this case myself. I too was accountable to two superiors, both however on about the same level: the procurator general, by name Dom Deodat, who was from Flanders and who was the superior for the curia section, and my former master of studies, Father Basil, who was in charge of the student section, except for the household and maintenance. They left me largely in peace, something it was not possible to say about the chief accountant Dom Louis de Gonzague who—despite his Spanish-sounding name—was totally French. Dom Louis, formerly abbot of the great monastery of Melleray, was a so-called higher prelate and seemed to believe that his title and his position as financial administrator made him more my superior than was actually the case. Why he had lost his position as abbot was not clear, although I suspected it might have had something to do with a certain tendency to be one-track-minded. He could talk the hind leg off a donkey. So much so, that if it were possible to do so without being noticed, I often vanished round some convenient corner to escape him.

Dom Louis was at the stage of emerging from what had been an important period for him: the funds for the implementation of the Monte Cistello project went through his hands, and, thanks to his excellent handling of the spending operations, our generalate could rely on the accounts balancing when all expenses had been settled. I say 'all expenses', for we are in complex Italy. Despite the fact that I tried to avoid it, it was my fate to be constantly fed with information by him, not least concerning the irregularities related to the disposal of the two houses from which the generalate had moved: the one on the Aventine and the one before that again near to the Lateran. The abbot general, as the embodiment of uprightness, had long ago found out that Dom Louis must be given all necessary powers if these operations were to be carried out according to plan.

My commercial aptitude (so far untried), traditionally attributed to those from Bergen, 'the city between the seven mountains', was to have a chance to blossom here in Rome, 'the city between the seven hills'. In a short time I rationalized all the buying wherever possible. Large-scale purchasing, strategic switching of suppliers, and the like became the order of the day. With Latin adaptability two of the Spanish lay brethren, who were also sibling brothers, had become fluent

in Italian. Now they were an indispensable part of the game—
for this was a sport they enjoyed![1]

Not that we were never cheated. One day I got a long-
distance call on a very poor line. The caller presented himself
as the parish priest of Radicofano, a mountain village north
of Rome. He cultivated olives to help eke out his meagre
income. This year he had oil (olive trees bear fruit only every second year), and of very good quality. He would be
happy to sell some to us. If I needed references—as would
be perfectly understandable—I could simply ring the abbess
of a named convent, whose telephone number he gave me.
She was a customer and could be depended on. The price
he mentioned was definitely favourable. Since in any case
the time for making the purchase was not far off, I rang
the 'abbess', who had nothing but praise for the product—
which I then ordered. The oil arrived and smelt reassuringly
of olives. When I met the cellarer from Tre Fontane and told
him of my bargain, he said: 'There are no olives in Radicofano. It's too high up. Besides I know the parish priest and
he grows nothing whatever.' I sent a sample to a laboratory
for foodstuffs control. The result showed 10 per cent olive
oil, 90 per cent sunflower oil, plus colouring. Fortunately no
one noticed the error, but the laboratory had acquired a new
customer.

I felt there ought to be a radical reorganization in the serving of meals. We were now many, and all of us, apart from
those who sat at or near the high table, had lukewarm if not
cold food because everything was set out ready on plates.
Moreover, those served last often got too little. The change
to serving-dishes with lids, to be set out just before mealtimes,
could not be effected without a flurry of minor objections—
what about the time-honoured traditions of the house? But
before long everyone was pleased with the change, particularly
the lay brethren who sat lowest; now they too could eat in
peace, with ample hot food.

The tranquillity of the monastery was subjected to many
strains. Agents of all categories found their way to my office

in such numbers that I had to remove the sign ECONOMATO (bursar's office) which I had put up. Some of these people were useful: one could be played off against another when it came to prices, but I risked being dragged into a world of salesmen who seemed to live at subsistence level and were correspondingly importunate.

Many who actually lived in dire poverty found their way here too, as it seemed they systematically did to all the cellarers in the papal city. I learned to distinguish between those who were genuinely in need and those who simply said they were. Their professed poverty was not always the whole picture. Dom Louis had ruled—wisely, as I soon understood—that a maximum of 100 lire could be given to individuals in need. I kept a supply of such coins in my petty cash, and consoled myself with the thought that the genuinely poor would probably get sufficent to live on in the course of wandering from door to door.

It was only now I realized fully how much psychological pressure many of our students were living under. Most of them seemed to dread the forthcoming examinations. Cramming led to increased insomnia as the fateful hour drew nearer. Life in the Cistercian monasteries strikes a balance between physical and spiritual activity. The body is accustomed to tough demands. However, in the course of the one-sided term of study here, this side withered, even though everyone had jobs to do in connection with the household. As the year passed, I was more and more frequently approached by Father Basil or his assistant about these problems of stress and anxiety. To some extent I recognized myself from the year before, although perhaps I had been more fortunate in keeping the bogeys at bay. We were good customers at the nearest chemist's. Usually we could get medicines, normally only obtainable on prescription, and even with a 10 per cent rebate. After all, were we not in Italy?

There was still a lot to be done before we would be able to say that Monte Cistello was finished and furnished. I was constantly out and about with my list of problems, which never seemed to get any shorter, since new ones cropped up never-endingly. Faithful Eliseo was always in full swing. If he had not been a Jack-of-all-trades from before, he certainly was so now. And although everything was new, it was clear from an early stage that quite a few improvements would have to be made. Italians as a rule build well and solidly, but are less interested when it comes to maintenance, while we northerners attend to the paint and putty from the start. Sad to say, the building complex at Monte Cistello bore evidence of being a rushed job. With the trace of Nordic perfectionism I possessed, it was my ambition to keep everything in tip-top condition. And in this I had at any rate the aesthetically minded Dom Gabriel on my side.

John XXIII has succeeded in giving the papacy a human face—indeed at almost eighty years of age he has become a father figure for the world: wise, kindly, and revered. The public audiences in Saint Peter's attract growing crowds. Everyone who possibly can wants to experience being in the presence of this man—sensing his charisma. There are always new anecdotes about him, some of them probably true.

The Council now being prepared has sent a silent quiver of emotion through the Church—and not only through the Catholic Church. The pope has given the lead with some key words: *aggiornamento* (updating), *pastoral council, ecumenism* (the word that reputedly made Pius XII see red), and, not least, *dialogue with the world.* The Council is to draw up guidelines for contemporary and future Catholics. No special item is given priority, however, for no less than the whole life and teaching of the Church is to be taken up for thorough discussion by the world's episcopate assembled in Rome under the leadership of its pastoral head.

The pope had begun by appointing a Preparatory Commission of bishops representative of the whole Church. The Nordic countries also had their man: Bishop Suhr. He telephoned one day, having just arrived at his order's Roman monastery, San Girolamo, where he had been prior when in 1939 he was appointed bishop of Denmark. He wanted to visit me now and see how I was getting on.

In the months and years that followed, either Bishop Suhr was my guest at Monte Cistello or I was his at San Girolamo where his old rooms were still at his disposal, unused by anyone else. Bishop Suhr and I hit it off very well together. He kept me informed of the preparations for the Council, now and then with details which fortunately seldom found their way into print. He made no secret of his lack of enthusiasm for certain leading figures in the papal curia in whom he saw power-conscious people who wished to decide things themselves— regardless of the Preparatory Commission. He believed that attempts were sometimes being made to out-manoeuvre the pope himself, even in areas which were of particular concern to him. If so, 'these gentlemen are not going to get very far', declared Suhr with determination.

He and I had an experience that seemed to illustrate this, during a ceremony in Saint Peter's. The Italian curia cardinal Bacci was a well-known expert on Latin who had under-taken to renew the language by thinking up equivalents for words and expressions which had come to the world after Latin's last gasp as it were. During his energetic campaign for the renewal of the language within the Universal Church, he had persuaded John XXIII to issue an authoritative cir-cular (in this case a 'papal constitution')—actually written by Bacci himself—obliging the Church to restore various Latin regulations which in the course of time had been more or less shelved. During the ceremony, at which parts of the text were read aloud, came the solemn moment when the pope with raised quill-pen—but perhaps with some hesitation?— signed the original, carefully inscribed on parchment. It may be that he felt himself in a way cornered, for what followed was strange, perhaps even provocative. He turned, and sitting with his back to his signature which was hardly dry, he gave a fine sermon on what seemed a completely different subject— in Italian!

★ ★ ★

Bishop Suhr was able to tell me more about developments on the Nordic diplomatic scene. As already mentioned, the pope had sent an archbishop from The Netherlands, Martin Lucas by name, as apostolic delegate to the Scandinavian countries. After having decided against Stockholm, the prelate had searched all over Copenhagen hoping to find a suitable residence, but in the end, urged on by Bishop Suhr, he had decided on an imposing house surrounded by old trees in a park between the capital and Helsingør. 'Far out in the country, then?' I asked. 'Yes, you can be sure of that', answered Bishop Suhr, 'far enough, I hope.'

One of the first things the apostolic delegate had done was to summon the bishops in our five countries to a meeting for the formal establishment of a Scandinavian Episcopal Conference. Only a few countries as yet had such a forum, and one jointly for several countries had scarcely been heard of. Lucas must have felt the urge to act, for only two months after he was more or less settled in, the assembly was at work—in my hometown Bergen (my heart beat faster). Bishop Suhr had been unanimously elected chairman.

On the day before Christmas Eve in 1960 it fell to me to celebrate the Christmas Mass for the Norwegian colony—as usual in the Saint Olav chapel in the large central church of San Carlo al Corso. Few of those who were present were Catholics, perhaps not even practising Christians. There were people I knew from wartime days, as well as quite a few who had come to spend their Christmas holiday in Rome, just as I myself had once done. Nevertheless, it was obvious that for some the real event came after the service at 'coffee time', when not only coffee was drunk.

At Monte Cistello I introduced an innovation: on Christmas Eve a real Scandinavian 'julegløgg' of hot spiced wine was ladled out. There were no objections, and it may not just have been a flight of fancy that the subsequent singing swelled in volume.

★ ★ ★

A new friend was now to enter into my life, unlikely though this was under the circumstances. Robert (Bob to everybody) Usher was an American architect who had worked for many years as an art director at Paramount. He had several friends among the brothers in a Californian monastery popularly called Vina (after the place). He turned up to visit two of them, at present students at Monte Cistello: Fathers Anselm and Herman Joseph. And it was they who wanted the two of us to meet. The reason soon became clear.

Bob had given up his architect's office after an uncle had left him a useful inheritance, and had decided to live in Rome, as near as possible to Monte Cistello and his friends there. Truth to tell, he had found an existence full of social commitments empty and meaningless. Now he wanted to give himself time to think over what he would do with the rest of his life. He had come across a roomy apartment not far away, but needed the help of someone who mastered Italian—not only as or-dinarily spoken but, because of all the red tape involved, also as used officially. Like most Americans, Bob wanted every-thing done straight away. I soon found it was almost a sport to protect him against abuse, for it was easy to see he was well-heeled while at the same time he seemed almost too trusting.

Bob's way to Rome had been across Germany, for he was determined to have a car, and it had to be a Mercedes. In the event it proved to be a long, silver-grey, custom-built two-seater that made people turn and stare.

Bob, who was old enough to be my father, didn't take long to find out that I had a background in films and made me feel like an old colleague. I thought him an unusually interesting acquaintance: an American totally at home with European culture, something which could hardly be said of all our students from 'over there'. As a former art director, one of the things he was best at was stylish interiors. Sometimes I was struck dumb by his over-inventive ideas. Then he would laugh with delighted amusement.

But Bob was deeply religious, a convert who loved his Church and could not do enough for it. And he loved the Cistercian community in Vina, situated at a manageable distance from his own home in Eureka. He had been commissioned by the abbot to plan their monastery complex, for the foundation was still so recent that the monks were practically living in temporary work-huts. And what planning! His apartment was awash with drawings and models, which I had to show an interest in and comment on as much as if it were my own abbey. But there was more. During his years in the film world Bob had got used to going right to the top in important matters. So now I was to open the way to the abbot general, whom he assumed he needed to win over for the project. Bob spoke only English and the abbot general only French, so I had to be their interpreter.

It was a memorable performance. One after another, Bob spread out the large sheets of plans in front of Dom Gabriel, following them with various cardboard models. None of this, however, reminded the abbot general of the Vina he remembered from his visitation there shortly before. *It* lay flat and in a (for him) rather undistinguished area. Bob's project, on the other hand, showed a fertile landscape with a number of ponds (you could see the fish), canals, and well-designed bridges, and with low monastery buildings in natural stone blending into the landscape. Dom Gabriel glanced over at me a couple of times as though wondering whether we were discussing the same monastery, while I discreetly strove to stick to my rôle as the impartial middleman. Finally Dom Gabriel threw up his hands: Yes, this was obviously interesting, even impressive, but what did Vina's own abbot, Dom Eusebius, think about it, for the commission must come from him, must it not? Monsieur Usher, he concluded, could certainly explain to him that the project had been presented to the abbot general who had found it remarkable—but beyond that he would not say anything, since it would conflict with normal practice. I could hear Dom Gabriel give a sigh of relief as we went out of the door. On later occasions, if Bob Usher's name cropped up, he would humorously pull a face in my direction to remind me of the audience I had involved him in.

Bob is more European than a European, but with an American's unspoilt way of looking at things. One Sunday when we are both free he takes me along in the afternoon to an exhibition in the grotesquely antiquated Gallery for Modern Art, which I have sworn never again to enter. (Since then the Gallery has been totally modernized.) It is a retrospective exhibition: Henry Moore. I have certainly heard the name, but without connecting it with anything in particular. They say the works have been brought in by twenty railway-freight trucks, which I can well believe. Moore is represented here with a considerable share of his output, from some enormous works (including a series of skyscraping totem-poles) to quite small pieces—and in addition a fascinating collection of graphic art, especially from wartime London, in a direct and intensely personal style. Quite overwhelmed, I remark that he must incontestably be the sculptor of the century. We wander around for a long time, enjoying the exhibition to the full: I at seeing the works for the first time and Bob at seeing them again.

The spring of 1961 was cold and unpleasant. Mother visited me again in May, staying at the Pensione Norden and freezing. The Scandivian guests seemed to believe they had decreed once and for all that there was to be delightful, warm weather in Italy at this time of year. On the days when the sun appeared and the temperature was rising, they set off sightseeing in blouses and short-sleeved shirts, despite warnings from the Pensione's 'Aunt' Ciss. True it was warm in the sun, but it was cool in the shade, and it got cold early. Half the guests had colds and if possible stayed in bed. I say 'if possible' because, excepting breakfast, meals were not served. Mother too caught a cold, but could take it less seriously because Ciss brought her all her meals in bed, loading her with well-meant advice and good works.

Mother wanted to meet this Bob whom I had written about. And he, who had seen a picture of her and noticed the likeness, was very pleased that they were now to meet. We were to be his guests—no, not in his apartment, but at a good restaurant. It was the Ristorante Alfredo, not far from the Pensione Norden. Bob was at his liveliest—and very gallant. He talked without stopping for breath, and I noticed Mother's rather cryptic smile. I realized that Bob probably struck her as being more out-of-the-ordinary than I had depicted. It was when he was going to order the wine that he was clearly less sure of himself, for wine was something he knew little about, and now here he was with a mature woman of the world. Slightly confused, he passed the list over to me: 'You two decide on the wine.' Mother was amused, that I could see.

A few days later there was an alarm. Mother had developed double pneumonia and had to be sent post-haste to hospital, that is to say to the clinic that Ciss 'advised'. But in Mother's opinion, it was intolerable to be in a place with staff who only spoke Italian, despite the good nursing. It helped a little that she had had a 'delightful visit' from a young Norwegian woman who was visiting her father, our Ambassador Prebensen, who by chance was in the same hospital.

I realized now that it was very important for Mother to be moved to an institution where the staff spoke English or German. I knew of such a place, the Salvator Mundi hospital on the Gianicolo Hill. It was largely staffed by American nuns, partly with a German background. It was also the hospital most English-speaking patients were sent to. I managed to arrange for her to be transferred there that very day, despite the fact that her doctor advised against a radical break in treatment. For Mother this was a new and better life. Not only was the nursing first-class, but here she could talk to everybody. The sister in charge, Mother Johanna, became her good friend, and she recovered remarkably quickly. Nevertheless, she wanted to get back home. Possibly everything was done too quickly, for in Oslo she had to go back to hospital for more treatment, which did not bode well.

The hot weather came suddenly. Now nature was going to make up for what we had missed. At Monte Cistello two newly arrived black theology students from a monastery in Kenya went past me groaning. They were to take their examinations in Rome, but felt the weather had taken everything out of them. 'Italy is so much hotter than Africa', said one, the other only nodding silently.

Bishop Suhr is back for further preparations for the Council. He brings with him to Monte Cistello a Benedictine colleague, Dom Jean Leclercq, not unknown to us, for in monastic circles he is both admired and respected as a researcher, author, and lecturer. Behind him he has innumerable publications on medieval spirituality, monastic life, thought processes, and theology, as well as the leading religious figures of the Middle Ages: pioneer work which it would be hard to overestimate. Each time a new number of a periodical connected with monasticism came out, it was Dom Leclercq's name you first looked for. His capacity for work was legendary. To attend retreats or lectures given by him was a privilege. He was French, but spoke fluent English, and spent a large part of his religious life addressing monks and nuns all round the world. At Monte Cistello, where introductions to monastic spirituality, along the lines of a retreat, were included in the syllabus for students, we had already a couple of times succeeded in getting him to come as a lecturer.

In Rome he always lived in the Clervaux foundation, San Girolamo, and then it sometimes happened that it was my duty (for which I was grateful) to drive him to and from Monte Cistello. We talked freely, not least about our shared monastic heritage—I asking, he answering. Dom Leclercq's memory was a fund of detailed knowledge covering a wide field. Once when I voiced my impressed admiration, he said:

'Yes, I was born with a capacious memory and easy powers of association.'

Bishop Suhr and Dom Leclercq had been novices together in Clervaux in Luxembourg and felt close to one another. In the evening the latter might drop in on his Danish friend for a chat that could last into the small hours. It struck me that there was the same sort of closeness between him and Bishop Suhr as I myself shared with my fellow novices in Caldey—like real brothers in the same family.

And now Dom Gabriel, his secretary Father Clément, and I were invited to lunch in the San Girolamo monastery. Neither Bishop Suhr nor the French abbot would take no for an answer. We were given a heart-warming welcome. Dom Gabriel had to inspect the monastery from attic to cellar, not forgetting the church and sacristy. I saw that he was tired, walked slowly, and was breathing heavily. It was clear, too, that he did not consider the complex—erected as it was from insufficient funds at a period lacking architectural inspiration—any sort of aesthetic revelation. Ordinary maintenance, as well, left something to be desired.

The meal itself was not without problems. We were given some huge slabs of meat, elegantly served on individual plates by a lay servant. I observed Dom Gabriel making the special gesture he used when things were getting out of hand. He would lift his hands chest-high and look up to the ceiling as if seeking help from above. He and I had certainly been served the most generous portions of an aged cow. I myself sawed away at it with my knife, and chewed for all I was worth, but to little avail. When I discreetly looked around to see how far the meal had progressed, I saw Dom Gabriel simply sitting there, staring motionless into space. His plate was empty. I was full of shame at leaving half of my portion untouched, but my jaw was numb. Later in the car, when I asked him how he had managed it, he replied: 'Yes, wasn't it awful? And we who are not used to meat! I managed to cut the steak into a couple of big pieces and swallowed them whole one after the other—and I can tell you they're still as whole as ever!'

I mentioned nothing of this to Bishop Suhr, who could be trusted to pass on the story to advantage during recreation.

In the summer of 1961 Dom Gabriel looks far from well. July and August are the months the Romans hate: extremely hot, with little fresh air. Monte Cistello is almost empty of staff on both the curia and the student side. But our abbot general is still here, because he has a great deal of writing and planning to do, and is therefore glad so many are absent. Also the lay brethren and I myself are still at our posts, for this is the time for renovation. Not only a thorough cleaning, but in addition, all the planned repairs, improvements, and changes must necessarily be carried out in this period.

One day Father Clément comes to me with a conspiratorial look. The abbot general is suffering, but in silence—or near silence. The secretary thinks he knows what is the matter. Do I know of a good urologist? He himself knows of none. Nor in fact do I, but the Yellow Pages should have the answer. Many grand names and even grander titles. But I have learnt the trick in another context: find a university professor, they know their stuff. Together we persuade Dom Gabriel to let us make an appointment for him with Professor N. whose consulting room is on the Aventine—not far from our former generalate, which he finds reassuring. While I wait outside, I hear Dom Gabriel yell with pain. A little later he comes out slowly. It is obvious that the consultation has made things clear. 'I have to have an operation', he says. 'And as soon as possible—everything is blocked.'

With the professor's help we find a clinic run by nuns. Instead of celebrating his silver jubilee as an abbot and his tenth anniverary as abbot general, Dom Gabriel has to submit to being laid on the operating table. Father Clément and I alternate in spending long watches at his bedside in the following days. The pain is intense and lasts longer than expected. But in the end our abbot general is restored, to the extent that he can set out on his postponed round of visitations. Many people notice, however, that things are not the same as before.

★ ★ ★

Towards the end of the heatwave we can at last close down
the establishment—now that all is ready for the influx in the
autumn—and go our various ways. My temporary goal is the
Cistercian abbey of Tamié in the French Alps, 950 metres
above sea level. I feel exhausted and in need of a retreat—
longing to find spiritual peace and devote myself to religious
matters. A former fellow-student in Rome, who belongs to
the Tamié community, has arranged to let me have a week
with them. But I have hardly arrived before my ex-colleague
drags me off on a long mountain tour—1800 metres up—to
the edge of the perpetual snow with Mont Blanc glittering opposite against a blue sky. Unforgettable, even for a Norwegian!
Next morning: intense stiffness in my legs, ankles, and feet, so
that I only just manage to crawl out of bed and down to the
church. I had forgotten to tell my hosts of the more spiritual
purpose behind my wish to stay. I therefore do so now, and
the rest of the time can be passed in rewarding peace.

On the way to Caldey through a London crowded out with
visitors, I make a brief detour to Knightsbridge to see if I can
find the monastery's newly opened perfume shop. I do. It is
opposite Brompton Oratory—in a dream of a location as far
as tourists are concerned. I do not go in.

On Caldey, which had finally reached a state bordering on
economic equilibrium, there were many visible improvements—or *were* they improvements? Among other things, the
roads for the 'duck' were now concrete-surfaced. There were
a few new faces, others had vanished. As a whole, however, the
community was growing and there was a feeling of optimism.
I myself was treated rather too much like a holiday-guest.
It was certainly with the best of goodwill, for signals from
Monte Cistello had let it be known that Father John was
tired and should ideally be given the opportunity to build
up new strength for the busy autumn ahead. Nevertheless, I
had plenty to occupy myself with, for the 'duck' required a
number of complicated adjustments. But what was especially

exciting, and enriching from my point of view, was to take over the organ again to accompany the services of the Divine Office and High Mass.

Very soon Monte Cistello faded into the background. It was here at Caldey I belonged and was at home, and it did me good to know the brethren felt the same. I should add by way of explanation that Caldey was still the monastery I was bound to for life (no one was bound in this way to Monte Cistello, except possibly in a sense the abbot general). In other words, Dom Samson was free to call me back, had he wanted to. However, not a word came from him to say that my trial year in Rome was now over.

Signals from Mother, in more dramatic tones than was usual for her, made it clear to me that she was seriously ill, bedridden, and in great pain, which necessitated frequent morphine injections. Could I come? Dom Samson thought I should go, since I was soon to leave for Rome anyway. So in mid-September I flew to Oslo.

When I came into the hall at Grav, Mother was standing there, dressed, but extremely pale. I was not to hug her, hardly take her hand. She had a blood disease and could develop an infection from almost any physical contact. Nevertheless, she was allowed to be up for a few hours every day, and the next morning I took her to hospital, where she had an appointment with her doctor, a professor who was a specialist in such cases.

Father wanted to take the opportunity to see me during this short visit to Oslo and announced he would be coming that same morning. I had actually said that I could not meet him at the airport because I was taking Mother to the doctor. But she insisted that I should meet him, and she herself would manage to get home in a taxi. So that's how it was. Later I learned that the professor had hoped to have the chance of a conversation with me in a separate room—unknown to my mother. At home, Mother told me that she was said to be getting better, but was to have some blood transfusions and a course of injections. I felt reassured, for was I not used to the way she had for years overcome all illnesses and always regained her strength? I stayed only a short week in Oslo, most of the time talking with her and fixing this and that in the house, for she still lived alone, although now with a nurse looking in daily. So reasonably at ease about her, I set off on the long train journey to Rome.

Two important events put their stamp on the coming study year, one internal to our Order and one to do with the whole Church. The first was the Order's General Chapter, which for the first time was held in Rome, and the second was the Vatican Council, the preparations for which were now crystallized in the form of concrete drafts for discussions in the Council aula. Thus the year promised to be different from the normal—if indeed such a thing existed.

The first fact we had to face was that the number of enrolled students at Monte Cistello had dropped to only sixty-five, as against more than one hundred, two years earlier. This ought really to have been foreseen, for several monasteries now had sufficient numbers of qualified teachers. The largest dormitory could be closed down. The calculated purchases would have to be reduced. Each student would now on average cost more. No great disaster, but naturally the question hung in the air as to whether Monte Cistello might not in time become something of a white elephant. (The answer came sooner than expected, and only a few years later the Order found it necessary to sell both the church section and the student section to a sister order, which also used it as a generalate.)

Dom Louis, for his part, could rub his hands: he had succeeded in selling the other former generalate, where the interior was half in ruins. For a long time it had been rented out to a film company that did not feel obliged to take care of anything. The buyer was a speculator with plans to renovate it as a hotel, which—we surmised—would be resold at a good profit. He had been through an endless round of public offices and had obtained the necessary permits for alteration in use. However, even when changes in usage had been regularized, it was never permissible to alter the façade (for instance, by setting in new windows) nor to make any substantial changes to an interior deemed conservation-worthy. If the notorious *bustarella* was generous enough, certain concessions could be counted on, as well as a more prompt expedition of the necessary documents. The latter was particularly important. We others were as pleased as Dom Louis, for he had persisted for years without giving up.

The Cistercian Order has held its annual General Chapters in Cîteaux ever since its inception in 1119. Sometimes, even for lengthy periods, they have had to be dropped due to *force majeure* such as war and revolution. I think the reason why the present assembly of the Order's leading superiors, as an exception, was to take place in Rome was Dom Gabriel's desire to give the abbots the opportunity to visit our new generalate and student residence. It would also make it possible for them to attend an audience with John XXIII, since no one prophesied any long pontificate for him.

Dom Gabriel, who disliked leaving things to chance, gave much thought to the arrangements and called in our little staff to many meetings. In addition, he often summoned his body of definitors in connection with the Chapter's heavy agenda, which in turn led to a mass of correspondence with the monasteries. Owing to the circumstances, I came closer to him during this time than would otherwise have been the case—for everything of a practical nature had to go through the cellarer. Our largest room, the refectory, was to be turned into a conference hall with simultaneous translation facilities from and into French, English, and Spanish. The students' large cloister, which was open towards the monastery garth, would be used for meals. This and much more had to be carefully gone into and organized, because once the meetings had begun, everything must function perfectly.

Bob suddenly looks me up, worried. And this is the reason: his own home for many years lay in the middle of a splendid property in the California Redwoods area, near Whitehorn, whose beauty was enhanced by the giant trees. Some time before, through the monks in Vina, he had heard that a community of Belgian Cistercian sisters were trying to find a suitable location for a foundation in California. He had offered them the property free, his own villa included. The sisters had moved in and were already planning to make extensions, for which funds were needed. The Mother Superior decided how to raise the amount: the sale of an important quantity of big trees would go a long way towards financing the programme. And this was what had reached Bob's ears. A hastily arranged meeting in my office with the theologians from Vina resulted in a telegram to the prioress: DO NOT SELL TREES STOP AM ON MY WAY STOP BOB. Shortly afterwards the no-longer-so-happy donor was winging his way to San Francisco and Eureka. There were apparently some hot exchanges of views when he got there, for the giant trees were his favourite treasures.

A letter with a Swedish stamp arrives from Mother. So then she is well again and can travel! But my relief is short-lived. The writing paper is from the Red Cross hospital in Stockholm and the message is worrying. To combat her blood disease her professor in Oslo had prescribed an intensive cure for which she had to be an in-patient—in a ward: there was no avoiding it. Mother had immediately left for a Stockholm hospital where she knew private rooms were obtainable. And now she's installed there. Her handwriting is as good as always. All things considered, I'm pleased that she is now in safe hands.

Then one day her sister Emy telephones from Stockholm. Can I come? Mother has acute leukemia and is dying.

Dom Gabriel is temporarily in Paris for observation. I contact the procurator general, the Belgian Dom Deodat. He is clearly full of sympathy, but says, as I knew he is obliged to, that alas, I may not leave. I emphasize that my mother is in a hospital abroad—and dying. He shakes his head. I leave the room, well knowing that this is how it is with us. But I had to try, if only for my own sake.

A little less than an hour later Dom Deodat comes to me. 'I have had a meeting with the definitors,' he says, 'because I felt this is too sad, with your mother about to die alone in a foreign country. We have agreed that you should go to her. But we must keep this to ourselves.'

Only a few hours later I was on board the aircraft. When I came into Mother's room in the late afternoon, it was difficult for me to recognize her. To my relief she signalled that she knew me, although she could no longer speak. Emy had come over, was staying in a hotel, and kept all in order, which was a good thing. The nurses were like angels—doing far more than duty required. They had in fact lost their hearts to this cheerful, unselfish, and happy patient—'and so beautiful!' confided the sister in charge.

For my own part, I felt it essential that Mother be given the sacrament of Extreme Unction, well aware that this is not infrequently done for non-Catholics if they are known to be disposed for it. I telephoned to priests I knew. The Jesuit superior in the Eugenia church hurried over with the ritual and the essential oil, and stood beside me while I conferred the sacrament. Mother lay there perfectly still, full of reverence I felt. And so she passed slowly away in the course of a few hours.

We managed to gather her old friends in Stockholm for a farewell ceremony in the hospital chapel. For the first time I led the service for the closing of a coffin. The next occasion would be ten years later—in Bergen.

Emy and I together saw to the thousand tasks which suddenly needed to be dealt with. I needed clearance from Dom Gabriel in Paris to be able to arrange the funeral and formalities in Oslo.

My brother Jens could not come, because he was ill in Lima. But Father, quiet and pale, came and helped. As a Catholic, I was not allowed to conduct the funeral service. Emy was a fine support, since from her husband's death a few years earlier she was familiar with all that had to done.

I returned to Rome, confident that we could tackle the complicated problems we had always known would arise as

soon as Mother was gone. For now it was the turn of Sigurd Kloumann's family. After Mother's death the Grav estate
belonged to them.

At Monte Cistello only a few people had been informed about
where I had been or what had happened. On grounds of
precedent it was better like that, and besides a mass of con-
dolences was not what I most wanted.

But Bob, back from the USA, came to my door and looked
at me searchingly. He did not know where I had been, but
he had guessed—and guessed right. My mother had won his
heart. His own mother was still alive and well at eighty-five
years of age. (She had recently declared that she wanted to
take her pilot's licence, for she had now been up in an aircraft and had become air-minded after years of refusing to
travel by plane.) Bob was brimming over with accounts of his
skirmishes with Mother Prioress. But a settlement had been
reached and legally registered, which meant that his beloved
trees would remain unscathed, apart from one or two which
would have to make room for the needed extension. And
he was still doggedly working on his project for a new and
different Vina monastery.

On a visit to my office Bishop Suhr tells me that our apostolic
delegate, Archbishop Lucas, has had to stand down for health
reasons. He has been replaced by a *chargé d'affaires*, the Swiss
Bruno Heim, who is said to be an eminent expert on heraldry.
He has designed the coat of arms for our new pope, so it is
no doubt true. (This is someone with whom, it transpires, I
shall have quite a lot to do later.)

Suhr gives an interesting account of the meetings in the
Preparatory Commission. It is obvious that two tendencies
(one might say factions) are making themselves felt, the conservative and the progressive. The spokesman for the first faction is the curia cardinal Alfredo Ottaviani, the supreme head
of the Holy Office—the congregation over all congregations
—whose mission is to watch over the purity and unassailability

of the faith. With him he is said to have various formidable personages, mostly Italian cardinals (such as Archbishops Siri of Genoa and Ruffini of Palermo) and prelates who fear the danger of a falling away from the faith and morals on all sides.

In the opposite camp, to which Bishop Suhr reckons he belongs, there are Cardinals König (Vienna), Alfrink (Utrecht), Döpfner (Munich), not to forget the well-known and respected German biblical expert Cardinal Augustin Bea. Cardinal Bea is the head of the Pontifical Secretariat for Promoting Christian Unity—and is regarded uneasily by a number of his Roman Curia colleagues because of his ecumenical zeal. 'Between the committee meetings', sighs Suhr 'while the majority of us are in our dioceses, draft texts are formulated in the Vatican by theologians under the constant influence of the conservative faction. They are not people of ill-will, heaven knows conservatism is no sin, but it does not lead to any *aggiornamento*.' When it comes to this aspect of the Council, Bishop Suhr is eloquent, even persuasive. Suddenly he gives me a cryptic look and says: 'Won't you say *du* to me?' Nothing could have surprised me more, for although he said *du* to me and to many others, there were few, if any, who addressed him in this unceremonious form. He was twenty-five years older than I and had a natural dignity which in no way induced familiarity. The first time I was to address him thus, my tongue almost curled up in my mouth. Gradually it went better. To call him Theodor was so difficult for me that I avoided it entirely.

Some time later, also in my office, and during the delivery of a new report about the tussles in the Preparatory Commission, Bishop Suhr's violet skullcap fell on to the desk. After a moment or so, when he picked it up to put it back in place, he changed his mind and put it on my head instead. Almost horrified I tore it off, as if some desecration had taken place. The interpretation of signs was never my strong point.

The person I saw most of was Eliseo, our general handyman. It was to him I listened most as well, for he loved to talk, even though he worked willingly and carefully enough. His hobbyhorse was wine; not that he was more given to drink than others were—if anything, the opposite—but he was passionately interested in the production process, all the way from the grape to the finished product. Before he went off to his own affairs in the evening, he could stand in front of my desk for up to an hour and talk about wine—or olive oil, another foible. He was interested, not least, in our purchases. He disliked the vine-grower from the Albano district whom I had taken over. 'Ranchella is no vine-grower', he would say with superior scorn, 'he is a *magazziniere*'. He had thus said everything that was to be said, for while those in this category possibly cultivated some vines themselves—if only for the sake of appearances—in general they bought from others and then rounded off the wine in their own barrels. That, too, was for the sake of appearances. After a while I got rid of Ranchella.

Wine then was drunk at Monte Cistello? Indeed it was, for wine is the drink of the country, and moreover about the cheapest beverage you can serve. What is more, it is nutritious. A little carafe at each place. And everyone—from the abbot general to the youngest lay brother—got the same quality and quantity. Always white, because in central Italy wine means white wine. Just as in Tuscany it means red wine. Everybody sticks to the local product—at any rate for everyday use— which in Rome means *i Castelli Romani*, the hills to the north and east. Some names are widely known: Frascati, Olevano, Velletri, San Marino. The buying had to be done at the right time and in large quantities, for only then can you drive a good bargain. But naturally it was very important to choose a product suited to storage. We made several wine-tasting expeditions as close as we could to the best areas, where the prices would be more favourable. And now Eliseo gained in stature, for this was his strong point. We took care not to be cheated. The wine we approved of was the one we made sure of taking with us. Each barrel had to be tasted before we nodded our acceptance. After that we saw that the wine was taken down by the shortest route to Monte Cistello—with ourselves vigilantly behind. We were always eager to see whether the monks noticed that the wine on the table was different. It did not always happen, but the worst thing was if someone we respected wrinkled his nose, as if to say the old wine had been better.

One day Eliseo has something he is longing to tell me. Yes, the fact is that he is thinking of getting married. A new light shines out from his whole being. This must be serious, the real thing. Congratulations, explanations as to who the bride-to-be is, and much else. But then there was—of course—one thing more: where to live. Both of them are still at home with their respective families, so there are no possibilities in that direction—what with all the brothers and sisters.

When Monte Cistello was built, it had been one of Dom Louis's pet ideas to include a dwelling for the general handyman in a piece of garden off on its own. But Dom Gabriel had refused. He knew Italy, and was not inclined to have family, children, grandchildren, and distant relations in and out of the grounds. It was, after all, a monastery. Eliseo, aware of the proposal, had had to swallow his disappointment.

But what now? Should he give notice, find himself an apartment in a poor quarter and hope for a job as a carpenter? Or could we help him to find a place to live near enough so that he could continue here where he was so happy in his job? I feel that in a way I have the fate of a human being in the palm of my hand. But the future of Monte Cistello's maintenance is also involved, for Eliseo is perhaps the most indispensable of all of us. However, no one has told him that.

The decision taken by Dom Gabriel with his council means that an attempt will be made to follow up a proposal I put forward, namely that the generalate buy an apartment as near as possible, which Eliseo shall then rent from us. He is to have a pay-raise, for there may well be new mouths to feed. Little do I guess what I have set in motion. The same property agent who had found Bob's big apartment for him is also able to find the small one needed for Eliseo, and even within a reasonable distance from us. We agree on the price. The apartment building's regulations, however, require that only a named person may be the owner, and moreover that this person must reside there.

A new council meeting; Eliseo as *owner* is quite a different matter! Perhaps all can be arranged by taking out a mortgage? But what happens then if Eliseo gives notice? Or if he is *given* notice? It falls to me as middleman to pass these views back and forth. The situation becomes even more complicated when Dom Louis is drawn into the matter, for he has opinions about almost everything. But Eliseo also has something to say: he does not want to have such a large loan unless he has adequate guarantees. This is understandable, for unemployment is Italy's nightmare. A resolution is hammered out: Eliseo is to borrow the purchase sum from the generalate, against a deduction in his pay, for interest and repayment instalments over twenty years. He for his part gives a written undertaking to remain in the job for the whole of this period. The agreement is mutually terminable, but then the apartment will be able to be taken over by the generalate against the restitution of the amount paid in.

Everyone is relieved! But we have forgotten to allow for Italy's all too well known bureaucracy; the most complicated part was still ahead. In the Mediterranean countries the law demands that all contracts concerning the purchase and sale of property must be handled by a notary who (to put it in simplified form) is responsible to the authorities for seeing that formal agreements are both in accordance with the law in force and entered into according to correct legal practice. Weeks of meetings and discussions followed where the notary, the sellers, the purchaser (Eliseo), and myself representing the lender, as well as at least one person representing the co-proprietors of the building, sat round a table and discussed this—in most people's eyes—strangest of all strange contracts. That we had gone too far to be able to turn back went without saying, not least because Eliseo was firm as steel here, since it was his future that was at stake. We sweated away under the suspicious hawk-like gaze of the notary—who was a university professor into the bargain. That he was constantly interrupted by telephone calls or by secretaries pushing documents in front of him for his immediate attention served to drag the process out unbearably. But finally the agreement, as long as a shipbuilding contract, could be signed by all parties, on each single page as required. The only one apparently not exhausted was Eliseo, who in an extraordinary way seemed to thrive on the situation. Perhaps because for once he was the centre of attention? I can round off the story by adding that our good man kept his part of the bargain to the letter. He is still employed at the generalate, but sold the apartment promptly twenty years later.

In reality, as time passed, I was only moderately contented with myself. In the first years at Caldey I had longed to go more deeply into things than circumstances permitted. But later, during the work on theology and especially on Holy Scripture, vistas had opened which, given time, seemed to promise more profound insight and a richer spiritual life. In Scourmont I had observed the fathers who year in, year out, had had the opportunity to become enriched by silent meditation and their theological pursuits: they all possessed something indefinable that seemed to be worth striving for.

At Monte Cistello I had become a sort of Martha, 'busy with many things', while the one essential seemed to escape me. That was because here I was not under sufficient monastic 'pressure' to strive systematically after spiritual renewal and theological understanding. I went along with it all, as they say, studied my Greek New Testament, prayed regularly, took part in the liturgy, tried to keep abreast of monastic publications. Even so I experienced—deep inside—a widening gap between the active and the contemplative life, the sense of a disturbing lack of continuity that lurks somewhere all the time even in classical monachism. Was it not that my practical self—here where all the duties were on that level—threatened to take over? My old temptation—to ask to be transferred to Scourmont—doubtless sprang from a longing after monasticism's real aim: union with God through self-effacement, obedience, and contemplation.

What was it Our Lord wanted of me?

Twenty

BEHIND MY BACK

THE YEAR 1962 was to be a year of upheaval. Not only in a welter of outward events, but also because, behind the scenes, my own fate was in the process of being transformed radically.

The temporary *chargé d'affaires* with the apostolic delegation in Copenhagen, Bruno Heim, had become delegate for Denmark, Iceland, Norway, and Sweden, as well as nuncio for Finland, and had been consecrated titular archbishop. Now he appeared and invited me to visit him in the old-fashioned but splendid guest residence in the generalate of the Sisters of Saint Elisabeth. Deep red velvet and a great deal of gold! All the motherhouses felt themselves 'obliged' to have such accommodation, since after all, a pope might come one day, or at least a cardinal.

Heim was relatively young for his post, 'only' fifty years old, and tackled his mission with determination and imagination. What he wanted from me, however, was not clear, even though he casually mentioned that Bishop Mangers was beginning to get on a bit in age. That my name was already included in a list of his possible successors was totally unknown to me. Had I had any idea of it, I should no doubt have thought it only logical that the archbishop felt obliged to look me over.

Here, in parenthesis, I must mention that the Holy See had long since followed the practice that neither Carthusians nor Cistercians of the Strict Observance were to be appointed bishops. Their form of life and education were too exclusively directed toward other goals than ordinary pastoral responsibilities. Therefore it was something that was simply never done.[1]

I liked this dynamic but informal diplomat who had a number of unorthodox ideas about how the Catholic Church could win ground in the North. He told me that he was already engaged in establishing a supportive organization in Switzerland for our dioceses, and that he would also do what he could to get the German bishops to lend their support, too. Moreover, Heim could tell me that a new bishop would soon be appointed in Stockholm after Knud Ansgar Nelson, who had had to retire—'for health reasons', as the phrase goes.

At that moment the delegate had no opportunity to tell me who the successor would be, but I could tell from his expression that there was a surprise afoot.

The General Chapter in September went off well. I had been worried about what we would do if it rained at mealtimes, with water pouring into our cloister-garth 'refectory'. I need not have worried. If anything, the weather was almost too good, with abnormally high temperatures. The delegates sweated more than usual and consumed huge quantities of mineral water, much more than our otherwise capacious cool storage room could manage, so my Spanish lay brother assistant had repeatedly to drive off for replenishments. The abbots showed the best side of their nature, however. Everyone was patient, no one complained.

We, 'in the house', kept at it round the clock, for there were not only many mouths to feed three times a day, there were also abbots with problems, because only a few knew the city and even fewer the language. So here I had to help, functioning as a telephone exchange and a miniature travel bureau, with messages to and from the five continents. There was no time to interest oneself in what the Chapter actually dealt with.

Some of the abbots I knew already, which meant hours spent in greetings and mutual updating. Dom Eugene Boylan, now abbot of Roscrea, was in excellent spirits and even helped every day with the washing up—which not everybody did. Also Dom Guerric was of course there, together with the new prior of Mokoto, Scourmont's foundation in the Belgian Congo, who could tell us that Dom Albert, our former prior on Caldey, was now with them, restored and clearly in the right place. It hurt me a little that he never answered my letters.

When the Chapter was over and the abbots had left, Dom Gabriel and those of us 'at shopfloor level' were tired out, but pleased that everything had gone so smoothly. Yet we had to keep at it, because soon the new batch of students would be arriving. The whole procedure of setting things up for the Chapter now had to be carried out in reverse. But the plans were in place, so at the beginning of October we were ready to receive the new group, which yet again was smaller than before.

The first Sunday after the normalization I hinted to Dom Deodat, our procurator general, that the lay brethren and I would have nothing against a brief pause at this stage. The lay brethren much appreciated a *gita* (Italian for a trip in the country) from time to time. The student bus was then lent to us for half a day. I was given clearance, and off we went, relaxed and cheerful to be free. Picnic lunch on a hillside with a wide view over green hills. It did not take more than that to get us back into form again. We visited two Cistercian abbeys from the Middle Ages: Casamari, where our cousins the Cistercians of the Common Observance gave us a warm welcome, but best of all, the older Fossanova, the abbey with Italy's first Gothic church—intact and captivatingly simple. The place had long since fallen into disuse, but you are admitted to the death-room of Saint Thomas Aquinas, the Dominican Order's great theologian. In the year 1274, just fifty years old, he spent his last days here, *en route*—he thought—to the Council of Lyons. Many theological pilgrims find their way here and—so I am told—like to spend some minutes in the room in silent prayer. The spartan cell certainly seems the right setting.

Bishop Suhr arrived, this time not alone. With him was the new bishop of Stockholm. I liked him immediately. The appointment had indeed been almost sensational, for John Taylor was from the USA and the only American head of a European diocese. He belonged to a mission congregation, the Oblates of the Immaculate Heart of Mary (OMI), which had only recently come to Scandinavia. He seemed to me—after my Roman experience—to be a different and refreshing sort of prelate. He and I were later to become firm friends.

Brother Sylvester, our lay brother from Ireland's largest abbey, Mount Melleray, was an unusual person even for that country: a man in the prime of life, tall, thin, and a sharp observer (and commentator), who here in Italy gave increasingly free rein to his tongue. He said aloud what most of us thought, so he was someone we were prepared to like—as long as we were not his targets. But in an amazing way the brother represented the personification of common sense—with a scale of values not learnt from any textbook. In his home monastery he was responsible for the wardrobe, and with us he combined the same job with that of doorkeeper-porter. The porter's lodge bore all the evidence, with piles of clothes—from both the generalate and the students—for inspection, patching, and repair. The sewing machine was always on view. The brother—as much loved as feared—was a bundle of energy, who almost never relaxed, who talked non-stop while he worked, and whose comments could make you want to bless yourself when you heard them, though they were without malice, being based on an inborn, discerning insight into everything human. Even Dom Gabriel could be the target if Sylvester thought he deserved it. But no one had any desire to see him recalled to Ireland.

★ ★ ★

The Vatican Council, which everybody talked about and looked forward to, opened on 10th October 1962. Dom Gabriel was a member in his capacity as abbot general of the Order. This meant that he had to be driven every day to the meetings in Saint Peter's, generally by Father Clément or me. It meant, too, that he felt obliged to give lunches for the bishops from all the sees in which there was a monastery of our Order, and they were many. Other prelates came as well, mostly those who had a special relationship with our definitors. Our lay brethren, particularly our two American cooks, had almost more than they could cope with. And poor Brother Sylvester, who had wretched knees, tottered shakily under the weight of large food trays through the long subterranean corridor linking the kitchen to the generalate section where the guests were served. One day, when we had the leading Nordic prelates to lunch (Dom Gabriel thought that I too must be allowed to invite 'my' bishops), just at aperitif time, there was a heavy thud followed by a clatter of breaking plates from the stairwell. 'Well, there goes lunch', remarked Bishop Suhr. He was quite right. When I arrived on the scene Brother Sylvester stood, pale and out of breath, with the tray hanging from his hand; and everything that had been on it strewn down over the steps. He had fallen over when his knee suddenly failed him. It was a long aperitif.

Naturally everyone was discussing the Council; it was the first time for almost a hundred years that the episcopate in communion with Rome was assembled like this. It was impossible to estimate how many matters would have to be addressed. Not least the bishops felt the burden of pressure inherent in Pope John's wish that everything should ideally be concluded by Christmas—in other words, inside ten weeks! I heard various bishops say that this was an impossible challenge, as indeed soon proved to be the case. And now there was real trouble afoot in several areas. The reason was that the discussion on the *schema* for a decisive dogmatic constitution 'On the Sources of

Revelation', which dealt with the sources on which Catholic teaching is based, the Bible and the tradition of the Church, had reached a total deadlock. This basic document, formulated by Cardinal Ottaviani's theological commission, quickly led to a marked tendency for the Council fathers to divide into 'conservative' *contra* 'progressive' camps.[2]

When a vote was to be taken as to whether the *schema* could be accepted as the basis for further discussion, it was given a 'thumbs down': 1,368 voted against and only 822 in favour. When the minority demurred that a two-thirds majority was necessary to reject a text, Pope John resolutely solved the problem by withdrawing the document for a new scrutiny by an *ad hoc* commission that was to represent the golden mean. It had two chairmen: the Cardinals Ottaviani and Bea. (Even so, it took a great deal of time and trouble to produce a text on which the Council could agree.) After all that, the pope ordered the assembly to continue with its programme. 'Now we can see with our own eyes how essential it is to have a pope', commented Bishop Suhr. And it was obvious to everybody that the Council would need to have one more session—at least.

Rome is the focus of the world's attention now. Media representatives from the five continents are everywhere. One of these representatives knocks on my door and I find outside a smiling Father Rieber-Mohn, our widely known Dominican author from the St Dominikus monastery in Oslo. He is here in his capacity as editor of our Catholic periodical *Sankt Olav,* and also to some extent as a contact person for our apostolic delegate, Bruno Heim. I have only a fleeting memory of the father from the jubilee in Trondheim in 1953, where he gave the impression of being a rather blasé intellectual. Nothing like this shows in him now; on the contrary, here is a man of unselfish disposition, a cultivated sense of humour, and unusually keen intelligence. Soon Rieber-Mohn and I are deep in a conversation that I find enrichingly full of information. A new friend? I hope so. We talk about more than the

Council, for he has much to report, also about church matters at home. I gather that many are hoping Vatican II will bring about a thorough renewal here, too. We have to smile when we talk about the father's 'distant aunt in Rome', as he likes to call Ciss, and we readily agree on her fabulous, even infamous, ability to characterize people—mutual acquaintances not excepted—in a few words. The father describes *her* in a nutshell, as he seems able to do about most things.

In the course of the session Rieber-Mohn comes to visit me a couple of times. I see him as Bishop Mangers's obvious successor. But he himself knows more about this than I could have supposed.

Our new apostolic delegate invites me to lunch, just the two of us, in a restaurant revamped as a grotto of stalagmites and stalactites, all rather pathetic except for the food. I cannot quite grasp what the motive is, for Heim does not give the impression of being somebody who would do something just for the sake of giving pleasure. However, towards the end of the meal he manages—more openly than last time—to convey the impression that Bishop Mangers has definitely seen his best days and yes, that he (Heim) has had to begin to interest himself in the question of a successor in the long view. Rieber-Mohn, I think to myself: the delegate wants to quiz me about my opinion of his possible candidature. But there was no quizzing.

Some weeks later there is a telephone call from the papal congregation Propaganda Fide, also called the Sacred Congregation for the Propagation of the Faith. It operates like a widely branching department of state and has all Catholic mission areas under its wings, including the Nordic countries. 'Father Gran?' 'Speaking.' 'His Eminence Cardinal Agagianian would like you come to his office on the Piazza di Spagna for a talk.' The voice mentions a time and asks if that would suit. I answer that it would. What does the 'red pope' want with me?[3] Perhaps he wants to ask something about the Catholic Church in Norway. Yet deep inside myself, I have the

feeling that the interview possibly concerns me myself, for signals that have reached me might perhaps be interpreted in that
way. In particular I remember a meaningful look from Archbishop Heim when he spoke to me about Bishop Mangers.
But I brush the thought aside—not wishing to understand.
Whatever it is, I feel uneasy, for I am not used to being sent
for by cardinals.

I am at the Piazza di Spagna in good time. Behind the tall col-
umn topped by the Madonna with a wreath of stars around
her head lies a large, well-kept baroque palace. Here the
Sacred Congregation for the Propagation of the Faith has
been housed since its inception in 1622. Without ever having set foot in the place, I know well that it is here that the
people who are in charge of our Nordic churches have their
quarters. Inside all is silence, but at the top of a very long
and broad flight of marble stairs a small group of people talk
together in subdued tones. A liveried receptionist sitting at
a solid table deals with telephone calls in a low voice. The
windows are not only high (we are on the 'noble' floor), but
are also hung with heavy lace-net curtains through which little
light passes. After I have presented my identification papers,
I am shown into a waiting room, almost a formal reception
hall, with heavy, plush-covered chairs along the walls, and in
the centre a table as big as half the room, bearing mission
publications from every continent. There are no other visitors. After a time a door opens and someone else in livery
beckons me into a somewhat smaller reception room. More
waiting on red plush. Yet another door is opened by the same
person, who shows me into a spacious, massively furnished
room where the curtains are completely drawn together, so
that what light there is comes from various lamps. At a desk
sits the famous Cardinal Gregor Peter Agagianian. Famous,
in that he belongs to the uniate part of the Eastern church
(he is a Russian-Armenian) and wears the 'patriarchal' robes,
complete with cylinder hat from which a red cloth covers
his back and shoulders. (The cardinal with his long, majestic

beard regularly makes 'spectacle number two' when the pope
appears together with his curia.) Still sitting, he motions me to
sit down at the opposite side of the table, which is completely
bare. A well-organized prelate, I can see!

Which language are we to speak? I suggest French, why I
don't know. He speaks the language fluently and goes straight
to the point: Jacob Mangers, bishop of Oslo, is close on
seventy-five, and for that reason he has asked the pope if he
may have a coadjutor bishop. So, I think, it must be that
I am now to be asked to give my views on the proposed
candidates. Nevertheless I have to struggle against my inner
unrest and nervousness. 'We have had the question examined
and reported on by our apostolic delegate to the Scandinavian
countries, Archbishop Heim. You know him perhaps?' I nod.
'The Congregation has assessed the proposed candidates, and
I have personally placed our choice before the pope, which
he has approved. You yourself.'

His words almost paralyse me, for although there has been a
hint of this in the air, now suddenly a radical challenge threat-
ens my present existence—with the sole purpose of hauling
me out of it.

I protest: 'But the Church never takes Trappists [for once
I use the word] as bishops!' 'An exception can be made',
answers the cardinal. 'But I have never been involved in any
pastoral work. I hardly know what it means to be a spiritual
adviser, nor anything at all of what is required!' I am frightened
by my own realization. 'Bishop Suhr didn't know anything either', answers the cardinal, to calm me. 'If he could learn, so
can you.' To liken me to Bishop Suhr seemed to be hitting below the belt. But there was also something else, and I brought
that up now. I knew that candidates to appointment as bishops
were required to have led evangelical lives. 'It is possibly not
known, but I am a past sinner', I said hoarsely. The cardinal
was not to be put off: 'That must have been a long time
ago, and that is over now. Furthermore, we discussed several
candidates—and you came out top.' (That my own chosen
candidate has not been preferred seems to me a mystery.)

Half-dazed, I request time to think this over—two days? 'I'm sure you know', answered the cardinal, 'that according to canon law the Holy Father is the supreme superior for all religious orders. In that capacity he has decided that you are to be coadjutor bishop in Oslo—with right of succession.' That too!

He adds some practical information: 'It will all take some time. The Council is in progress and nothing will be done before this session [I prick up my ears] is over. It is hardly necessary to say that this is to be regarded as strictly confidential. Nothing must leak out before the official announcement.' I gather the audience is over. The cardinal rises, lays his bearded cheek majestically against mine, and leads me to the door. A nervous priest of my own age is standing outside the door waiting his turn.

On the way to Monte Cistello feelings of dismay and reluctance fought against a dawning sense of flattered vanity. No matter how things were, they could never be the same again. I felt an acute need to talk, to have someone to consult about all this, but whom? Obviously no one at Monte Cistello. Strangely enough, not Bishop Suhr either, not in this connection, for I felt he might have had a hand in it. Moreover, my mouth was supposed to be sealed with seven seals—seven papal seals! Suddenly I glimpsed a way out: I could go to confession, and talk about the matter inside that hermetically sealed framework. But to whom should I go? All at once the answer came: Jean Leclercq, who was in Rome in connection with the Council. I wondered why I had not thought of him immediately. I was given an appointment straight away. That is to say, I was told simply to come. He must have noticed my disturbed state of mind.

During the confession in his room I presented my problem as concisely as I could. I had not become the God-devoted monk I had intended to be, but a mediocre organizer of daily trivialities. How could I take on a position as a religious leader for a whole diocese, priests, nuns, and many involved lay people? Added to that there was my total lack of pastoral experience. I had never seen other church activities than Masses and ordinary services, not even a christening. Could he not give me any advice as to how I could get the pope to change his mind? Spiritually I felt myself at the lowest possible ebb, and Dom Leclercq must have realized this. By giving me time and being completely at my disposal he became my sheet anchor. He sat for a long time, just thinking, uttered no confessional clichés, but opened our talk with words full of wisdom and humanity. The drift of it was that, despite my feelings of unworthiness and inadequacy, in the end I would be able to do a fair job where the Church now intended to send me. Someone had to take on the work, and I could be sure that Rome, never mind what I myself thought, had sought out the least unsuitable. 'Take heart and go into this with fresh courage!' he said.

Exhausted but relieved, I felt I had done whatever could be done. At all events it now seemed less of a burden to go round with a secret of this nature sealed within me.

I met Bishop Mangers several times in the course of this first session without his giving the slightest sign of knowing what was afoot. Nor did Bishop Suhr. *A fortiori* neither did I.

The Scandinavian bishops I got to know during this Council period struck me as a somewhat peculiar and ageing assembly. The exceptions were Bishop Suhr, who stood out with a clear Nordic profile, and the American Bishop Taylor, who in this setting was like a breath of fresh air.

At the beginning of December, John XXIII concluded, not the Council— as he had hoped—but only its first session. No further significant progress had been made, no text had been finalized, and the pope was not well. It was an open secret that he had cancer, and could hardly be expected to see the Council through to its completion.

I had a telephone call from Cardinal Agagianian's office, with the cardinal himself on the line. On Friday he was to have his monthly audience with the pope. (The curia cardinals have regular audiences during which, like cabinet ministers, they present the pope with lists of proposed decisions for final approval.) He would like to have me with him and introduce me to the Holy Father. It was not absolutely certain, however, that the audience could take place. I understood, and said I would await a further message. It came with regrets—that the pope was not well.

The Council fathers had left, and life was falling back into its usual routine. We knew that another plenary assembly would probably be arranged for the following autumn at the earliest—if at all, owing to the pope's progressive illness.

At the beginning of January I received an open postcard from Bishop Suhr: 'I hear that the date for the publication of your appointment is to be 17th January.' I had not received any message to that effect myself. The day came, and I was no wiser. I knew that the Holy See's new appointments are first announced in the Vatican radio's midday bulletin, but at Monte Cistello we had no radio. Dr Mostyn, however, had one. So I rang and made an appointment to visit him in the Vatican. The elderly prelate and his Irish housekeepers were always hospitability itself. When the time drew near, I asked as casually as I could if we might hear the Vatican news. 'We certainly can—Your Excellency', said John Mostyn with a knowing smile and turned it on. I pretended not to have heard, but it came at once as the first item of news: His Holiness . . . has appointed Father John Willem Gran . . . and so on. I remembered that something similar had happened to Bishop Suhr twenty-five years before, when the Holy See had 'forgotten' to inform him of the appointment, which was announced in Denmark, but not in the Roman monastery of San Girolamo where Suhr was prior. (He told me later that it was precisely this experience which had occasioned his postcard to me.)

Dr Mostyn offers us *spumante*, excited at having the new appointee in his drawing room. We have hardly lifted our glasses when someone knocks on the door and in comes Bishop Smit, Bishop Mangers's predecessor, exultant: 'There, what did I tell you?' Then he notices me and throws his arms round me. 'Yes, I was so sure that it must be you!' He, too, is given a glass. I myself am more dazed than happy, but now at any rate there is no way back.

I telephone to Monte Cistello, which presumably has not yet been informed, because the abbot general is on a visitation in Normandy. Dom Deodat comes on the line.

'What?'

I have to repeat. He can't believe his own ears. 'Come quickly!' he says, obviously affected by the news, and puts down the receiver. At Monte Cistello I knock on the procurator general's door. Dom Deodat, glass in hand, opens it. He has had confirmation of the news by telephone from an officer friend in the Papal Guard. I see that all the definitors are gathered here, clearly celebrating the occasion. 'Come in', he says, 'come in—there's still something in the bottle.' There was perhaps five drops. I was still dazed, and understood that so were the others, for it was the first time for over sixty years that a member of our Order had been made a bishop, and it was almost incredible that it should happen with a perfectly ordinary monk—hardly five years a priest. Had it only been an abbot from a large monastery! I agreed heartily. The reaction among my fellow brethren was about the same, but all of them said how pleased they were and wished me all the best. Nevertheless my lifelong monastery existence was all of a sudden practically over, which was a painful realization. Already I missed the feeling of only being one among many brethren.

There was a telephone call from my father in Bergen: 'What's this—are you to be a bishop?' 'Yes.' 'Does that mean that you'll be coming home?' 'Yes.' 'Why haven't you said anything?' And so on—all very understandable. Father is in quite a state and tells me that there is some confusion at home, for the radio has spoken of the appointment of a Cistercian father by the name of John Willem Nicolaysen, actually my (maternal) middle name. Now he calms down and says how happy he will be to have me back again.

I still fail to understand why I was given no information about the date for the announcement of the appointment. By telephone Propaganda tells me that in accordance with usual practice, the message was sent to the abbot general asking him to pass it on to me. Dom Deodat remembers the communication which came by courier from the Vatican. He had opened it and inside found a sealed envelope addressed to the abbot general personally and stamped 'papal secret'. This he sent unopened to the monastery in Normandy—and the delay had been in the post. Somewhat later I was told the following little story by Dom Gabriel's secretary. The papers about the appointment arrived the day after the publication. That evening when he addressed the community, Dom Gabriel began by saying that something important and remarkable had happened. They all pricked up their ears. 'Our Order has got a bishop.' Excitement. 'You know who it is.' Greater excitement. 'It is—Monseigneur Gran!' (Dom Gabriel had suddenly found it impossible to call a bishop simply 'Father John'.) Dumbfounded silence, since no one knew who this could be, because inside our Order surnames were never used. 'Yes, I mean Father John, our cellarer at Monte Cistello', he added quickly, amidst general laughter. He even had to laugh himself.

At this point I had to put all my energy into teaching Brother Antonio, one of the two Spanish sibling brothers, to take over the economics when I left. Things had to be kept going until someone could be appointed to the office.

Meantime post arrived, as was only to be expected. Bishop Mangers wrote, warmly welcoming me and saying he could now feel himself safe. Bishop Suhr let me read between the lines, confirming my suspicion, that my appointment had to some extent been his work. Dom Gabriel congratulated me—with an undertone of regret. There were letters from my family, from old friends, individual Catholics, congregations of nuns, people unknown to me . . . a lot of mail.

I felt I must pay a visit to the Propaganda Fide HQ to get some questions straightened out. Among other things, it had to be decided when and where my consecration should take place and who should conduct the service. All this, I was told, I could, according to canon law, decide for myself. But first I had to sign several declarations of loyalty, as well as the so-called antimodernistic oath by which I forswore all possible and impossible heresies. In this area nothing seemed left to chance.

I learn that from now on I may wear the violet skullcap as a sign of my new dignity, even if formally I am not yet a bishop. I buy one, and go around with it in my pocket—ready for the right moment. And that comes very soon. I have called in to see a Norwegian theology student at the missionary priests' college on the Monte Gianicolo when it happens that Cardinal Agagianian, the principal superior also of that institution, arrives on a visit. He is on his way to a special pontifical ceremony in Saint Peter's and, on seeing me here, he suggests I come along with him. He would like to make up for the fact that the planned audience came to nothing. I accept readily, for this may well be my last chance to see John XXIII (as indeed it was). But when we get out of the car at the Vatican, the guard on duty informs us, with some consternation, that the cardinals' procession is almost certainly already on its way into Saint Peter's. We are half an hour late. It must be the first time in this well-organized prelate's life that he has made a mistake about the time. So now begins a race I shall never forget. The cardinal in his multi-layered choir robes, the long train doubled up over his arm, rushes at full speed through a sort of labyrinth, a series of interconnected rooms I had never guessed existed. Fortunately he knows all the ins and outs, and heads for an elevator that takes us straight down into Saint Peter's, right beside Michelangelo's Pietà. On again into the basilica where the tail-end of the cardinals' procession is just moving up towards the altar in the tightly packed church, to the accompaniment of the Sistine Chapel choir in its high-pitched register. The cardinal, puffing and panting, follows and closes up—no longer conscious of me in my bizarre get-up of monk's habit and violet skullcap behind him. I find myself inside the cordonned-off section. What now? The only course of action open to me, apart from returning to our starting point, is to bow my head and follow the cardinals at a discreet distance—hoping to find a suitable place to step aside. But no such luck. When I am level with the main altar, the duty officer of the Papal Guard takes my arm and asks me where I think I am going—with a quizzical look at my (doubtless usurped) bishop's skullcap. All of a sudden he recognizes me, for we had off and on exchanged a few words when he visited his friend Dom Deodat at Monte Cistello. 'Yes, Monseigneur, I noticed your appointment in the *Osservatore Romano*', he says slightly abashed, 'and I'm sure you too will be part of the procession here one day, but not just yet.' 'I was brought here by Cardinal Agagianian', I say shamefacedly, 'but we had to hurry. What should I do now?' 'You may take a seat here', he answers in the polite tones of the Vatican. The upshot of it all is that I am seated well to the front among the multitude of bishops present. All's well that ends well!

A violet skullcap, however, is not enough. The full outfit is needed, and nobody at Monte Cistello knows how a Cistercian bishop should be dressed, except that it is probably all in white. Our French definitor knows what to do: 'Go to the generalate of the Cistercians of the Common Observance [they too were based on the Aventine]. They have a couple of bishops and the outfit is certainly the same.'

It was a very agreeable meeting with the members of the other Cistercian curia—intelligent, cultivated fathers, all with a quiet sense of humour. Some of them were of the optimistic opinion that our two Orders would almost certainly come to be reunited in the not too distant future. But, as regards my outfit! Yes, of course, the bishop's robes would doubtless be identical, but Gamarelli would have all the answers. Gamarelli?

I was given an address: Annibale Gamarelli, papal tailor, Piazza Santa Maria sopra Minerva.

It was busy in the tailor's, with many clerical customers. I stood there patiently and waited for my turn. In my monk's habit and beret I can hardly have seemed promising material. Some who arrived after me were taken before me. But when it was at last my turn, there were suddenly smiles all round: a newly appointed bishop! Ergo, the full works with plenty of money to earn. Gamarelli junior ('I am the fifth generation'), who was now full of attention and knew where everything was to be found, pointed out from the firm's design collection. I felt I was hooked, with no way of escape, for the duty of being formally correct was not one that could simply be disregarded. Dom Gabriel had honoured me with a cheque for a million lire which should cover everything. Robes for ordinary days, for feast days, for altar use, for choir use, and so on. And quite right: all in white except for the skullcap. Of course I had more stuff foisted on me than I really needed, for what did I know of all this?

I felt it went without saying that Bishop Mangers should be the principal one of my prescribed three consecrators. He and I agreed on the date, 24th March, for the ceremony— which would naturally be in Oslo: the first time since the Middle Ages that a Norwegian was consecrated a Catholic bishop in Norway. I asked Bishop Suhr and Bishop Wember of Tromsø to be co-consecrators. Both accepted. Thus the most important things had fallen into place.

Archbishop Heim wrote to say that on the way home I was very welcome to break the journey at Vedbæk, the rather imposing house between Copenhagen and Helsingör into which his predecessor had moved. There were various subjects we had to discuss. He himself would come to Oslo for the consecration.

I stayed on longer than foreseen at Monte Cistello, dreading all the fuss at home, but soon received a new letter from Heim about various decisions which required my participation. In addition he told me that Bishop Suhr had invited the president of the Pontifical Secretariat for Christian Unity, Cardinal Bea, to give an ecumenical address and conduct an ecumenically inspired High Mass in Copenhagen at the end of January. Bea had accepted. Could I arrange my journey so that I could take part in these events? The cardinal was to stay with him, but there was still plenty of room.

I flew to Copenhagen, and was driven to Vedbæk by the delegation's chauffeur. For this sort of attention, it was good to be near the top of the tree. I had understood from Heim—the expert in heraldry—that there was talk of a bishop's coat of arms. As soon as I came in, I was introduced to Hallvard Trætteberg, who for some time had evidenced professional admiration for Heim.[4] Here and now the decisions were to be taken regarding my—actually obligatory—coat of arms. Heim was to make the drawing and then arrange for the engraving and printing—and in addition pay for the whole operation (I remembered the vigor with which he went about setting up the new organization in Switzerland).

Tired after the journey I tried to interest myself in this medieval affair, which would naturally be first-class from the heraldic point of view, although neither Heim nor Trætteberg had any definite ideas as to the content of the coat of arms. On Father's side we had a sort of family shield: a fir tree (in Norwegian 'gran') with a star above on each side. Both agreed that this was heraldically correct and could be used. But what about the religious element? Trætteberg had brought along various existing coats of arms with Saint Olav and his two habitual heraldic axes, linked to his martyrdom in 1035. We sat gazing at them for a long time: it was important neither to be banal nor to tread on the toes of the Norwegian Lutheran church, from which these arms actually came. At this point I got my first and last heraldic inspiration: 'What about removing the cross and then bringing the axes [set on each side of the trunk with the blades outwards] closer together so that they themselves make a cross?' I could see that the problem was considered solved, and withdrew with relief from the rest of the discussion which concerned the purely technical aspects of the question.

Naturally I visited Bishop Suhr, who said he regretted not being able to house me as his guest: it was not posssible because his only guest room was a housemaid's room from former days, which he used for visiting priests needing overnight accommodation. And of course it was occupied now, owing to the numbers who had come to Copenhagen to hear Bea. But I am sure he still more regretted not being able to offer lodging to the visiting cardinal, a man for whom he felt a genuine friendship.

Parallel with the ecumenical arrangements, Suhr had invited guests to a Nordic interdenominational seminar. Our own 'chief ecumenicist', Father Finn Thorn OP, gave me a touchingly warm welcome home. My old acquaintance Gunnel Vallquist had come from Rome and interviewed me for the publication *Sankt Olav*. Also from Rome came Denmark's renowned ecumenicist, the Council observer Professor K. E. Skydsgaard.

Cardinal Bea, straightbacked despite his eighty-two years, stepped out of the aircraft wearing his prelate's robe and his customary winning smile. I knew him from photographs and at a distance, but now had a chance to see him at close quarters—up to several hours at a time. And I was able to have confirmed something that I had heard, namely that in his capacity as an expert on Holy Scripture he was the author of the draft for Pope Pius XII's previously mentioned encyclical *Divino afflante Spiritu,* which had revolutionized Catholic biblical science.

Bea, who in every way was an ecumenical pioneer in the Catholic field, radiated spiritual strength, culture, and humanity, as well as unmistakable intelligence. In the summer of 1960 he had persuaded Pope John XXIII to establish an ecumenical commission to work on the preparations for the forthcoming Vatican Council. When it was set up, there was nothing to suggest that this commission, the Secretariat for

Promoting Christian Unity, which was similar to a number of other preparatory organs, was destined to become a permanent papal forum. Yet this is what gradually happened. In the very first session of the Council, by a decision of Pope John XXIII, it was placed on the same footing as the conciliar commissions, and after the close of the Council it was confirmed as a permanent institution in the Roman Curia. As was only natural, Bea was appointed chairman, which he continued to be until his death. Today its designation is the Pontifical Council for Promoting Christian Unity.

At that time it was generally assumed that the Catholic Church as such in principle stood irrevocably fast against interconfessional *rapprochement*, although there were individual Catholics, even priests, who strove towards this goal, particularly in France where the two great names were Father Paul Couturier and the Dominican theologian Yves Congar.

Even before the Vatican Council, Cardinal Bea's attitude on grounds of principle was wholeheartedly ecumenical. That was why the Christian world was above all interested in the documents for which his commission had been made responsible, namely 'On Ecumenism' and 'On Religious Liberty'. Somewhat later a third was to be added: the epoch-making 'On the Relation of the Church to Non-Christian Religions' (the so-called '*schema* on the Jews'). In other words, it was these conciliar documents, above all, that were expected to come up with the great and revitalising impulses.

Bea's lecture, with an excellent introduction by Skydsgaard, made a deep impression. In brief, he based his position on the fact that all baptized Christians, whatever their faith, have much more uniting than dividing them. His theme was followed up in a lively and positive speech by the Lutheran bishop of Copenhagen (not all of whose colleagues were enthusiastic). This was a real widening of the horizon!

I could not know then that I should soon have the good fortune to work with this man—right up to the time of his death five years later. In fact, I had not yet realized that I myself should take part in the Council. Indeed, it was first in Oslo that Bishop Mangers made it clear that I too was a Council father and as such required to travel to the next session. It would be difficult to imagine a more fascinating challenge.

Archbishop Heim enjoyed the occasion, which he knew how to make the most of. The festive reception which he gave at Vedbæk was intended as a sort of apotheosis. As the French would say: *Tout Paris était là!* (everybody who was anybody was there!).

Heim had the idea of giving another reception in Oslo in connection with my consecration. Could I make a list of the people I should like to see invited? I worked on it, anxious not to hurt any feelings. To my surprise, our delegate also wanted to invite most of the diplomatic corps, although the diplomatic relations between the Holy See and Norway were nonexistent. But this was his way of doing things, and they all came.

Then there were the people who should be invited from outside to be present in church and at the dinner, German prelates and other clergy. I knew none of them, but began to learn. The other Nordic bishops were to be invited as a matter of course (thought Heim). I mentioned those I should like to have: Father Lowry, Dom Gabriel, Dom Samson, Dom Eugene, and one or two others.

After this foretaste of episcopal life, I returned to Monte Cistello. It seemed too soon to appear on the scene in Oslo, and besides there were still a number of things to be arranged and wound up before I felt ready to leave the administration to the overwhelmed Antonio, who still had a lot to learn. He and I spent days at the open archive shelves of the economic administration, and slowly but surely he became acquainted with our contacts, problems, responsibilities, and all the rest of it.

Bishop Mangers wrote regarding the festive dinner. His list of questions was long: for example, should the priests in the diocese be automatically invited (as if they should not)? Had I any more names I wanted to include? I had. There was no mention of my own family (as though I were a sort of Melchizedek without parents or relatives). I asked him to include my father, as well as three aunts. There could have been cousins and so on, too, but I knew that lack of space would be a problem, since the dinner was to take place in the parish hall, which cost nothing. But on second thoughts I had another request, and one that the good Bishop Mangers almost shied away from: the superiors of the women's congregations working in the diocese. It would be cramped at the feast, but the presence of these Mother Superiors was applauded with approval by this purely male (except for my aunts) gathering.

In mid-March I finally set out for Oslo, confident that Brother Antonio now had the wherewithal to manage the job.

The Bishop's House in Akersveien (Aker Road), in Oslo, which I had been in and out of when I was engaged in youth work, from now on was to be my home. Bishop Mangers welcomed me, simply and kindly as always. He wore his full robes indoors, so I had to do the same, or so it seemed to me.

The diocese had one of the four floors at its disposal. (The others were used for parish offices, priests' accommodation, the sisters' convent, the library, the parish hall, and other purposes.) Apart from a couple of short visits previously, this was the floor I knew least. It was, if anything, a depressing sight. Bishop Mangers had no aesthetic pretensions, and was frugal, to say the least, in regard to himself and his surroundings.

I mentioned the convent. Several Franciscan nuns belonging to a Dutch congregation, the Saint Anthony sisters, ran the establishment, always having to watch that the tight budget was not exceeded. Now they were hard at work round the clock. The consecration of a bishop entailed a thousand tasks over and above the usual routine. But the sisters were kindness itself, and could not do enough to help. The Mother Superior, Sister Intemerata (her religious name), was full of attention from the first moment—and indeed ever since.

Bishop Mangers had extended the premises considerably after his instalment in 1931, but since then it was obvious that not much had been done. My first thought on seeing it all was that a thorough facelift was necessary.

The approaching consecration occupied everybody's attention. Father Lowry came from London with his friend, Father Peter Anglim, master of ceremonies at Westminster Cathedral. These two had accepted my invitation to take care of the liturgy together. The guests from outside were lodged in Our Lady's Hospital, adjoining the bishop's residence. Being back in Akersveien made a greater impression on Father Lowry than he had expected: 'I should never have stuck it out', he murmured with a wry smile.

Father Hansteen Knudsen was still the bishop's secretary, with more than enough to do, because Bishop Mangers was somewhat helpless at the practical level. As for me, the days flew past, but very little could be properly planned because unforeseen things kept cropping up. It was clear, too, that the media saw the event as a newsworthy item.

Bishop Mangers felt that the foreign guests should be met by me at the airport. The diocese, however, did not own a car, and no one in the house had a driving licence except the German-born parish priest, who more and more often had to act as chauffeur. A car would really have to be allowed for!

Bishop Suhr arrived from the south and Bishops Rüth and Wember from the north. On D-day minus one there was to be a 'dress rehearsal' in the church. Those taking part appeared; only Bishop Mangers failed to show up, sending a message to say that he was behindhand with his sermon and that someone would have to stand in for him. The full Latin ritual, with its renaissance inheritance in all its grandeur, was used. (Vatican II was to simplify much in this respect.) Fathers Anglim and Lowry were as one and worked as if preparing a gala performance. Soon everybody knew what was required of him. The one who knew it best was (naturally) Bishop

Suhr. Yet of all people it was he who involuntarily almost wrecked the whole trial run. Towards the end of the ceremony the ordaining bishop has to seat himself on his throne so that the newly consecrated bishop may present himself to him, bow and chant the phrase 'Ad multos annos!' ('Many years to you!'). I had hardly chanted this before Bishop Suhr's voice was heard: 'Ad unum annum!' ('One year to you!'). A salvo of laughter put a stop to all further rehearsal. Bishop Mangers, who apparently was not thinking of retiring for a long time yet, remained happily ignorant of Bishop Suhr's fabrication.

Mangers wanted to give me an ordination gift, and from the old safe brought out a small blue leather box. Inside was a bishop's ring consisting of an incredibly large amethyst mounted on a gold ring with several rows of small inset diamonds. He told me that this treasure had once belonged to the famous Cardinal Merry del Val, secretary of state to Pope Pius X. After the owner's death it was passed on to Bishop Fallize by Pope Benedict XV. Since then it had come down the line, and now it was mine. Or was it? I wore the enormous ring during the ordination, but I don't recall ever having done so again. At any event it has long since found its way back to the old safe in the bishop's office—no doubt never to be worn again.

The ordination went off smoothly—some said even splendidly. The papal decree of appointment was nobly read out by the Nestor among our Norwegian clergy. Bishop Mangers was alarmingly impressive. He had prepared a very long (and to me, moving) sermon, which he delivered word-perfect and without any notes. Was I to be expected to do the same?

According to Catholic doctrine (as is also the case in the Orthodox church) episcopal ordination is a sacrament: that is to say, an outer action (gestures and words) instituted by Christ, which carries with it an active inner grace. Because it confers a 'character'—an inner seal—and a permanent grace, it cannot be repeated. Once a bishop, always a bishop.[5]

The moments when the consecrating bishop lays his hands on the head of the ordinand and follows this with the sacramental formula were naturally for me the highpoint of the ceremony. Flooded with a profound sensation of a sacred presence and with an awesome perception of time standing still, I finally felt myself wholeheartedly in accord with God's inexplicable hand steering my life.

Twenty-One

AN APPRENTICE AGAIN

CELEBRATIONS, SPEECHES, GIFTS, crowds of people, some known, many not known, all important. I was back in Norway, yes, but very much in Catholic Norway, which, to be honest, was of modest dimensions.

As foreseen, I was fundamentally unsure of myself, but realized I must not let this uncertainty be my trademark. I had not gone through any of the previous stages of experience that the position demanded, and which the older parish priests had long since mastered. Of these we had about twenty, together with several chaplains, as well as Franciscans, Dominicans, and Marists who had been in Norway for a long time (quite a few were even Norwegian-born), so there was plenty of expertise here—except for myself. (I often inwardly recalled the cardinal's voice: 'If Bishop Suhr could learn, so can you.')

Anyone visiting Bishop's House in Oslo today will find a multifarious centre of activity on both sides of the street. A good-sized staff, large, bright rooms, computers, and so on—in brief, a modern administration. Then, however, there was little of all this. The diocese was the bishop—and his secretary, Don Ivar (Hansteen Knudsen). Mangers himself did the bookkeeping, paid out as necessary, dealt with applications for annulment of matrimony, officiated at confirmations, carried out visitations in the parishes—and much more besides.

★ ★ ★

The bishop was revered as a person, totally unegoistic—a priest through and through. He had kept the organization going for over thirty years, but did not seem as fatigued as Heim had implied.

Bishop's House was built in the 1850s and already had a history that could have filled a book. Among other things it had been used as a boys' school. When Bishop Mangers extended the building in the 1930s, it acquired a relatively large assembly hall with a stage, kitchen, and ample cloakroom; a room on the street for a bookshop (first realized, however, after the war) and for the periodical *Sankt Olav;* and in addition a sort of club room where various associations and societies could hold meetings. A small caretaker's lodge had also been allowed for. The fourth floor contained the diocesan library and the convent for the Sisters of Saint Anthony—our 'good angels'.

The first floor was the bishop's quarters, although nothing to write home about. Bishop Mangers had the largest room, which served both as office and private sitting room. You could almost have called it ugly, but at the same time comfortable-looking in an old-fashioned masculine way. It smelt strongly of cigars. In beyond it the bishop had his bedroom and bathroom. Modest quarters for a modest man.

I myself had a room of passable size, with an alcove for a bed, on the far side of the long, greyish corridor. Otherwise on this floor there was the bishop's private chapel, a breakfast room, a secretary's office that was not in use, an archive room without any order or system, and a reception room in many shades of brown, with furniture inherited from departed Catholics. This room also served as an anteroom. In addition, there were two small adjoining guest rooms with a single shared door into the corridor, which had a window out towards Akersveien at the far end.

This was to be my home, for an indefinite period. Something I would just have to get used to as quickly as possible—for was I not an apprentice?

Don Ivar did his office work in his sitting room on the floor above, which was otherwise reserved for the parish. As well as his job as secretary, he had a great many irons in the fire, and I could see how eighteen years of this had taken their toll.

For a couple of days I sat at my little desk and wondered what I should start on. Seemingly it did not cross the bishop's mind that I should be taught anything or be informed about anything. No doubt he thought all would be understandable in due time. It gradually became clear to me from our conversations that he had not requested a coadjutor at all (contrary to what Cardinal Agagianian had led me to assume). My appointment was a Roman initiative, and besides, Mangers felt that Bishop Suhr might have played a part in it. But he was neither upset nor unfriendly on that account. We got along very well; indeed, there were never any problems between us. The bishop felt and behaved like a kindly uncle. When I asked him if he would be my confessor, however, he seemed to be knocked off balance for a moment and stammered something to the effect that that would hardly be natural. But my confessor he became, and I feel certain that neither of us regretted the arrangement. After a time I found out how I could learn something 'on the job'. Particularly during breakfast after early Mass I asked him about all sorts of things I wanted to know. And he answered fully and frankly, sometimes giving me information that was certainly not supposed to go any further.

One day he said to me: 'Well, from now on you are my vicar general.' So, that was a worthwhile piece of news. Unfortunately the bishop forgot to pass it on to the people necessarily concerned, so it took some time for my new authority to make itself felt.

I did not have a telephone, which was a problem. The bishop had his, and there was a sort of public apparatus, with coins, on the parish floor. I asked if I too might not have a telephone, but Mangers felt that was out of the question, since it was impossible to arrange for new lines at that time in postwar Oslo. But I had read somewhere about systems allowing for several telephones on the same line, managed by buttons on each apparatus. Could that be an idea? The bishop had never heard of this, but all right: 'Find out about it!' A visit to the right quarters proved that one could indeed have four or even more telephones with one and the same number. I think I paid for the installation myself, from money given to me at my ordination. It was a proud moment when I could ring from my own desk, both in to Bishop Mangers and up to the secretary and to the sisters on the fourth floor—and, not least, out to the city and to the world. Bishop Mangers had some trying days with the light-signals and buttons, but he was soon pleased to escape all the running up and down the corridors and stairs.

Now my blood was up, and I reacted eagerly to an exciting item in the press: a copying machine. A demonstration proved that you could put a sheet of paper into the little machine, and out would come a duplicate (or several if desired). The copy was yellow (slowly darkening to brown) with the text actually burnt on to a type of heat-sensitive paper. This device, the ancestor of the photocopiers so common today, was long ago, happily, much improved on.

I had occasional visits, frequently from parish priests on trips to Oslo wanting to tell me about their situation, which was often far from congenial. Apart from the refugees fleeing after the invasion of Czechoslovakia and the revolution in Hungary, this was before the big wave of asylum-seekers, and the diocese still had fewer than four thousand inscribed members (in 1999 some ten times more). Of these, at least 16 per cent were sisters belonging to religious orders; I shall come back to them later.

Spring was just round the corner and with it the time for confirmations. Bishop Mangers looked forward to my taking on as many of these as possible, so that he would be relieved of the duty and at the same time I would get to know the local circumstances at first hand.

It was during one of these rounds that, in Bergen, I followed the news of Pope John XXIII's worsening illness and death.

Little of international interest happened around late May and early June, therefore all the more interest was focused on the events in the Vatican. It was obvious that most people, whatever their religion, felt deeply for the dying old man, and many followed what was happening from hour to hour. Questions were constantly addressed to me, because people mistakenly believed that as a bishop I could be assumed to have inside information about the state of the pope's health.

John XXIII passes away on Whitmonday. To hold a service of mourning during the Octave of Pentecost is contrary to all liturgical rules; nevertheless we do exactly that—anything else seems unthinkable at the ordinary human level. Still in Bergen, I conduct the service in Saint Paul's church, which is full to overflowing. The silence is impressive. A period, as short in time as it is rich in content and devotion, is over for Christianity.

And immediately afterwards one question becomes all-important: Who is to be the successor? The question is particularly urgent because any ecumenical council automatically comes to an end with the death of a pope. Suddenly we no longer have a Council. Or do we?

Less than four weeks later we have a new bishop on Peter's chair: Giovanni Battista Montini, who was formerly archbishop of Milan and before that one of Pius XII's two secretaries of state, is now Pope Paul VI.

The first announcement he makes to the world is 'The Council will continue'. It is necessarily a race against time, because during Pope John's illness the preparations for the second session have lost their impetus and died—with him. The vast machinery starts up again, so cumbersomely you can almost hear it creak. I too receive a formal summons and begin to read conciliar documents at every available moment. There is much more to familiarize oneself with than I had ever understood at Monte Cistello.

In connection with my diocesan visits, it was taken for granted that I should call on our Catholic institutions, of which there were not a few at that time. Most often it was a hospital or a clinic, but we also had a nurses' college, another college for nursing auxiliaries, three primary schools, a number of kindergartens, and some homes for the elderly. In Bergen, as mentioned, there was the motherhouse of the only Nordic congregation of sisters, founded there at the turn of the century by our first bishop in modern times, Johannes Olav Fallize.

The total number of sisters in the diocese was remarkable—around 550—most of them belonging to active congregations with backgrounds in the Netherlands, Germany, or France. None of this was actually unknown to me. What was new and interesting, however, was to experience it from the inside, to be shown round, to have things explained, to gain insight into already increasing problems, due not least to a significant fall in the number of vocations, reflecting the tendency in the rest of Europe. It was especially hard on our Norwegian congregation, which without the security of international backing was none the less dependent upon new blood from outside. The sisters therefore had their own house in Bussum (Netherlands) from which they organized recruitment campaigns. Yet there, too, the decline in response was appreciable.

The parish priests, above all, had many worries. They struck me as men ready to give generously of themselves, who lived out their lives in—by normal standards—comparatively straitened circumstances, despite the constant help of the sisters. I was told the following story from the earlier pioneer time: A bishop was sent by Rome to Norway on a visitation. He came to a tiny parish which, apart from some sisters, consisted of only a handful of Catholics. The bishop, more used to visiting missions, tackled the parish priest: 'You have been here for almost twenty years now, Father, and not a single convert. What have you to say for yourself?' 'My Lord Bishop', answered the priest quietly, 'I have stuck it out.'

There was more to get to know than I had imagined. I met with goodwill everywhere, however, even from those who had hidden hurts, or who harboured bitterness as a result of a frustrated life or from having been shackled all too long to the same place. For the priests who belonged to a religious order (for example, the Franciscans) it was much easier, thanks to their common life, no matter how primitive compared to the wide options of the world at large. Several of our secular priests had a harder time of it and could be more scarred by their isolation.

It was clear that the Catholic Church in Norway rested on the shoulders of the women religious. It was in their institutions that the greater part of the Church's contact with the outside world was taken care of; this was where the unbelievable (sometimes the almost superhuman) feats were performed, and this was where the economic fundament of the diocese was to be found. Indeed, without the sisters I think it would have been difficult for the Church to have existed; if at all, it could only have been with solid financial backing from outside.

Slowly I began to feel more at home with things and I even had to discipline myself and rather draw in my reins, for I still lacked the competence to suggest solutions, let alone to put them into effect.

During my visits to Bergen I lived at home with Father (and the housekeeper, Marie). It was both pleasant and to a large extent 'normalizing', for during this running-in period my head was so full of things Catholic that everything else had to be temporarily ousted. Now it did me a lot of good to be together with my family and childhood friends. I began to put on weight, which wasn't to be wondered at, perhaps.

Mother had had a small villa built at some distance from the main residence on the Grav estate which now belonged to her late husband's family. She had looked forward to spending the evening of her life there. Jens dropped his option on the villa in favour of the house down on the south coast, which he later sold.

What did Bishop Mangers think? Could I have the villa finished and move in there? Yes, he thought that ought to be all right, provided I came in every day. I was happy at the thought of not having to live any longer in Akersveien, which in my mind's eye, however, I had already begun to plan as a new complex rising like a phoenix from the existing layout.

Bishop Suhr is on the line from Copenhagen: 'You and I are invited to participate in an advisory meeting in the German Bishops' Conference in Fulda next week.'

'What?'

'Cardinal Döpfner [archbishop of Munich and Freising] says they are to discuss the conciliar *schema* "On the Virgin Mary" and he would like to have the Scandinavian Episcopal Conference on his side—so that his proposal for incorporating the *schema* "On Mary" in the constitution "On the Church" will win through, as he hopes it will.' I am certainly getting involved in things quickly! That Bishop Suhr, as our chairman and also a member of the Council's Preparatory Commission, has been invited is hardly surprising. That he wants to have me with him might well be for the sake of company. The reason he gave me was that this would give me a useful foretaste of the Council. Yes, I should certainly like to come.

Suhr and I drove south, he at the wheel of the same car we had used in Trondheim ten years before. We arrived in the lovely old town of Fulda where Germany's patron saint, Saint Boniface (the Englishman who had christianized Germany), lies buried, and where the Bishops' Conference met annually. Soon we found ourselves in the middle of the meeting, with Cardinal Döpfner as its main driving force. (The chairman of the German Conference was the archbishop of Cologne, Cardinal Frings, and Döpfner succeeded him, as was only to be expected.)

Döpfner certainly had a dynamic and winning personality emanating a sense of inner power—beyond all doubt a born leader. He was concerned at the thought that the Council had far too many items on the agenda (originally about seventy *schemata*, although some of these had now been deleted, and certain others were combined with related themes). The *schema* 'On Mary' therefore ought to be dropped, he argued, for what was there that was new to say on the subject? If the subject matter *had* to be retained (as Döpfner reckoned it would), the relevant text should be incorporated as a last chapter in the *schema* 'On the Church'. He would like to see their own Bishops' Conference, ideally supported by the related conferences (Austria, The Netherlands, France, Belgium, Switzerland—and Scandinavia?) go in for such an idea. But there was no time to be lost. If we were to have a chance of winning through, the proposal must be put forward immediately.

It was here I experienced my first hint of laughter in a Council setting. The French episcopate was represented *ad hoc* by the auxiliary bishop of Strasbourg who naturally spoke fluent German. The cardinal asked: 'Bishop Elchinger, what would you say the French Episcopal Conference think about this matter?' 'Herr Kardinal', answered the young bishop, 'I don't know. You Germans have an episcopal conference; we French have only free-wheeling bishops.'

After a short debate it was resolved to support Döpfner's plan. Was there an inkling of conspiracy in the air? I heard later that the good cardinal had been taken to task in Rome and been asked to explain himself, which he is said to have done with bravura.

The time to set off for the Council is getting closer, and my plan is to visit Britain, in fact Wales, *en route* for Rome. The newly elected archbishop of Westminster, John Heenan, is to be installed in Westminster Cathedral, and I have been invited to attend. As well as that, I feel the need to bid farewell to my community, so I arrange to visit Caldey briefly on my way to Westminster.

To come to Caldey under these circumstances is a strange experience, almost painful, for now I myself am the honoured guest who is not needed for anything. I pass my couple of days in wandering around, greeting and saying goodbye to many and to much. My 'home for ever' is no longer that. That my brethren take a certain pride in the fact that the community has fostered the Order's only bishop in modern times is under-standable. Smiles and friendliness everywhere—nevertheless it all underlines the end of my existence as a monk, for my binding promise to belong here for the whole of my life was annulled the very moment I was consecrated a bishop.

Caldey disappears in the fog, and the journey continues, but now in an unusual manner. The archbishop wants to have his car with him at the Council, but cannot waste time in driving across Europe. A priest in Heenan's chancery is to drive the heavy Daimler to Rome, but half the distance will be covered by air. The archbishop has offered to let me join in on this drive—it is safer to be two. At Southend-on-Sea the secretary and I see the limousine being driven up into the clumsy-looking aircraft of the type then used for such transport. A few hours later we are able to manoeuvre the car ourselves down on to the runway—in Basel.

Even with this shortcut it was a long trip—the two of us alternating at the wheel over the Alps, via Saint Gotthard to Lugano and on by the Aurelian Way along the Mediterranean, with an occasional swim on the way. On arrival I had to wake Brother Sylvester, who had not been told I was coming. I was now a Council father and was to be among those deciding the orientation of the Church for coming generations, but the brother was not impressed. To him I was still 'Father John'—as if I had expected anything else.

I note with satisfaction that two Council reporters from the North, Sweden's Gunnel Vallquist[1] and the Norwegian Do-minican Erik Gunnes, are already in Rome. Also that the reformed Taizé monks are installed for the session.[2]

Ecumenism is in the air. Oscar Cullman, the renowned Protestant theologian, is due to arrive. I am full of anticipation.

Dom Gabriel and I agreed upon the driving schedule to the Vatican, a routine we were to adhere to with few exceptions. The transportation plan included a rather special personal-ity: the Vietnamese archbishop of Hué, Ngô Dinh Thuc. As brother of South Vietnam's recently murdered President Ngô Dinh Diêm, he had been ousted from his see by a coup. His other brother was murdered with the president. A bitter man now, whom I had sitting beside me every day while I drove. Through him I was able to pick up a lot of interesting information from his part of the world, not least regarding his famous, ambulating sister-in-law and the rest of the family.

Dom Gabriel always sat behind in his billowing choir robes (which took up the whole seat), while I myself was still in my monastic habit, since anything else would have been impractical. We regularly parked at about the same place in the Vatican with the car pointing toward the north side of Saint Peter's. Now, standing behind the vehicle, I had a chance to change into the prescribed choir robes (which, like many colleagues, I eventually learned to simplify somewhat).

The archbishop of Zagreb told me a long time afterwards that he used to park his car beside us, and had always been amused at the sight of the young monk who changed from his habit to bishop's robes (and vice versa) in full public view.

As might be expected, the first day of the Council was a tremendous experience for a newcomer, and one which more than anything else imparted the feeling of belonging to a universal church. To accommodate the 2,300 or more prelates, Saint Peter's vast central nave, in its entire length, was built up with massive stands to permit seating along both sides. This, then, was the Council aula, our great gathering place, and here we sat rank upon rank upwards, facing our colleagues opposite. I was placed near the bronze gates towards Saint Peter's square along with the other newly ordained bishops. The First Vatican Council (1869–70), with its 700 participants, had had a similar seating arrangement, but contenting itself with the transept.

The special stand, far up near the high altar, was an impressive sight, for here were the places for the observers from other denominations, a highly colourful gathering that included Eastern exarchs and metropolitans; archbishops, bishops, and prelates from the Anglican churches; delegates from the Lutheran, Calvinist, Zwinglian, Methodist, and other denominations, many from remote parts of the world, who had accepted the invitation to be represented. They were all here, from high-ranking prelates in magnificent vestments to simple pastors like Sunday-school teachers in dark suits.

It was a vast enterprise that was now getting under way. A presidency of twelve cardinals sat at a long table placed across the church with their backs to the high altar under the baldaquin. At another smaller table—with their backs to the twelve—sat the cardinals who would take turns to lead the meetings, always the same four—my 'friend' Agagianian being one of them. The others were Döpfner, Lercaro (Bologna), and Suenens (Brussels and Malines). The system of having such moderators, which was new that year, was intended to do away with the difficulties that arose during the previous session when the curia had too much influence.

At another special table (with their backs to the venerable bronze statue of Saint Peter!) sat the five uniate patriarchs of the Eastern Rite churches, all with imposing beards and splendid attire.

In the gallery directly behind my place sat a handful of laymen (thirteen in all), the so-called *auditores* (listeners). It was said to have been the previous pope's good friend, the French author Jean Guitton, who had managed to bring about this innovation—and he himself was naturally among them.

A rostrum, placed on high like an old-fashioned pulpit, was reserved for the Council's secretary general, the Italian curia cardinal Angelo Felici, who spoke fluent, comprehensible, and extremely audible Latin.

Unfortunately, the whole episcopate of the Catholic Church cannot participate in this collegial brotherhood. Many are missing from Eastern Europe and the Far East. The reality of the Iron Curtain is patently demonstrated. The many apostolic nuncios and delegates (all archbishops), posted all over the world, were entitled to participate but were not obliged to do so, and only attended ocasionally; whereas other bishops who did not wish to attend had to obtain formal leave of absence.

It is the first time our new pope, with visible emotion, opens a Council session. Some weeks earlier in a remarkable address to his own curia, he has argued against the conservative— not to say foot-dragging—attitude in regard to the Council's aim that still characterized many an otherwise loyal curial servant (read bureaucrat). The keywords in his address had been *reform, supra-nationality, ecumenism, simplification, decentralization.* Today the pope's main theme is *The Church.* The reason is that the first session, which at the eleventh hour was presented with the Council's most central *schema* 'On the Church', had rejected it by a large majority because of its legalistic and narrow-minded basis. Now there is a new draft—worked out by theologians, mostly from the university in Louvain (Belgium)—revised, however, yet once again by the Council's theological commission.

Paul VI speaks appealingly of the Church in general, using terms like *God's people, house, vineyard, bride, Holy City,* and also, very beautifully, of the Church as the *Ecclesia caritatis* (the Church of love). It is heart-warming and promises well. He also touches on a subject which, in particular since the meeting with Cardinal Bea in Copenhagen, has fired my interest: ecumenism. He not only stresses the importance his predecessor, John XXIII, attached to it, but emphasizes that it is also his own view that the Catholic Church should be open for compassionate and close cooperation with 'the separated brothers and sisters in the faith'. To the surprise of all of us, the pope goes so far as here and now to beg these brothers and sisters for forgiveness for all the Roman church may have been guilty of in regard to the split in Christianity. Such words give pause for thought.

The main themes for the near future are announced. We are to consider the *schema* 'On the Church' and its theological doctrine concerning the episcopal order, and further to consider the proposed introduction of the diaconate as a permanent clerical grade. After that, finally, we're to start the debate on the *schema* that is so often the subject of discussion: 'On Ecumenism'.

The First Vatican Council was cut short in 1870 as a result of events in international politics (the Franco-Prussian war, Italy's war of independence resulting in the dissolution of the Papal States). The Council was just in the process of drafting a decree on the hierarchic structure of the Church and had come to the rôle of the episcopate, when the delegates had to disperse in haste. Vatican II aimed particularly at taking up the matters which had been on the abandoned agenda. And so, what absorbs us all here and now (also the observers) is the text 'On the Church'.

It is also the Council's longest and weightiest, so far, which among many other subjects is to define the theology forming the basis for the sacramental ordination to the diaconate, the priesthood, and the episcopate. There are so many comments, however, necessitating so many revisions, that two of the Council's four sessions are used up before a final agreed-upon text can be hammered out.

My new travelling companion, Archbishop Ngô Dinh Thuc, is one of the first to comment on the Church *schema*. Not entirely without pathos he advocates an in-depth discussion on Adam (but not Eve!). How can the Council treat the question of the Church without discussing the person who is the antecedent of us all? What is more: the Holy See should have invited observers not only from the other Christian denominations but from *all* the other world religions. (Not a very brilliant contribution, I think to myself.)

Of the speeches that follow, some strike me as promising and forward-looking, while others are more like deliberate brakes on the whole process. I note the trend towards polarization, just as Bishop Suhr has described it.

Many listeners prick up their ears when the Ukrainian archbishop of Winnipeg in Canada (later supported in this by Cardinal Liénart of Lille) introduces a proposal for the establishment of a 'senate' consisting of democratically elected bishops from all five continents. These must be regularly summoned to Rome, he says, to be ready *as a group* to assist the pope in his administration, for the bishops are not only leaders of their respective sees, they also have a *collective responsibility*, together with the pope, for the *whole* Church. A memorable speech, particularly because Paul VI later suggests the establishment of just such a forum, provided the Council requests it. The Holy Father had in fact himself touched on the possibility of such a 'senate' during his speech to the Roman Curia referred to above. He said then that—provided the Council was in favour of such a forum comprising bishops from the entire world—his own curia would certainly not oppose it! This veiled challenge to loyalty was acted on by the aula fathers with growing courage. And the pope kept his word after the end of the Council by establishing the *Synodus Episcoporum* (the Bishops' Synod) mainly composed of freely elected participants from bishops' conferences worldwide. Since then they have convened every third year in the Vatican for protracted plenary meetings with the pope, with in-between special synods of specific categories.

Our working day begins with High Mass, celebrated by a high-ranking prelate with many attendant clerics. We also sing the office of Lauds, naturally in Latin, which has been the language of all the Councils since the schism with the Eastern church in 1054. The work routine, which is inherited from previous councils, functions satisfactorily. Every member bishop has the right to speak in connection with a text under discussion, although not more than 5 per cent at most actually make use of it, while some are repeatedly on their feet. The cardinals have priority, as do those who speak on behalf of an entire bishops' conference.

In principle, only *one* basic text is treated at a time: a principle which more and more often has to be disregarded owing to the shortage of time.

The *schemata*, of which everyone has a copy and which have been drafted by the Preparatory Commission in cooperation with a comittee of experts, are used as a helping hand—more or less as a basis for discussion. The chairman of that committee first gives an account of how it has been arrived at, drawing attention to the central issues and the main problems. The General Secretariat for its part has drawn up a list of those wishing to speak, who now take it in turn to use the microphone closest to their place.

I have not been very long in the Council aula before I note with relief that here everybody may say whatever he wishes, provided he keeps in the main to the matter in hand. Fortunately the time limit is ten minutes, and the presiding cardinal, called moderator, is required to break in, first with a warning that only two minutes are left, and then by declaring that time is up. With increasing frequency, as a last resort, he even switches off the microphone in the middle of a sentence. On precisely that point the assembly hardly ever disagrees.

It is only natural that certain basic texts are considered more important—and of more consequence—than others, although all are regarded as significant in themselves.[3]

In practice the routine procedure means that a *schema*, which with the Council fathers' consensus had been declared at that point to have been thoroughly debated, is removed from the agenda for revision. Because anyone expressing the wish to speak has been obliged to hand in his speech in advance, it is regularly insinuated that controversial comments are placed so low on the list of speeches that they are never heard at all. Be that as it may, our attention is routinely drawn to the fact that also those who have not expressed the wish to speak are welcome to hand in written observations which will be dealt with on a par with speeches, whether actually given or not.

So, what happened to all these verbal—and written— comments?

The commission responsible for the basic draft, without giving undue consideration to its own text, now had to formulate a new working document—which of course took time, often weeks. The assembly would therefore take up the next subject, the secretary general having already informed us well in advance which this would be, so that we could do our homework.

As soon as the new working document on the recently debated *schema* was printed, it was delivered to us, whether it was to be treated afresh now or later. This enabled us to study our own improved (or perhaps even completely new) version, as well as—often equally important—allowing our theologians to do the same, for it was not against the rules to have advisers, rather the contrary. These private experts, or *periti,* had no conciliar status, however, although they were occasionally permitted to follow the discussions from a separate gallery.

The Council had its own permanent staff of about 380 appointed theologians attached to the various commissions and select committees. There were well-known names from many countries: Karl Rahner, Yves Congar, Jean Daniélou, Henri de Lubac, Hans Küng, Gregory Baum, John Courtney Murray, Lucien Cerfaux, Romano Guardini—to mention a few. These men were often to be seen in the aula, which led to their being frequently accosted by bishops keen to sound them out on their views.

As may be seen, there was a lot going on at once, but the work schedule was reasonably well organized. Thus it was disappointing that the first period had not managed to produce a single text ready for promulgation. During the ongoing session (also regarded as the last!) it therefore became obvious that, if we adhered to this traditional procedure, there was no hope of finishing before Christmas. Other councils had been able to round off so because the subject matter had been limited, but this time vast areas of the traditional life and teaching of the Church were to be reviewed. In addition new fields were to be opened up: ecumenism, relations to the non-Christian religions, religious liberty, the mass media, and not least, 'The Church in the Modern World'. Moreover the Council fathers showed no signs of being in a hurry to round matters off. As expected, one day we were told that the pope had convened a third session for the following autumn. With this, it was declared, the Council would be concluded (except that, once again, the calculations proved wrong).

For the record, I think it should be added that not all the bishops made speeches that were notably constructive. Some seemed to be speaking for domestic consumption—*pro domo,* as the phrase goes: it was to be reported back there at home that this or that had been said by their bishop in Rome. There were more than a few speeches of this type, although it was clear to everybody that the Council's precious time was being wasted and that a speech only gained attention by virtue of its relevance at the universal level.

The star speaker, if I may use such a presumptuous term, was the eighty-five-year-old Maximos IV of Antioch, one of the five uniate patriarchs. He was the only Council father who ventured to speak a modern language, in this case French—no Latin for him! He spoke with authority in a sonorous voice, always having something to say that was worth listening to. And he was never cut short. (One refrains from interrupting a patriarch, especially here right in front of so many alert Orthodox dignitaries on the observers' stand.)

To take an example. During the ongoing, sometimes ac- rimonious, debate concerning the *schema* 'On the Church' he showed little clemency. Whoever had prepared this draft, he thundered, must have imagined that the Church of Christ consists of the pope and the Roman Curia. The episcopate has a *collegial* responsibility for the Church as a whole. Yes, in governing the Church the pope must naturally share the responsibility with the College of Bishops. The special 'Ro- man court' must not be allowed to replace the College of the Apostles. The Council must now take the necessary steps to throw light on this truth which the custom of several centuries has overshadowed to such a degree that 'more and more of us have ended up regarding the prevalent situation as normal'. In Rome, he continued, there ought always to be a *synod* consisting of a nucleus of members of a Supreme Council made up of (1) the Patriarchs, (2) those cardinals who govern an archdiocese, and (3) elected representatives from the bishops' conferences. These must do duty in rotation and always be available to assist the pope in word and deed. The papal administration must be subordinate to this Supreme Council, whose members, thanks to their ambulant status, would not take root in the Vatican, and thus would be unlikely to decide all types of questions in a one-track and often narrow-minded manner. That he was referring to the curia was not missed by anybody, not even by the curia itself. Paul VI is said to have remarked later that it was the most important speech of all during that session.

The pushing conservative wing had its obvious (apparently self-appointed) spokesman in the archbishop of Palermo, Cardinal Ruffini, whose theological competence, however, was beyond doubt. Many of us could indeed disagree with his views, but this did not mean that we any the less enjoyed his logic, his elegant formulations, and his sharp sense of humour. It was otherwise no secret that the Italian episcopate under the leadership of the archbishop of Genoa, Cardinal Siri, with few exceptions (one being Cardinal Lercaro of Bologna) represented a not inconsiderable proportion of the conservative wing, where also Marcel Lefebvre, later so famous for his break-away, obviously belonged. Their closest 'allies' were the Spanish and Portuguese bishops.

It was not difficult to perceive that the greater proportion of the future-oriented progressive wing, comprising the Council speakers who were most attentively listened to, were from Europe.[4]

Amid the flood of words, the organizers of the Council, with well-advised common sense, had set up two large coffee bars, each with an entrance from its side of the aula. In general it was a relief to be able to quench one's thirst with coffee, tea, or mineral water and to have something to eat. Most of us visited them every day—even twice, for we also had afternoon meetings. (Against that, we had both Saturdays and Sundays free.) To my question about his coffee-bar habits, Bishop Mangers replied—without the slightest hint of superiority—that he had never set foot in either of them and never intended to do so.

We went home to lunch and, in our opinion, a well-deserved siesta. Then back to a new round. And we were not free to skip our duties, for every meeting began with our having to sign a punch-card collected at each place. Absence had to be granted by, or as the case might be, reported to, the General Secretariat, even in the event of *force majeure*.

I felt I had virtually landed in the ideal situation, for a young bishop could not have participated in any more instructive seminary in preparation for his duties. The discussions which eddied back and forth in the aula were, as stated, about the episcopate, both theologically and formally. The situation to which Patriarch Maximos had drawn attention was that the bishops as a rule governed their sees with a feeling of doing so on behalf of the pope (it was, after all, he who had appointed them in the first place). That they should have a wider responsibility in common with other bishops, for example within the same country or region, was not normally seen as a matter of course—nor that they should share a divinely ordained responsibility for the Universal Church. The reason for the uncertainty was that there was as yet no clear doctrine regarding the extent to which the consecration of a bishop was or was not a sacrament. I was now witness to a series of theological and practical developments that I found fascinating.

Not least important was the rediscovered teaching on the College of the Apostles—because it naturally led to the doctrine concerning the collegiality of the bishops. After lengthy debates almost in a state of deadlock (clearly drawn out by parts of the curia), our four moderators—in order to proceed further—sent four written questions to the assembled Council:

I. Is episcopal ordination the highest grade of the sacrament of the priesthood?

II. Is each validly consecrated bishop a member of the College of Bishops?

III. Is the College of Bishops a continuation of the College of the Apostles, and as such has it together with the Bishop of Rome, and never without him, the full and supreme authority over the Universal Church?

IV. Is this authority divinely ordained (*de jure divino*)?

It was particularly the last two points that in speech after speech had been contested by the conservative block, and by virtue of the sheer accumulation of their spoken comments they certainly seemed to represent an overwhelming majority. The enquiry, however, produced an entirely unexpected voting result (I omit the invalid votes):

I: 2,123 for—34 against
II: 2,049 for—104 against
III: 1,808 for—336 against
IV: 1,717 for—408 against

Admittedly the ballot was intended to be no more than indicative and was clearly announced as such, but even so it proved to be a watershed in the debate. For most of us the voting results opened up new perspectives pointing towards a theologically based apostolic fellowship and global co-responsibility, giving us a sense of liberation combined with an increased sense of responsibility. At the same time, it cleared the way for a theological basis for the bishops' conferences. Such assemblies had certainly existed in various countries, even for a considerable time—both in Ireland and in Germany for over a century, and in the Nordic countries since 1960. Nevertheless, the bishops' conferences were regarded as a purely practical arrangement for discussing common problems, with no significance in terms of ecclesiastical law.

Now the bishops felt themselves to be bound ontologically as much to one another as to the Holy Father. Many eyes shone with a new light, and there were many smiles to be seen in the aula that day.

As for the hotly debated *schema* on Our Lady, regarding which Bishop Suhr and I had witnessed the attempted 'torpedoing' in Bonn, there were many tough confrontations between the two sides before it was incorporated, by a narrow majority vote, as a chapter in the constitution 'On the Church'. The members of the German bishops' conference could be seen exchanging knowing looks.

It was one of the foreground figures in this ponderous assembly who produced the 'bomb' of the session. The ageing archbishop of Cologne, Cardinal Joseph Frings, was blind. But he compensated for his lack of sight by an extra acuteness in the other senses. As a member of the Council's presidency he had become all the more irritated by the systematic obstructive manoeuvres by the Ottaviani group, most recently by the fact that these gentlemen now openly denied the significance of the ballot concerning the College of Bishops, maintaining that the theme belonged to the theological commission's area of competence.[5] The voting, which after all was only in the nature of an orientation, was therefore, acccording to them, formally of no consequence.

In polite and measured tones, but with freezing scorn, Cardinal Frings set himself up against not only the aforementioned commission, but also the whole congregation behind it—the so-called Holy Office. Was this to say, then, that the almost unanimous opinion of the Council meant nothing? he asked. The truth was that also the theological commission was subordinate to the Council and obliged to implement its intentions. As for the Holy Office, its methods had long been in contravention of contemporary concepts of law, indeed it was no less than a scandal in the eyes of the world. (At this point the assembly burst out in applause.) The cardinal went into further detail on this score, demanding the revision of both the regulations and the procedures of the congregation. He also advocated that the number of bishops in the papal curia be drastically reduced: in many cases they could to advantage be replaced by competent lay persons. (More applause.)

I admit that after this salvo, of which I have only quoted small snippets, I felt so shaken that I escaped to the asylum of the coffee bar, which was then practically empty, but soon filled up with smiling bishops who were mentally and physically rubbing their hands. At last somebody had dared to speak out!

Later the same morning, the shock-stricken Ottaviani made a counterattack. The cardinal—who was likewise blind—improvised in perfect Latin a highly justificatory speech in defence of his holy congregation (which at one time had taken over from the Inquisition). His voice trembling with indignation, he declared that to attack it was tantamount to attacking its prefect, the pope. He himself was only the pontiff's deputy. The speech seemed strangely pathetic—and moreover unconvincing, as was evidenced not least by the apparently indifferent fashion in which it was received.

It is part of the story that a day or two later we could observe these two cardinals, Ottaviani and Frings, strolling back and forth in the wide space behind the high altar, to show that there were no ill feelings. 'Just look', said Bishop Suhr to me, 'the blind leading the blind.' The remark went the rounds both inside and outside Saint Peter's.

On a November afternoon Bishop Suhr arranged for all of us Nordic bishops to foregather at the Brigittine Sisters' generalate on the Piazza Farnese—my first bishops' conference. The tone was informal, almost convivial. Most of the bishops smoked large cigars, slapping each other jovially on the shoulder every time something amusing was said. Bishop Suhr, who neither smoked nor had the habit of making jovial gestures, was unaffected by this tone, which he was used to. We had no set programme and no secretary taking notes. We just had free discussions on a couple of Council questions. Suhr kept the matter he cared about until the end: he felt we should draw up a joint Nordic pastoral, naturally about the Council—and preferably about the liturgy. His reason was that the session had now approved its first decree, *De sacra liturgia*, which would decide the orientation and development in this area for ages to come. He believed that our faithful—through such a pastoral, read aloud from the pulpit during Sunday Mass in our five countries—would clearly and authoritatively receive the necessary introduction to the many liturgical innovations. Everyone considered this a positive step, and so it proved to be.

When the pastoral was read out on the first Sunday in Lent the following year, it was very well received but unintentionally led many Catholics to infer that the Council's programme for liturgical reform would now be co-ordinated in the North, something which disquieted those who specialized in the liturgy.

Dom Gabriel sprang a surprise on me. Suddenly there was to be a celebration for the Order's newly fledged bishop. The invitation indicated that my episcopal robes were to be worn. When I entered the rearranged dining hall, I saw a sort of 'bishop's throne' rigged up for the occasion, to which I was now conducted, though with some embarrassment on my part—unaccustomed as we were to such formalities at Monte Cistello.

Sitting there I had to listen to a long, though well-phrased, panegyric that Dom Gabriel, with his appreciation of style, probably felt himself obliged to pronounce. Much of it concerned the good relationship between us over the years, a relationship he hoped would last. He then turned towards a table on which lay a box covered in crocodile skin. From this he lifted up a magnificent pectoral cross made of huge golden yellow topazes mounted in gold and fastened to a long, elaborately wrought gold chain. There was also a bishop's ring, this too in gold, with a large, sparkling topaz. It was obvious that these were not modern work. After enjoying the general atmosphere of surprise, or perhaps gaping amazement, the abbot general recounted the history of these treasures. Both had been given to the Cistercian abbot Augustin Marre when in 1900, as the only bishop in our Order in this century, he was consecrated in the cathedral in Reims. After his death— then as abbot general—it had remained in the keeping of his successors, yet without ever having been worn by any of them. Now 'Monseigneur John' was to have both pieces—for what could be more fitting? He then hung the cross round my neck and placed the ring (which was much too large) on my right hand. My guess is that neither Dom Gabriel, nor I myself, nor the kindly applauding brethren really thought that I should ever wear these ponderous objects. During a General Chapter in Rome many years later—when I was no longer Bishop of Oslo—I hung all this finery back on the then newly elected abbot general amid amused rejoicing.

In mid-November the long-promised and—for many—the greatly longed-for *schema De oecumenismo* ('On Ecumenism') was at last laid before us. When it had been given to us in June, the difference then had been that, unlike the *schemata* we had been issued with previously, it was incomplete. Of five chapters, the last two were missing—precisely those which were awaited with the greatest eagerness, both inside and outside the Council. Now at least the fourth chapter (that on the Jews) was in place. The one on religious freedom was still ominously missing.

The Commission for the Catholic Eastern Churches had for long struggled with its own ecumenical draft, but under pressure from our presidency had agreed that its draft be incorporated in Bea's text.

Everyone was aware that we were experiencing a turning point in the history of Christianity as a consequence of the fact that John XXIII had felt the urge to initiate a radical new orientation of the Catholic Church's relations to the other Christian denominations.

In addition to his commitment to ecumenism, Cardinal Bea had for many years been taken up with the Jewish question, appalled as he was by the inherited 'Christian' attitude which held that the Jews *as a people* were to be considered guilty of the crucifixion of Christ. He had obtained Pope John's promise that his own commission, the Secretariat for Christian Unity, should also be instrumental in clearing up the Catholic Church's hopefully final position on this question. Thus the document on ecumenism had an addendum 'The Catholic Church's attitude towards the non-Christian religions and in particular towards the Jews'. That it took so long for the *schema* to proceed from Bea's commission to the Council was mainly due to the complexity of this issue, about which not only the curia but also the world at large felt deeply. Divers Arab states had also in various ways used pressure in an attempt to have this controversial theme removed from the Council's agenda. And so, serious tension had built up in Christian, Jewish, and Muslim circles concerning the wording of the declaration.

Normally Cardinal Bea would have presented the *schema*. This time, however, the procedure was unusual—unusual because it was the Holy See's secretary of state, Cardinal A. M. Cicognani, who was a member of neither Ottaviani's theological commission nor the Secretariat for Christian Unity, who did the presentation. Cardinal Cicognani was president of the Council's Central Committee and as such its most influential person after the pope. It was assumed therefore—and not incorrectly—that there had been quite a tug of war behind the scenes.

Although it is not possible here to go into detail on this long and disconcerting course of events, where we witnessed from the outset the most stubborn anti-ecumenical attitudes in open confrontation with the unreservedly positive, I think it is worth giving some fragments from what went on.

With few exceptions, the first days' speakers, who had apparently applied far in advance, were all anti-ecumenical— naturally from deep conviction. A couple of Spanish bishops, seemingly in cooperation, strongly advocated that the Council should reject the entire proposal, as being of a type designed to spread disquiet among God's people (the Catholics). What was regarded as particularly dangerous was the *schema*'s enjoinder to pray together with non-Catholics—something which

moreover 'was contrary to canon law'. Protestant proselytiz-
ing is gaining ground, they said, so we must be on our guard.
Yes, the *schema* speaks in far too positive tones about the non-
Catholics—'as if the Holy Spirit were at work outside the
Church, and one could find the virtues of faith, hope, and
charity in non-Catholics!'

Among those on the positive side, Patriarch Maximos, as
usual, made an impression. He took the content of the *schema*
to his heart: it was the expression of sound doctrine and was
to a high degree suited to ending once and for all the sterile
polemics, the proselytizing activity, and the spirit of competition that reigned between the different churches. Here the
way was opened both for healthy missionary zeal and for the
open profession of faith in love. He had his reservations about
the chapter concerning the Jews—not against its content but
rather against its being placed in this context.

As the discussion developed, it became clear that more and
more speakers shared a favourable attitude towards the main
points in the *schema*, even if they might have reservations
concerning details. In line with the patriarch's objection, a
growing number of voices were raised against the 'enforced
incorporation' which appeared to have taken place in regard
to the two (originally independent) *schemata* concerning the
non-Christians (particularly the Jews) and concerning religious liberty. The fate of these chapters was thus increasingly
uncertain, at all events within this framework. But the debate
demonstrated with growing clarity that the Council fathers
were in the course of swinging in the direction of a positive
attitude towards the separated brethren in the faith, as they
were then called.

The observers were now in quite a different way in tune
with the situation and could in their turn be observed in
the wings debating with one another and with their Catholic
colleagues.

So it was Cardinal Bea's turn to speak—for the first time in
this debate. He had in fact given up the general introduction,
in order to be able instead to present the chapter on 'The

attitude of the Catholic Church to non-Christian religions and in particular to the Jewish religion'— a matter so dear to his heart. The cardinal stressed the purely religious character of the text and precluded all political implications.

The Christian church, he said, rests on a Jewish foundation; Christ himself was a Jew, and so were the apostles; the original church was spread among Jews. It is impossible to contend that God rejected the Jews *as a people*. To lay the guilt for the death of Jesus collectively upon them all is untenable because of its inherent unreasonableness. For example, Matthew says that the leaders of the Jews did not dare to allow Christ to be arrested during the Passover celebrations 'because there could then be unrest among the people'. This showed that the majority of ordinary Jews were *for* him. Those who called out 'Crucify him!' were in the minority. And what about all those Jews who were not then in Jerusalem—let alone all the later generations? Regardless of the question of guilt or lack of guilt in this matter, concluded the cardinal, 'as Christians our guiding principle must always be forgiveness and compassion'.

It was transparently clear after Bea's fascinating presentation (fascinating—not least due to the noble fashion in which he tackled his subject) that the content was good, right, and timely (even though there were many suggestions for various minor amendments), but also that the whole subject of the non-Christian religions belonged in another context.

The debate was almost finished—there was a risk of time running out—when at the last moment we were presented with the final chapter, 'On Religious Freedom', this time by the bishop of Bruges, Émile-Joseph De Smedt, one of the two vice presidents of the Secretariat for Christian Unity, whose area of responsibility—and favourite subject—it was. Solidly behind the text, besides Bea's Secretariat, stood—interestingly enough—the hierarchy of the USA. The draft of the *schema* had been drawn up, in fact, in committed pioneer spirit by one of America's most significant (and most likeable) theologians, the Jesuit John Courtney Murray (apparently a particularly black sheep according to the Holy Office). So there was something explosive in the air here too.

The traditional Catholic teaching is that the individual Christian cannot decide what to believe solely on the basis of his or her own judgement. Consequently the Inquisition had firmly indicated (and more than *indicated)* the duty of Catholics to believe blindly in the Church's teaching *in toto*. Here, conscience had to come second. The Church therefore was in duty bound to engage itself in missionary activities—and to fight, in armed combat if need be—for the preservation and propagation of the true faith. Many questions were repeatedly posed regarding such oversimplification; and many years of theological deliberation—not least against the background of the United Nations' Declaration of Human Rights—had led to a demand within the Church itself for clarification by the Council of the fundamental problems related to the *free* exercise of religion, precisely as a human right. That it was Bea's commission that was made responsible for the handling of the subject can only be termed a heaven-sent stroke of fate, for Cardinal Ottaviani's theological commission would have been more than glad to get their hands on this particular matter. Now they had to content themselves with dragging things out as long as possible, until a direct order from Paul VI put it on to the current agenda.

In her book about this session of the Council, Gunnel Vallquist has with admirable brevity reiterated the content of De Smedt's speech introducing the *schema*:

> The bishop went straight to the most sensitive nerve-centre when he stated that many non-Catholics suspect the Church of Machiavellianism: that we would plead for religious freedom when we are in the minority, but oppose it when we are in the majority.
>
> The Church dissociates itself from all doctrines of freedom which maintain that mankind is independent not only of all exterior instances, but also of God. It is for this reason that previous popes have expressed themselves so negatively on the subject: they spoke out against

philosophical theses which propounded such a total independence. A development which has taken place in the thinking of the Church means that today we can formulate the Christian position in a different way. When the Church now (in particular John XXIII in his encyclical *Pacem in terris*) defends the absolute sovereignty of the individual conscience vis-à-vis external authorities, it is thus propounding mankind's total dependence on God alone. The Catholic Church of course still believes that God has revealed his truth in and through the Church, but that this truth may never be forced upon anyone; it must be recognized in freedom. Indeed, anyone who honestly follows the voice of his own conscience is following God's voice—even if his conscience should lead him out of the Church.

Such a person must be respected and venerated by all Catholics.

This view on the sovereignty of the conscience, however, makes firm demands on one's spiritual honesty.

It is the duty of the public authorities to protect this right and to ensure that every citizen's free exercise of his religion is respected by his fellow citizens.

(After his introduction to the *schema* there was loud applause.)[6]

John Courtney Murray, the chapter's driving power, said that in his opinion Bishop De Smedt's presentation was even better than the text itself. Would that all theologians were so unegoistic!

I received a letter written on the Hotel Hassler note paper. Large handwriting, discreetly scented. The sender's name was given as Vera Zorina. I had seen her in the leading rôle in a musical at the Coliseum in London in 1936. What could she want with me? Yes, she and her Norwegian mother, she wrote, had spent a few days in a fjord hotel in Norway at the end of May. A seminar was taking place that I had attended (this was so). Being a Catholic she had been tempted to greet me, but had refrained, since she did not actually know me. This she had later regretted. Now she was in Rome. Could I think of joining her for lunch?

During the meal, she told me something of herself and her varied career. She had finished with the ballet, musicals, and a film career in Hollywood, all of which lay in the past. Afterwards she had recited with orchestras in larger works such as *Jeanne d'Arc au bûcher* by Honegger and *Persephone* by Stravinsky—both in French and in English. She had also been responsible for several productions and had recently directed Poulenc's opera *Dialogues des Carmélites* in Santa Fe, New Mexico. She was, she said, a committed Catholic, which explained her contacting me. After that we talked at length about religion, something for which she clearly felt a deep need.

With dessert I switched themes: 'I have seen you perform.' 'Oh, in what?', she asked hopefully. 'In *On Your Toes*', I replied. (*On Your Toes* by Rodgers and Hammerstein ran for a long time at the London Coliseum and in New York, with Vera Zorina playing the principal rôle in both cities.)

She lowered her head in obvious disappointment, for her years in musicals were not those for which she wished to be remembered, and especially not in the company of a prelate when *Jeanne d'Arc* would have been more fitting. She told me that Vera Zorina was the professional name she had adopted when she belonged to the Ballets Russes de Monte Carlo, where everybody had to have a Russian name. In fact, her original name was Brigitta Hartvig. Her father was a German opera singer, and her mother was from Kristiansund in central Norway; she herself had been born in Berlin (all this I already knew vaguely, but let her tell me). She was first married to George Balanchine (one of the world's leading choreographers, at that time artistic director of the New York City Ballet), but after a separation by agreement, the marriage had been declared null and void because he had already been married before. Later in New York she married the composer Goddard Lieberson, who had moved into gramophone records and was now the president of Columbia Records.

They had two sons; the elder of whom is the composer Peter Lieberson.

A few days later Brother Sylvester came to my door: 'A lady is here asking for you.' 'A lady?' 'An American, I think, very beautiful—smells lovely.'

I understood: 'Show her into the visitors' parlour.'

'She's there already; I said that you would come.'

Mrs Lieberson felt the need for clarification of some spiritual problems, and to deepen her religious life. There was no doubt that she was a genuinely committed Christian. We had another hour-long talk. Before she left, she said that if I happened to be coming to America, I should let her know. She and her husband would be able to show me things which would otherwise be inaccessible. I could not know then that this was an invitation I should later have the pleasure of accepting.

At the Council, the discussions (speech after speech) concerning ecumenism continued, now about the document in its entirety. I shall limit myself to referring to some of the views on religious liberty. One on the negative side (Archbishop Florit, Florence): 'Can there be any right, even in good faith, to disseminate a false religion?' Someone else wished to cut out both the chapter on religious liberty and the one on the Jews. Instead, the Council should without any dissimulation declare that there is no salvation to be found outside the Church (the papal church, naturally). It is outrageous (insisted Bishop Carli of Segni) to speak as if the Holy Spirit should also be at work in non-Catholic communities—as if God would wish to legitimize the split!

A sizeable group of Italian bishops led by Cardinal Ruffini now met regularly once a week to compare and harmonize their views and endeavours. The progressives did the same. None of this was considered disloyal, let alone illegal. However: the last working day of the session was marked by an unusual episode in this connection. When we arrived, we found that on each seat lay a pamphlet written by several Italian bishops who strongly criticized everything in the chapter on religious liberty. It was one thing that such a distribution of material in the aula was forbidden, but that it could apparently be effected with the tacit compliance of the administration was another. Normally behaviour of that kind would be stopped in good time. Here no one had intervened!

Nevertheless, the majority of the speakers were now positive to ecumenism, even if basing themselves on different points of view and assessments of several questions involved. Some people felt that the chapter on religious freedom should come first, since this was the real point of departure for both the spirit and the active realization of ecumenism. Others— the majority—maintained that this particular text ought not to have been included here, but rather have remained an independent document (and it was the latter who would carry the day).

In the middle of this imbroglio, President Kennedy was murdered in Dallas. The days that followed seemed to bear the stamp of horror, but also of a sort of unreality, as if we could not quite grasp what had happened. Something of the same feeling had gripped the world at the news of President Roosevelt's death in April 1945. As in those days, we asked each other: the new president, who is he? The difference between then and now was that while Roosevelt was ill and well on in years, Kennedy had been the image of 'the man of the future' for a large part of the world. The uneasiness was palpable even in the heart of the Council, where many American bishops had to request leave of absence in order to be able to officiate at mourning ceremonies at home. Cardinal Spellman of New York conducted a grandiose, almost pompous, Requiem Mass in the Lateran basilica with guards of honour from all branches of the US defence forces, the entire diplomatic corps, 1,700 bishops, and 10,000 other people present. For a brief interval we had to forget the Council and let the outside world take over.

I have mentioned that I was to work with Cardinal Bea. This happened towards the end of the session. Once again it was a matter of chance. In Oslo we had a community of contemplative Dominican sisters, mostly French, who had originally come from a convent in Lourdes. Because they were subject to a strict rule of enclosure, the sisters had to have a grille dividing their visitors' parlour. I had promised that during my stay in Rome I would try to obtain a dispensation in this respect for them, granting permission for the room to be divided by a counter, with the sisters on one side and the visitors on the other, but without a grille.

What happened is this: during the ongoing session the Council also addressed a whole complex of problems under the heading 'On the Adaptation and Renewal of Religious Life'. The broadminded and energetic French Bishop Gérard Huygue (Arras) was in charge of the preparatory procedure, and the thought struck me that raising the grille problem with him would be to take the bull by the horns. To track down an unknown prelate was not difficult; everybody knew somebody who knew other people. He and I soon had a constructive conversation. Yes, indeed, he would take up the matter, for he heartily agreed that such grilles were not in keeping with today's mentality. It took the intervention of the Holy Father himself, but eventually the grille was removed.

What happened next was quite unexpected. The pope suddenly decreed the enlargement of all the conciliar commissions. The scarcely camouflaged reason was that Ottaviani's theological commission had made no progress whatever, neither with the previously mentioned constitution 'On the Sources of Revelation' nor now with the one 'On the Church'. The members were divided into two even factions. To reach a solution, Paul VI, who never liked to tread on anybody's toes, decreed that all conciliar commissions should forthwith be increased by five new members, four chosen by the Council and finally one appointed by himself—making a total of thirty members each instead of twenty-five. Proposals for candidates would be put forward by an *ad hoc* panel which should first consult the larger bishops' conferences. During an afternoon meeting with the German bishops, I learned that my name was third on the list of candidates proposed for the

Commission for the Religious, something for which Bishop
Huygue must have been responsible following our talk, for
nobody else could have known me. But the Germans agreed
that this would not do, since they themselves had a candidate
whom they most definitely wished to have voted in, while
the other names at the top of Bishop Huygue's list should not
be displaced. Thus I was out again, as fast as I had come in.
A German cardinal, however, thought that to rule out the
only candidate from the North could seem like a disavowal
of the Scandinavian Episcopal Conference, with which the
Germans wished to maintain good relations.

In a deft move, which I witnessed, the cardinal entered my
name on the list of proposed candidates for Cardinal Bea's
commission. When shortly afterwards in the aula we were
issued with lists of proposals for candidates, I again found
my own name suggested, but for the Secretariat for Christian
Unity, still as number three. After my neighbour—an American bishop—had approved suggestions for that commission,
he turned to me: 'Well, if I haven't just voted for you—you
character!' And so it must have been with most of the aula
fathers, contenting themselves with putting crosses beside the
names at the top. Thus, at least in my case, somewhat over
2,000 Council members voted for someone they could never
have heard of. This was more or less how it came about that
I became a member of Cardinal Bea's Secretariat.

No more enriching experience has ever come my way than
participation in Bea's Secretariat, for this establishment was
responsible throughout for the Council's three most pioneering and remarkable drafts, all of which led to texts which we
finally—not without many ifs and buts—managed to bring
to a successful conclusion.[7]

From the Secretariat for Christian Unity I was summoned
to a plenary meeting, my first. It was certainly a mixed assembly! Cardinal Bea cordially received those of us who were new
members. It felt good to have known this leader from before.
His right hand throughout many years' work on ecumenical
matters was the Dutch Monsignor Jan Willebrands, secure in

his position as secretary and second fiddle. As for the rest of the gathering, they could be divided into three components: (1) the staff, (2) the members, of which I was now one, and (3) the counsellors, all priests. The last two categories were appointed for the duration of the Council. In full sessions, as now, there were many of us, but we managed to squeeze ourselves in around one table (admittedly of fair dimensions) in the main hall. The adjacent rooms were for subcommittees, since we were often divided into language groups to facilitate working.

Cardinal Bea opened, but soon handed over to Willebrands who normally led the meetings. The approved languages— apart from the official Latin—were Italian (the curia's daily language), French, English, and German. Anyone who was disadvantaged language-wise sat beside someone who was not. You could hear the sound of all the whispering.

We were, to a man, convinced that it was here that the real dynamite of the Council was concocted. It was not only that the *schema* 'On Ecumenism' represented a U-turn in our Church's history. In addition the declaration concerning the Church's attitude to the non-Christian religions, and in particular to the Jews, was so combustible that single words, sometimes even a comma, could cause an outbreak—both inside and outside the commission itself.

The declaration 'On Religious Freedom', which was the very thorn in the flesh of Ottaviani's theological commission, was no less controversial. Actually, in the end, we had as much trouble with this text and as many revisions to make to it as to each of the two others, so that it could not be put up for the final voting until the very deadline in the last conciliar period.

It is impossible within the present framework to give an adequate account of the enormous amount of patient effort put into this work, or to describe all the setbacks and the many disappointments which complicated our Secretariat's awkward path, or to tell of the outside world's different attempts to torpedo our efforts. Countless drafts and revisions had to be drawn up, reworked, and adjusted in accordance with the bishops' many comments, both verbal and written.

It was impressive to observe how everyone in our commission, from the cardinal to the lowest ranking secretary, adhered to the goal with unwavering persistence. Bea's working slogan was: The Council has given us an assignment, and we are going to honour it—cost what it may. With ever-growing wonderment I registered, from the inside, this series of intensive endeavours that had already extended over several years.

For me to be allowed to join in on this, virtually straight after my episcopal consecration, was a welcome and useful training in endurance and religious priorization at the highest level—but also an extraordinary enrichment. Not least I considered it a great privilege to have the chance of working so closely and for so long with several of the most significant figures of the Catholic Church.[8]

It is a special pleasure to recall the mini-holiday Bishop Suhr and I spent together in Assisi. Towards the end of the session we were tired and glad to take the opportunity of a few days' relaxation away from Rome. This chance was due to the fact, quite simply, that even if the Council was working internally under high pressure revising drafts, no new text was up for debate and comment, since there was now too little time for that. A short break was thus possible for many of us, even for the Secretariat's episcopal members.

Bishop Suhr knew an elderly priest who had founded and now ran a large institute in Assisi: Pro Civitate Christiana. It had, he exclaimed, a building for seminars with plenty of accommodation, so we could come if and when we chose. 'Any time?' 'Yes.' So that settled it.

We drove north, pleased to leave the Council and all its affairs momentarily behind us. When we arrived at Don Giovanni Rossi's institute, which was as large as Suhr had said, we found a motley assembly and great activity. The amiable Rossi welcomed us with open arms assuring us that of course there was room and, besides: for bishops always! What was going on? Well, actually a seminar arranged by the International Catholic Film Institute. Bishop Suhr pointed at me and said something to the effect that this must be of interest to Bishop Gran, for he had been connected with films. 'Only as an assistant director', I hastened to add. 'But then' exclaimed Rossi, 'you absolutely have to be in the adjudication committee.' 'What is to be adjudicated?' I asked cautiously, with little enthusiasm for any new challenges. 'We're going to decide whether Pier Paolo Pasolini's newest film, *The Gospel according to Saint Matthew,* can make the top of the list for next year's International Catholic Film Award.' Pasolini was gifted in a variety of fields—as a poet, a novelist, and a film director.

'You must be in on this!' declared Bishop Suhr. So that very afternoon, I sat together with the assembled jury and viewed a masterpiece, as yet unknown to a world that so far knew Pasolini mainly as an author, as well as a Marxist and an atheist. He was present himself, and in the jury sat a number of well-known film people. I myself had an agreeable time afterwards talking to the actor Tullio Carminati, now old but a gentleman full of the spirit of life. He was the famous actress Eleonore Duse's leading man for many years, and after her death had a career in films in Hollywood and England, and later in Italy. I was tempted to whisper to him that I had read what a critic of standing had written twenty years earlier, that he was 'the only gentleman in the Italian film world'. But I desisted.

In the middle of the night I was woken by a knocking on my door. Outside stood Rossi in his long nightshirt. 'Bishop' he said, 'as a former film man you must obviously celebrate the Sunday Mass in our chapel tomorrow—at eight o'clock. Everyone will be there, Pasolini and his wife, too. Yes, and so you must preach a fine sermon; that will do them good; probably most of them don't often go to church.' Now I was awake, but a moment too late because before I had gathered my wits to react to this strange improvisation, Don Rossi had shuffled off again in his slippers on his way back to bed.

At crack of dawn I sat down at my desk and noted the main points for my homily. Bishop Suhr seemed slightly nonplussed on discovering that it was I who was to celebrate Mass and even preach, ignorant as he was of the nocturnal corridor 'agreement'. Not unnaturally, I remember almost nothing of what I said, apart from 'casually' including some elements from my own time with films. Otherwise I only remember Tullio Carminati's dominant figure agreeably nodding in the front pew.

The jury's views on Pasolini's film were largely positive. Quite a few of us had this or that minor objection, mostly concerning unhistoric or para-evangelical details, which we pointed out to Pasolini saying that we would like see them adjusted. In any event we voted that *The Gospel according to Matthew* should be put forward for the first prize, since we were convinced it possessed exceptional qualities. A new meeting, with Pasolini himself present, decided the matter. He was willing to make the recommended alterations, for it was obvious that he greatly desired the award. The story ended with his receiving the prize the following year—although without having made the slightest change. We were still in Italy! (Pasolini's ending was a macabre one: twelve years later he was murdered in a Rome slum.)

At the very end of the conciliar session several things happened. One important event was the ballot on the epoch-making *schema* 'On the Sacred Liturgy'. It had been discussed in depth during the first session, but—despite generally positive acceptance—had been complicated by so many suggested amendments that it was only now possible to present it for the final voting. To the relief of the exhausted fathers it was approved by an overwhelming majority: 2,158 to 19 votes.

No less important for us was the (arranged?) voting on three out of the five chapters of our *schema* 'On Ecumenism'—in one go. The voting concerned only the extent to which these three could be accepted as a basis for further detailed treatment next year. Into the bargain it was announced that neither could the last two chapters be voted on before then 'due to shortage of time'. I noticed during the announcement of this bizarre procedure that several heads nodded sagely ('Wasn't that just what I knew would happen!'). We in Bea's Secretariat, however, noted with relief that the ballot resulted in a total of 1,966 votes in favour and only 86 against. The many negative interventions in the aula had led us to expect a much more even result.

Suddenly the session was over. Pope Paul VI himself celebrated the closing solemn Mass. In a finely balanced address, using unexpectedly positive phrases, he gave a summary of the results so far. He dwelt particularly on the broadly worked-out but still far from finished constitution 'On the Church', and called the Council fathers' endeavours 'a vast meditation on the transcendent character of the Church'.

As will be remembered, the text for this dogmatic constitution had been slaughtered by the bishops when it was presented by Ottaviani during the first session (1962): slaughtered, in the sense that the large majority found the draft so traditional as to be quite pointless. A completely new text had been prepared by an expanded *ad hoc* commission, and during the present session it had been thoroughly commented on and improved, although much still remained to be done.

The pope likewise emphasized the inherent values in the two documents which had so far been promulgated (*On the Sacred Liturgy* and *On the Media of Social Communication*). In particular, he underlined the importance of the liturgical decree with its wise rating of priorities: God first, then the liturgy as a source given by God for the promotion of mankind's supernatural life, and as a school in spiritual and religious self-realization. Last, but not least: the liturgy as God's primal gift to his people.

But it all showed clearly, as we were all painfully aware, that precious little had actually been completed, with correspondingly much left to do.

Towards the end of his speech the pope announced—totally unexpectedly—that in January he intended to make a pilgrimage to Palestine to honour the holy sites connected with Christ's birth, life, work, death, resurrection, and ascension. And there, in the Holy Land, he would present the Church as a sacrifice to God, and at the same time invite back into the one fold the separated brothers and sisters in the faith. And there he would pray with all his might for God's merciful intervention in the cause of peace among mankind.

Paul VI's words released an intense and prolonged applause of the kind only a good surprise can give rise to. No pope had ever made a pilgrimage to the Holy Land, and besides, what but an initiative like this could so well illustrate the noble content of the Church's new attitude on ecumenism?

It was in private with Cardinal Bea that we now for the first time learned that he and his closest colleagues had for long been playing a rôle in the many complicated and delicate Jerusalem negotiations—with contacts that had also involved considerable numbers of civil authorities.

We members were told that before the next session we would be recalled to the Secretariat for more commission work. I did not find the thought distasteful, for Rome was still, above all others, very much 'my' city. But more important still: like the others in Bea's commission I had had my appetite whetted and was eager to strike while the iron was still hot!

Twenty-Two

THE END OF THE BEGINNING

T HE YEAR 1964 was to be my last year as coadjutor. Bishop Mangers had his seventy-fifth birthday in March and had hinted that he now would like to retire before the end of the year. He would then return to his homeland, Luxembourg, where he had been given the opportunity to spend the evening of his life in the same convent in which his predecessor's predecessor, Bishop Johannes Olav Fallize, also from Luxembourg, had spent his retirement. At all events, this was a question that lay with the pope, since the decision had to be his.

Something exciting was under way in Oslo. The Dominicans there had had several Norwegian vocations, and the level of quality was high. Among the 'new blood' was the young, gifted Father Erik Gunnes, who had been a correspondent in Rome during the previous session of the Council, and who had specialized in Bible scholarship and church history during his long period of study in France. Parts of his translation, already begun, of the Gospels from Greek to Norwegian had been placed before Bishop Mangers who, pleased with what he saw, had assigned him the responsibility for a new version of the New Testament to meet contemporary scientific criteria. This would be our third Catholic New Testament translation in modern times.

Gunnes based his work on the best Greek texts, and added commentaries with the backing of the Ecole Biblique in Jerusalem, which was run by French Dominicans and enjoyed high international prestige.

I became involved in the project and was delighted that we were here preparing a worthwhile publication which would definitely be able to win a place for itself, even in 'Bible belt' Norway where we were still without a translation that was up to standard.

A deputation of leaders for our youth work, all of whom I know from my time in that milieu, have an urgent need: a youth centre. The Young Norwegian Catholics' League arranges seminars and camps. It is true they have been allowed to take over the Sisters of Saint Francis Xavier's now disused novitiate, pleasantly situated in the country not far from Oslo, but the road has recently been rerouted and is now lying so close to the buildings that the place is virtually unusable for this purpose. A tour of inspection proves this to be the case. We will have to find something else.

A veteran among the youth leaders, Kjell Ruyter, undertakes to find a property within a radius of fifty kilometres from Oslo, preferably with suitable buildings, but above all in a peaceful situation protected against incursions. He combs the market from end to end. We look at several properties and are finally almost on the point of giving up because nothing seems feasible.

Suddenly Kjell, his voice full of urgency, rings to say he has come across an advertisement in a local newspaper: a small farm for sale near Lake Øyeren. He has studied the map: it is at the lakeside and has its own private approach-road through the woods. But we must hurry, for there is a buyer on hand and the farmer is thinking over the offer. That same afternoon Bishop Mangers, Kjell, and I go to take a look.

Holmen farm has at some time been separated from a larger estate that is still fully active. The landscape is hilly, about eight acres with woods behind, tall trees, a dwelling-house, a barn, and some cultivated land, a splendid view over the water, its own shoreline. Admittedly it is rather far from Oslo: 60 km. Never mind, anything better we could never hope for. The farmer feels honoured—two bishops. He has, however, another interested party: a nudist association! They have offered him the proposed price of 75,000 kroner, but have not managed to come up with the money by the agreed deadline. He therefore feels free to sell. He has indeed developed moral qualms about dealing with nudist bathers, so if we make a definite offer, he would rather—much rather—sell the place to us. And we can have it for 70,000 kroner! The bishop, Kjell, and I agree with a look at one another, and Mangers nods: 'We'll take it.'

There and then we draw up and sign an agreement for the purchase. We are pleased, and the seller is happy—and not least relieved. On the way back we begin to discuss what we shall call the place, for 'Holmen' (meaning *holm, islet*) seems rather uninteresting. An idea comes to me: 'What about Mariaholm?' The others think it a good suggestion, so even its name has been settled—all in one afternoon.[1]

Bishop Mangers and I were conscious of the fact that a lot of money would be needed to turn the place into an up-to-date youth centre. We engaged an architect, who proved to be the right man for the job. He had great respect for nature, was eager to keep the small pieces of cultivated land untouched and to make the buildings fit into the landscape.

But then the money! Mangers suggested I go on a begging trip to the USA, as he himself had once done when there had been the same sort of need. We also had an elderly Norwegian priest who had more than once successfully undertaken fundraising journeys 'over there'. If a young bishop came to beg for the establishment of a youth centre, he reasoned, there should be a chance of a good response.

Because the Nordic Catholic dioceses were still subordinate to the Congregation for the Evangelization of Peoples (Propaganda Fide) and were thus considered as mission areas, we enjoyed the privilege of being able to give mission sermons during the holy-day Masses throughout the USA. The apportioning of time and so on was arranged centrally from a New York office where the celebrated TV-Bishop Fulton Sheen was 'boss'. There ensued a great deal of correspondence between us to coordinate the travelling and dates, arranging for me to give sermons in a number of parish churches all over the country.

So as early as April 1964 I was airborne for New York—the first time I had travelled outside Europe. In New York City I was to stay with my new acquaintances, Brigitta (Zorina) and her husband Goddard Lieberson. I had at first declined their invitation, but changed my mind after having received a friendly and amusing letter from him urging me to accept. Otherwise it was the normal practice to ask for lodging in houses belonging to religious orders or in the rectories. Staying in hotels was never considered, for economic reasons.

In New York, where I was to spend two weeks and preach in that part of the world, I was given the full treatment. The Lieberson family lived in Manhattan. Goddard turned out to be one of the most interesting people I could ever remember having met. He was a 'ball of fire', full of knowledge and a perpetual source of intelligence, with brilliant observations about everything and everybody. As his name suggested, he was Jewish. He had been born in England, practised no religion, and had few, if any, taboos. He was generous with his time, showing me round in the incredible city where you could get a crick in your neck from no more than the view, which in general ran straight up into the sky.

The afternoon of my arrival we were in the new concert hall in the Lincoln Center where Rubinstein played *both* Brahms piano concertos. Every morning I went out with Brigitta and said Mass in a neighbouring church. Her religious needs were both genuine and intense. Every evening I was taken out to something different: concerts, plays, operas. The Liebersons were at the centre of cultural life, knowing about the 'in' events and the 'in' people. I soon found all this unaccustomed hurly-burly something of a strain, however, and was content when I could continue on my begging tour. At all events I was very grateful for having been welcomed so warmly and generously to the New World. This was not, in fact, my last visit in connection with Mariaholm, and each time I enjoyed the same hospitality in the Lieberson home.

My assignment was to make an appeal during every single Sunday service, which quite often entailed a Mass or two already on Saturday evening. I remember particularly well what a strain it was the first time I had to undergo the ordeal. It was in Philadelphia. The church was not only large and constantly full, it had an equally roomy chapel directly below, where Mass was also celebrated. Nine times that Sunday I went up and down the stairs to be presented to the congregation by the officiating priest—in the wake of his own sermon—before I had the chance to make my appeal. Regardless of all else, first there was an ordinary collection, followed by a second collection for the Church in Norway with Mariaholm as a tailpiece. The heat was increasingly unbearable, and I was bathed in sweat already after a couple of efforts. But then the weekends were my only real working days.

I visited as many Cistercian monasteries as I could manage in this unbelievably vast country. Fortunately I knew most of the abbots from the General Chapter. I always had to give an address to the community one evening before Compline, and thus I could put Norway and Scandinavia on the map for the brethren. In Gethsemani I found myself on the same wavelength as the best-known monk of that time, Thomas Merton, whose books—published in huge quantities—attracted many young men to our American monasteries, with the result that the older houses constantly had to make new foundations.

At some periods I had my base in Massachusetts, in Spencer Abbey, which with Gethsemani was among the largest monasteries in our Order. There, I was at least able to do something in return by ordaining one of the young monks to the priesthood.

Slowly but surely I moved westwards, ending up in California and our most westerly abbey, Vina, where the welcome from my old friend Bob Usher was overwhelming. He had now settled there for good and was just starting on the construction of the monastery he had once described in the 'purple passages' that had astounded Dom Gabriel. Now it was taking shape in a considerably more modest form, albeit in fine taste.

Back in Oslo, the house I had inherited finally landed in my hands more or less overnight. My American tenants had suddenly left for home. I felt this was destiny and used the chance to move in myself. Everything went smoothly, because I had rented it out fully furnished, including bed linen, kitchen equipment, even gardening tools, all brought in from the neighbouring Grav estate. It was wonderful no longer to have only one room right in the noise of the city centre. Here, where I was to have my home for the next five years, there was plenty of room, a garden, and fresh air.

To many people—especially to Catholics—the name 'Caritas Norway' is closely associated with aid to the Third World. That year I was to play a part in the birth of the organization. Our Norwegian-born parish priest, Harald Taxt, became more and more involved in the postwar problems related to the growing stream of refugees in the wake of the communist take-over of power in Eastern and Central Europe. This practical and caring priest found himself constantly organizing aid projects.

An organization called Catholic Refugee Aid had been founded by Taxt in 1956 with himself as leader. Its office was on the ground floor in our Bishop's House. He himself still remained in his parish, for no clergy could be spared from their ordinary pastoral duties. Now, however, circumstances indicated that a new man should be appointed in his stead, while at the same time—particularly in East Norway—there was a growing consciousness of the lack of a full-time priest for refugees.

A question of reshuffling? To a certain extent, yes. I decided on the following: as already mentioned, our Norwegian Francis Xavier sisters had their recruitment house in the Netherlands, from which most of their vocations came. The Dutch Marist, Father Rommelse—a much appreciated former parish priest in our diocese—held the post of rector for the sisters. I very much wanted to have him back, and for this purpose I went to the Netherlands and visited St Olavshuis, as the recruitment centre was called. The father lit up with pleasure when I mentioned the idea. To resume his Norwegian pastoral work was his dearest wish.

When it in fact proved possible to find a replacement for him from the Marist fathers in the Netherlands, it was easy to have Rommelse appointed parish priest in Father Taxt's stead. The next step was to draw up the necessary guidelines for the work of the organization. The name 'Caritas Oslo' was chosen, and suitable offices were found. Eventually the project developed into an aid organization for both the Oslo diocese and the two vicariates apostolic of Central and North Norway under its present name of 'Caritas Norway'. This slowly but surely developed still further, to become a part of the worldwide Caritas Internationalis with its headquarters in Rome.

I receive a visit from Dom James Fox, abbot of our American monastery of Gethsemani. During my stay there, in answer to my insistant request, he had promised to make a foundation in Norway—at least twelve monks; that was something! Now he has optimistically come on a tour of reconnaissance, without there really being anything definite to look at as yet. Still, he was travelling in Europe anyhow, so it suited him to visit Norway now. I take him on various trips to give him a chance to form an impression of the country and the people. This serves its purpose. Dom James keeps to his intention, but of course there are many obstacles to overcome. He lays most weight on the possible location and the economic viability of the proposed monastery. He becomes doubtful when I give an account of our restrictive laws relating to the sale of land—especially of cultivated land, especially involving foreigners. The regulations in the American states are complicated enough, but these seem totally baffling! However, no thumbs down. I must just have a report prepared, explaining all sides of the question connected with a foundation out in the country by a group of foreign nationals. I groan inwardly, well knowing that such a proposal is hardly feasible.

Quite unexpectedly I get a letter from one of Mother's old friends, Countess Mannerheim; she is Norwegian-born, widow of the son of Finland's famous general, and lives now at her place in east Norway. She has heard (I don't know how) that I am on the look-out for a largish property for the foundation of a monastery. She could very well think of selling both the land and the buildings to us, for the purpose fascinates her. What is more, she is getting on in years, so that running the estate has become irksome. Dom James says he is interested and would like to come on a tour of inspection in connection with his next trip to Europe, asking me once again to have any related problems clarified. While I am still in the course of doing just that, a monastery in Belgium initiates a small experimental foundation with four young monks on the Danish island of Bornholm. Telegram from Kentucky: CANCEL PLANS REGARDING FOUNDATION STOP ONE MONASTERY OF OUR ORDER IN THE NORTH IS ENOUGH STOP SORRY STOP DOM JAMES.

No effort on my part could alter his decision, once taken. When I went to Gethsemani two years later to try to persuade him to resume his plans, I met with great friendliness, but no response. The Cistercians are still on Bornholm. Then there were four of them; today, their number remains unchanged.

As already mentioned, I was appointed vicar general for the diocese, and we were soon to have one more. It was now practically decided that Bishop Mangers would retire before the end of the year, when I would automatically take over.

The third session of the Council was about to begin, while at the same time it was evident that the bishop's secretary, Father Hansteen Knudsen (Don Ivar), was no longer well enough to keep things running as before. But Mangers now looked forward impatiently to his retirement and preferred to make no more decisions than absolutely necessary. I thought it essential that yet another vicar general be appointed, preferably one who would be reliable and capable of sorting things out. For example, Bishop Mangers had a desk bearing archaeological layers of business. No one—perhaps not even he—knew what was at the bottom. I suggested to him Father Gorissen, who had been parish priest in Bergen for the last twenty-five years. The proposal did not fill Mangers with enthusiasm, for that man could be a bit of a stickler in the Dutch manner. The bishop had had him as secretary thirty years before, and had mixed feelings concerning him. But Gorissen it was—and a clearing up was certainly undertaken. (Among other things which came to light in the deepest layers were letters with hundreds of Norwegian kroner in worthless banknotes, long past their redemption date of 1945.)

But I am anticipating. In March, Bishop Mangers had been able to celebrate his seventy-fifth birthday, which was the occasion for large-scale and well-deserved festivities, for few people were more beloved. To bring the priests together at that time, however, proved to be impossible. That autumn we were going to have a theological seminar for the clergy, an annual arrangement in which it was expected Bishop Mangers would now take part for the last time. That proved to be an appropriate occasion for the celebration. The lecturer was to be the young, highly respected American conciliar theologian, Gregory Baum.[2] The seminar was held—in German—in a small-town convent of the Francis Xavier sisters. Virtually all the priests participated, and the lectures were swallowed whole. As a pedagogical event, no one could remember having experienced anything quite like it.

And in the midst of it all, we celebrated Bishop Mangers's birthday. In its newly promulgated constitution *On the Sacred*

Liturgy, the Council had voted to reintroduce something called *concelebration*: a far-reaching liturgical reform entailing many consequences. Simply put, it meant that several priests celebrate one and the same Mass in common. But because the liturgical rules were not finally worked out, the implementation of the reform was not yet authorized. I had heard, however, that by telegraphing to the Congregation of Rites it might be possible to obtain permission to concelebrate *ad hoc*, if the occasion was of importance. We felt it was worth a try. I therefore cabled to Rome requesting authorization and explaining the circumstances. A reply came promptly. Authorization was granted, on condition that we sent back a detailed report on what we had done. Thus it was that the first concelebration of all time in the five Nordic countries took place in a modest Norwegian parish church. None of us had experienced anything of the kind before. Bishop Mangers, very moved by the occasion, was naturally the principle celebrant. After the ceremony there were festivities in a restaurant— already with a sense of farewell in the air.

I sat beside Bishop Mangers. 'You'll never be a proper bishop if you don't smoke a cigar', he said, proffering a box of Havanas, the largest on the market. To please him I took one and lit it. It was my first and last. I think I turned a little green—but fortunately it didn't make me sick, for I was still to make the speech in his honour.

We had some taxing meetings in the Secretariat for Christian Unity, where difficulties still kept piling up. Although we had been able to note, from the reactions of the Council fathers, that the opposition to the first three chapters of the decree 'On Ecumenism' was a thing of the past, this was by no means the case when it came to the last two (concerning the Jews and religious freedom). Here the objections and proposals for amendments were still legion.

Regarding the *schema* on relations with the Jews, attention was still focused on the vexed question of the alleged responsibility of the Israelites—as a people—for Christ's crucifixion. With my hand on my heart I would claim that our short document on the subject must be the most discussed, the most contested, and the most frequently drafted and redrafted, text in the whole history of the Church. And not only in the Church, for to the extent that the world at large interested itself in the Vatican Council, this question was certainly the focus of intense interest. And we had repeated evidence that both Jews and Arabs throughout the world continued to follow the matter.

What was so combustible here? Two phrases: *God's murderers* and *the condemnation of hate against the Jews.* The original draft, which had long prevailed, went like this:

> The Jewish people must never be represented as rejected or accursed or *God's murderers,* for what occurred in connection with Christ's suffering can in no way be blamed upon the people who then existed, and still less upon those of today. The Council, which most severely rejects all injustice, wherever it may be inflicted upon man, is keenly aware of the common heritage here. It expresses its deep regret and its *condemnation* of all hate and persecution of the Jews in former times as well as in our own. (Italics mine.)

It would take three full sessions, despite Cardinal Bea's introductory admonition, to change the inherited view of so many Council fathers that it was *the Jewish people as such* who had rejected Christ, who had brought about his death on Calvary, and who later had persecuted his church. The sad consequence of this attitude was of course that countless pogroms and sufferings in the course of the centuries had been inflicted on the Jews by Christians thirsting for revenge. It was a matter close to Bea's heart (likewise for our Secretariat) to have it laid down once and for all that although this was said over and over again—and far too often by ecclasiastical circles, even in Rome—it was *not* the teaching of the Catholic Church.

The aim of the debates that took place round the vast table in our Secretariat—and (back and forth) with Cardinal Ottaviani's watchful Theological Commission—was to repudiate, once and for all, the firmly rooted idea that the Jewish people were condemned by God because of their presumed collective guilt in the crucifixion of Jesus, and indeed that their history since Calvary indicated that Our Lord had vanquished them.

In the end, Bible in hand, the Council refuted all anti-Jewish pronouncements of this nature in Catholic teaching. It was laid down that Christ was not rejected by the *whole* Jewish people; he *divided* the people in two: those who were for and those who were against Christ.

In the declaration 'On the Relation of the Church to Non-Christian Religions', just before the session ended, we succeeded in having the following text—among others—accepted as Catholic doctrine:

> The Church, which condemns all persecution, against whomever it may be directed, can not forget the heritage it has in common with the Jews. Motivated by its religious and evangelical charity, and not for political reasons, it regrets therefore with sorrow the hate, the persecutions, and the expressions of anti-semitism which have been directed against the Jews, wherever they have occurred and whoever has instigated them.[3]

Admittedly a somewhat watered-down text, but one it was possible to live with—as was evidenced by the Church's subsequent improved relations with the Jews.

On the opening day, 12th September, the Council's third session focuses attention on the much-discussed liturgical innovation already mentioned: the Holy Father concelebrates the ceremonial Mass with twenty-four bishops from the five continents, as if in order to emphasize the significance of both the apostolic collegiality and the landmark of the liturgical reform. The Council fathers take part fully in the dialogues between the pope and the people, convincingly demonstrating the workability of the people's extended participation in the liturgy of the Mass.

★ ★ ★

Pope Paul VI had had a memorable meeting with the Patriarch Athenagoras of Constantinople during his pilgrimage to the Holy Land in January that year.

And now, for the first time, a personal envoy from the patriarch is present on the observers' stand in Saint Peter's.

Everyone is aware that time is short. In his inaugural address the chairman of the presidency, the French Cardinal Tisserant, stresses that the Council must make an extra effort if it is to meet the deadline. The permitted time for each speech is cut, the voting procedures are streamlined, the meetings are prolonged by half an hour. The coffee bars are not to open before eleven o'clock, and so on. But few of us are under the illusion that these initiatives will enable us to deal satisfactorily with the remaining *schemata* by the closing date of 22nd November.

Had the text 'On the Church' already been conclusively treated, the schedule might have been possible. But 'On the Church' appears first on the list, and it is clear from the start that this topic alone will take a great deal of time. What is disappointing is that, despite repeated warnings, so many speakers cannot resist repeating much that has already been said—*ad nauseam,* in fact—by others. They are cut short with increasing frequency.

The two-edged sword, however, is the voluminous 'Pastoral Constitution on the Church in the Modern World', the so-called *schema XIII,* which has already been delivered to us. Rumours say it will be 20th October before it is discussed. That in itself would occupy the rest of the session, packed tight as it is with comments on the Church's relations with contemporary civilization. It will therefore require deliberation on problems ranging from culture to nuclear warfare, from world economy to the international community, and from human rights to matrimonial fertility. And 'the eyes of the world' are now focused on this debate, according to our friends the journalists, who keep us informed—as we do them. The Council continues at headlong speed, aware that time is short, so that by halfway through the session we are all feeling the onset of fatigue.

Here, of course, I have to limit myself to events in which I was directly involved, either as a newly fledged bishop or as a member of the Secretariat for Christian Unity—the added bonus being that I was able to experience the Council from 'below stairs' as it were.

I am glad to note that, between the previous session and the present one, so many bishops have changed their views from a cautious, conservative stance, the tone that had originally characterized the large majority, to a clearly more progressive attitude. At the same time, the militant conservative wing appears to show signs of having lost, if not momentum, at any rate supporters. This was patently clear during the voting on forty specific points in connection with the now greatly improved *schema* 'On the Church'. Most of them would probably have been rejected by a large majority at the start of the Council: now they were approved with a reassuring majority. It is evident that we have made a marked breakthrough and can nourish a reasonable hope of making further advances.

Of the many proposed drafts which now come up for discussion, two are among the Council's most important: 'On the Apostolate of the Laity', and 'On the Church in the Modern World'—this last *(schema XIII)*, being perhaps the most hotly debated.

But first to the document originally called 'On the Sources of Revelation'. As already mentioned, it had been withdrawn during the first session by John XXIII after having met with bitter opposition. A new and entirely different text was begun, but was not finished until after the pope's death. Without being up for debate in the following session, it was sent to the bishops for their comments. The reaction, however, was that the text was now so abridged and vapid as to be meaningless. Many people, in any case, wanted to keep the vexed question of Scripture/Tradition outside the Council.

Since the *schema* had not been on the agenda during the previous period, we assumed that it had died a natural death. During his address at the conclusion of that session, however, Paul VI had not only inquired about it; he had demanded it be restored to the agenda. After a reproof of this kind, the dormant commission under the theoretical joint chairmanship of Cardinals Ottaviani and Bea pulled itself together and delivered a notably well-formulated and balanced text—renamed 'On Divine Revelation'—which now came up for debate. The two permanent theological 'brain-teaser' dilemmas (the sources of faith, and the relationship between Scripture and Tradition) were here treated warily at an elevated level. For while the basis of the original text seemed to have been that the theology related to revelation primarily derives from Bible passages and doctrinal tenets, the new *schema* radically identifies revelation with God's Word—our Saviour Jesus Christ. The perspective is no longer an attempt at a compromise between two schools, namely the Christocentric (soteriological) and the Counter-Reformation (Council of Trent), but the deeper concern of revelation—which is salvation through Jesus Christ. Nor is the problem now the question of one sole source versus two sources, but rather the handing down of supernatural knowledge disclosed to man by divine agency. The Council wishes to provide true teaching on the divine revelation and its transmission 'so that the world shall hear and thus be led to faith . . . and through faith to hope, and through hope to love'.

And the reception is now surprisingly positive. But of course the first speaker out is the Council's colourful *enfant terrible*, Cardinal Ruffini, who during the ongoing session made no fewer than twelve interventions. In his opinion the text suffers from one serious defect: it fails to state clearly that the *whole* of divine revelation is not to be found between the covers of the Bible. Thus he seeks to reopen the now partly healed wound from the first session, but fortunately does not succeed. The new *schema* deliberately shelves the still unsettled questions, leaving them open to further research and maturation. The objections to the text are now amazingly few and are possible to live with. (When the final voting took place during the last session, the text could be promulgated by 2,018 votes against 27.)

I found it rewarding to work on the *schema* 'On the Apostolate of the Laity', which gave me added insight and invigorating perspectives. True enough, the ground had already been well prepared by the text 'On the Church', which from the outset was focused on *God's People*: the whole Church with a place for everyone from the newly christened child to the pope in Rome. As well as that, for the first time in the context of the Council, it supplied a theological rehabilitation, virtually a restoration, of the status of the laity within the framework of the Church's hierarchical system. Instead of the 'voiceless masses' which it was up to the hierarchy to evangelize or educate, a different and older vision reappeared: everyone in a fellowship, God's People on the way to their everlasting goal. The laity, too, have an inherent priestly dignity, for everybody who has been baptized participates in the general (universal) priesthood. Our text took this as its point of departure, with the word *apostolate* as the central concept. Every Christian is an apostle by virtue of his or her baptism and confirmation. Indeed it is a divine injunction to take part in the Church's never-ending mission—not in competition but in *cooperation* with the hierarchy which has received the necessary powers from above.

Several different levels, areas of activity, and forms for the lay apostolate are analysed and described in depth. I recognized, from my own time in youth work, a great deal that recent generations with their steadily higher level of education had in fact practised, but which now for the first time received the Church's blessing. Also lay men and women are virtual envoys of Our Lord.

But most of all during this session, interest was centred on *schema XIII*: 'The Church in the Modern World'. It had come into being as a result of John XXIII's desire to bring about a fruitful dialogue between the Church and the international community. In his encyclical *Pacem in terris* (peace on earth), Pope John had already taken such an initiative, and—as the first pope to do so—addressed himself to 'all people of good-will'. An interesting point here is that the prelate originally made responsible for this matter—a previously unthinkable question for a Council—had been John XXIII's secretary of state, Cardinal Montini, now himself pope. As cardinals, he and Léon Joseph Suenens (archbishop of Brussels and Malines, and now one of the four moderators) had cooperated on the text and worked to promote it in the face of considerable opposition.

The burden of its message was that the Council must be on its guard against an introspective attitude, and avoid becoming occupied solely with its own problems.

One difficulty which perturbed many people was that we Council fathers naturally could not have a direct dialogue with the world, but had to limit ourselves to issuing guidelines for our people as to how such dialogues might be conducted. Yet at the same time it was important to draw attention to the most fundamental contemporary problems, so that 'God's people' should give them serious attention.

Here too, at quite an early stage, there was a tendency to divide into factions. This almost certainly hinged on theological views, but it was far from only that. On the one hand there were those who maintained that the world in essence must be good, because it is willed by a Creator whose nature is pure goodness, and because it is a token of the good that, according to revelation, is to come: the Bible's eschatological 'new heaven and new earth', or 'the new Jerusalem'. For that reason it must be afforded conscientious reflection. The world, they said (often quoting Teilhard de Chardin), is developing and in the course of entering into its maturity as regards both the natural and the supernatural. This text had to be able to 'interpret the signs of the times', as John XXIII had put it.

Contrary arguments were inspired partly by the belief that 'the world' stands in direct opposition to 'the kingdom of

God', partly from the conviction that 'sin' and 'the world' are intimately linked—not to mention that creation, according to the Bible, is heading for its own destruction. In the opinion of some, the present draft lacked any real theological foundation, chose to follow dangerous byways, and pandered openly to the very world from which it was supposed to save mankind.

Other opponents of the *schema* contended that none of this was in any way material for a Council, which must after all concentrate on the divine truths, on pointing upwards, and on seeking solutions to problems dealing with eternal values.

Slowly a compromise made itself felt, which was to win the day. The draft was generally considered both well-done and necessary, but there was room for improvement. This was largely because a number of problems, so far not touched upon, urgently needed to be taken up and, if possible, solved.

The Italian Bishop Guano, who was responsible for the work on the *schema*, agreed with much of this: the Catholic Church is active today on all five continents, it seeks to absorb—and itself to be absorbed into—innumerable cultures at many different stages of development. The problems are of great diversity, so let us have them presented, analysed, and clarified. The text can only gain from this. 'We must explain' he said, 'to what extent (and how) the Church in fact contributes to progress and development in our times, and how we Christians can and must help to solve the vast problems confronting the world at this point of history.'

A mission bishop, La Ravoire Morrow of Krishnagar (India), caused a hum in the assembly with the following modest question: 'How can a small child be expected to comprehend that our infinitely loving God would sentence to everlasting banishment and suffering—like the sentence for adultery and murder—a person who has only erred by eating meat on a Friday? No, Christianity is not a religion of fear but of love. And if we do not cultivate in our hearts the message of love rather than that of fear, I do not believe that a real dialogue can take place in the world as it is today.'

The debate became so heated, and there were so many speakers, that extra days had to be granted from the limited time allowed before the moderators felt it safe to ask the obligatory question: 'Is it the Council's wish that the present *schema* be accepted as the basis for further discussion?' It was, and far more than the required two-thirds majority voted in favour— 1,579 for and 296 against.

I myself was very much involved in this discussion. Not in the sense that I made a speech (some we could have been spared, for we had heard most of it before); but I submitted written observations, and used my free time to study and comment on the various subjects that arose, never doubting that these themes were of paramount importance for the Church itself.

After this, the fiercely contested theme 'On Religious Freedom' was once again up for general debate, now in a fully revised version, with partly new text. In our Secretariat we had worked ourselves to the bone in analysing, assessing, approving, or discarding the mass of incoming proposals for this famous additional chapter to the *schema* 'On Ecumenism'. One crucial statement was worded thus: 'Anyone who honestly obeys his conscience obeys God, even if this occurs in ways that are unclear to him and of which he is unconscious. If anyone honestly seeking to discover God's real will should be mistaken, no person and no human power has the right to make him act against the dictates of his conscience.' This was indeed new music!

Although few voices were now raised *against* the actual term 'religious freedom'—a term which, after all, several popes in this century had found acceptable—many people belonging to the conservative camp questioned whether liberty of this nature could be deduced from philosophical-theological principles as the text and the so-called progressive majority apparently contended.

A fiercely negative statement again came from Cardinal Ruffini: 'The truth is one and indivisible. Therefore the true religion can only be one, and it alone is entitled to make a valid claim for such liberty.' Another bishop went even further and wanted the Council to issue a declaration unilaterally defending the rights of the Catholic Church in all parts of the earth. And one inflexible comment was that a person's dignity does not depend on his freedom but on his adherence to the truth (clearly the Roman Catholic truth).

Those who belonged to this camp held that religious liberty cannot be argued on philosophical, let alone theological, grounds—but only for practical and social reasons, reasons stemming from the concept of *tolerance* and the various considerations the Church must take into account in today's pluralistic world. To go further than this would have been difficult for these 'fundamentalists'.

The 'liberals' for their part would have nothing to do with a view which implied that tolerance was a 'necessary evil'. Such an attitude where the Church's policy was concerned was unworthy of the Council. A staunch defender of the chapter as it stood was the newly appointed archbishop of Cracow, Karol Wojtyla (in whom scarcely anyone then could have seen a future pope). He emphasized that it would not be enough to find reasons for religious liberty in the Church's obligation to be tolerant, since such a standpoint was obviously too negative, 'for this civil right is based not least on the right which natural law gives to everyone to seek and find the truth'.

Among those of us who viewed the draft proposal in a positive light, many did so, naturally enough, in different ways and to varying degrees, yet it was clear that we all wished to retain the proposed text on religious freedom as a basis for further work on the issue. [4] More and more I understood the importance of a Council. Indeed, I now felt convinced that only within this age-old, sacred, and universally respected context could the Church's attention be focused afresh and its teaching progress in a decisive yet balanced manner.

Nevertheless, it could not be denied that a number of very conservative fathers—roughly 300 in all, judging by the votes—were still unreconciled to much that they considered far too new-fangled, unclarified, and dubious, and that they would prefer to see removed or at any rate kept at arm's length as long as possible. All in all, however, it finally seemed to lie in the cards that the Council was heading in the direction of updating, innovation, and reform. Fortunately the spirit of Pope John XXIII still—incontrovertibly—prevailed. So we believed! But without having sufficiently taken into account what could be engineered by a stubborn opposition in—or near—the papal curia.

Bishop Suhr, who had suffered and survived a serious illness entailing a long spell in hospital earlier that same year, was granted his application for retirement during this session, but was requested to continue to administer the diocese of Copenhagen until a successor was appointed.

Now he managed to drum together the Scandinavian Episcopal Conference to a meeting at the Brigittine Sisters on the Piazza Farnese. I could imagine what awaited us: cigar smoke, sacristy stories, and collegial joviality, as well as some non-committal talks about conciliar affairs. The Dutch Paul Verschuren, Finland's new coadjutor bishop, took part for the first time. He looked across at me once or twice with a look of wonderment, as if he wanted to ask: 'Can a bishops' conference really be like this?' I nodded an implicit answer: 'Yes, but you and I must do something about it.' It was not to last so long.

I am called in to a meeting with the secretary general of the Propaganda Fide Congregation, Archbishop Pietro Sigismondi, an unusually fine man full of warmth and humour, and easy to get along with. He wears his episcopal skullcap at a jaunty angle, no doubt unaware of the fact, but it suits him well. He wants to consult me—as he puts it in his man-to-man way of speaking—about my taking over the diocese. The Holy See, however, has had no wish to do anything about this during the present session, in order not to expose Bishop Mangers to something which might seem like a degradation.

The intention, therefore, is to keep the measures regarding his departure secret until the prelates have gone home. Bishop Mangers would like to retire before the end of the year, he continues (as everyone knows, I think to myself), so it is best that, here in Rome, he and I now agree on a convenient point of time for my installation. The formalities are indeed taken care of and in the right order!

Mangers and I have long since discussed all this between us and opted for a 'handover of powers' on the third Sunday in Advent. The reason for the choice was liturgical: since my consecration had taken place on Laetare Sunday in Lent, I had suggested that my installation be on Gaudete Sunday in Advent. The name of each of these days means 'rejoice', and each occurs half-way through an otherwise (liturgically speaking) solemn period.

The archbishop approves and will be pleased to inform Cardinal Agagianian who, if he agrees with the submission, will lay it before the pope.

Many of the bishops would gladly have seen that this was the last session and they sympathized with Paul VI who looked exhausted. On the other hand, there were not a few of us who still had texts to fight for—not to say push through—which we believed in and which our Secretariat considered to be the most important in historical terms. Many who belonged to commissions of the same category as ours—that is to say, whose *schemata* were still not finalized—were of the same frame of mind. We all believed that there should at *least* be a fourth session.

A turning point comes in early October, beginning in our Secretariat. An unusually sombre Cardinal Bea opens the working session, friendly as always, and goes straight to the point: 'We have had two letters sent on to us by the secretary general [Felici] on behalf of the Central Committee [Cicognani]. One concerns the chapter "On Religious Freedom".' It ran, in brief, like this: (1) The pope, who—on the basis of the debates concerning religious freedom—has had to take note of the fact that unusually recalcitrant differences of opinion reign in regard to several statements in this text, recommends a thorough revision of the *schema* so that it will be better enabled to fulfil its purpose. (2) In line with this, the Central Committee wishes to establish a mixed working party consisting of an equal number of members from the Secretariat for Christian Unity and from the Theological Commission (Ottaviani). Neither the number of members nor the name of the chairman of this select committee is specified. Bea adds drily that he will reply to the communication, about which our Secretariat actually can do nothing, since it comes from the Council's supreme authority.

The other letter contains a 'conciliar text' which is intended to replace the chapter 'On the Non-Christians and Especially the Jews'. This matter, according to the letter, should be taken out of its present context and be incorporated in the *schema* 'On the Church'. In an oppressive silence the cardinal loyally reads out the proposed version. We sit there appalled, for the content only in parts resembles the text which the Council and our Secretariat have produced after endless negotiations. Here a great deal is missing. 'So what do you think, gentlemen?' asks Bea with a strained smile.

I cannot contain my indignation at such a mean trick and explode: 'Cardinal, the Council has entrusted us to cooperate with it on an agreed text, and that text *we* cannot possibly replace with another!' The assembly expresses its massive agreement. Looking resigned—but far from displeased—Bea raises his eyebrows, nods, and lays the paper aside. 'So we recommence where we broke off', is all he says and calls on Monsignor Willebrands to take over.

In the break one of our theologians, J. M. Oesterreicher (a convert Jew), comes over to me. He still has tear-stains on his cheeks. 'Thank you, Bishop', he says, 'thank you for daring to say what we were all thinking.' I can still—over forty years later—feel his pathetically tense handshake. For my own part I do not doubt what would have happened in any case. The assembly would never have approved such interference, for in our opinion 'the Jewish chapter' had long since passed a point of no return.

This manoeuvre, however, had one positive outcome. Cardinal Bea promptly received Pope Paul's assurance that 'the text concerning the Jews will be neither amputated nor abridged'. What is more, the text succeeded in having its status radically improved, in that the cardinal obtained the presidency's approval for its removal from the *schema* 'On Ecumenism' (all parties were agreed on this), in order to make it part of a new, more universal document: the 'Declaration on the Relation of the Church to Non-Christian Religions'.

Uproar in the media! The text on religious liberty is yet again the focus of interest for the world outside when the following circumstances become known: Nine indignant cardinals (Bea, Alfrinks, Döpfner, Frings, Lefebvre [not Marcel], Léger, Meyer, Ritter, and Silva Henriques) had hurriedly assembled to assess the situation. Then and there they composed a letter to the Holy Father expressing their 'extreme concern and very great anxiety' regarding the fact that the text on religious liberty 'which had after all been ratified by an overwhelming conciliar majority' was now to be referred to a new working committee for revision. 'The entire world is well aware that the text has already been completed—and knows its content.' After having listed several similar objections, they implore that the pope allow the draft to follow the normal routine procedure through the Council. The letter is signed by all apart from Bea, who has sent the pope a separate letter. Another eight cardinals (including Lercaro, Liénart, and Suenens) sign the next day.

'The Seventeen Cardinals' letter' fell into the hands of the press, as might be expected, and was published in its entirety. An indiscreet cardinal had given a copy of the letter to an equally indiscreet reporter—with intent. The uproar, however, was out of proportion to the gravity of the matter. No real catastrophe was under way. It was clear to us 'insiders' that the Council sometimes functioned in this manner behind the scenes, and not seldom gained ground as a result. But it could not be denied that the atmosphere towards the end of the session was clouded by the concentration of such negative imputations. And there were more to come.

A further message from the pope seemed reassuring: Cardinal Bea himself was to be the chairman for the planned select working party concerned with religious freedom. It would consist of five members from his own Secretariat and five from Ottaviani's Theological Commission. Both fora were now requested to put forward ten names. The pope himself would then appoint the members from among these. (In fact the new working party met only once—under Bea alone. The existing text on religious freedom was scrutinized paragraph by paragraph and then approved almost unanimously.)

As usual in this type of crisis, the whole affair was settled amicably without anybody's feelings being hurt. The pope's main aim was to arrive at the greatest possible degree of accord. The solution, therefore, often lay in a compromise—if a workable result could be obtained without touching on the sensitive core.

'You and I are invited to Florence this weekend', said Bishop Suhr one day in Saint Peter's. 'Can you get hold of a car?' He took it for granted that I would come. I was allowed to borrow Monte Cistello's little Fiat, which I had bought and driven when I was their procurator, and we left as soon as we were able to get away.

There were actually two invitations to Florence. One came from the San Lorenzo basilica where centuries ago a Danish bishop, the Venerable Niels Steensen (later beatified by John Paul II), had been buried among a number of highborn Florentine citizens. Now a memorial service was to be celebrated for him. We were spoiled and made a great deal of, and were given accommodation in the canons' residence where Bishop Suhr was obviously a revered and popular guest.

The other invitation was from Giorgio La Pira, the well-beloved mayor of Florence—a man as highly original as he was deeply religious. He had invited a large group of Council fathers to a festive reception in the Palazzo Vecchio, the city hall. I had once paid a short visit to Florence and was delighted to come back to Tuscany's beautiful capital, so richly endowed with culture, which had been the Medici family's traditional bastion. Suhr and I wandered around in the fine weather, greeting our 'old acquaintances' from the Renaissance. Repairs and rehabilitation work were in evidence everywhere, for the city's war wounds were far from healed.

In addition to the festivities in the city's magnificent official reception hall, La Pira had invited a handful of us—all Italian-speaking non-Italians—to a reception in his office, also antique, where he talked informally with us about Florence's (and his own) problems, both economic and political. Before leaving we were presented with some excellent reproductions of works by Florentine masters.

Next day, just as Bishop Suhr and I were on our way into the cathedral to Sunday Mass, we met the same Giorgio La Pira on his way out. He gave a broad smile when he recognized us and told us, with many gesticulations, how rewarding his own visit had been—and that we would greatly enjoy the beautiful liturgy of the High Mass. I remembered that a mutual acquaintance had told me of something he had witnessed here. The city's easy-going mayor, in the very same cathedral, had been questioned by a total stranger as to how he should behave when going to confession—for he could at last think of doing so. La Pira had immediately proposed that he first confide his sins to *him*, so that it would be easier when he knelt in the confessional, which he discreetly pointed out to the man. Our friend could no longer remember whether the man utilized this unusual chance to make a trial confession. However, La Pira's delight at having been able to serve Our Lord in this small way had been very apparent.

Back in San Lorenzo, in itself a fascinating museum, we were given an informative tour, outside visiting hours, of the

Medici burial chapel that is part of the complex. It was here Michaelangelo left behind him the last and finest corpus of Florentine sculpture.

Despite the Council's hectic rush of activity as the deadline draws near, a morning meeting in mid-November is replaced by a High Mass of a very unusual nature (as transpires in the course of the service). The liturgy is celebrated in Greek according to the Byzantine rite, quite different from our Latin ritual. Patriarch Maximos IV is the celebrant, assisted by dignitaries from the same uniate church. A procession comes slowly up the nave of the basilica, with Pope Paul VI in all simplicity walking last. He attends, just like one of us, the— to our 'Latin' eyes—grandiose ceremony, where the idea of time seems to mean nothing. Towards the end he rises unexpectedly, steps forward, and with his own hands places his tall, heavy tiara on the altar, fraternally embraces the ageing but well-preserved Patriarch, and returns to his place.

Suddenly the secretary general's matter-of-fact voice comes over the loudspeakers: 'Many serious words have been said here in the aula about poverty and need in the world. The words of His Holiness earlier this year in Jerusalem, "My compassion is with the people", ring true here too—like an echo from *Him who became poor for our sake.* The Church is the Mother of all who are in misery. As evidence of his care for his people, His Holiness will let his tiara be disposed of in order to benefit the needy and impoverished people of the earth.' There is a murmur of wonder and admiration.

Naturally this was symbolic, in the sense that a tiara— whatever its worth—would only be a drop in the ocean of the world's suffering. We knew very well, however, that Paul VI liked to express himself in symbols. So this act represented much more: an implicit invitation to the prelates of the Church to do something similar with their often valuable rings, crosses, and chains—perhaps?

Some prelates found it remarkable that the pope had chosen to make this gesture within the context of a Mass in the Greek

rite. Here, in fact, the patriarch of the Latin rite laid down
his mark of sovereignty side by side with a Greek patriarch.
Was it to emphasize that Rome considered herself a sister
church? Be that as it may, it became subsequently clear that
the gesture had yet a further meaning: Paul VI, in laying down
his tiara, the symbol of the secular power of the Holy See,
laid it down for good. He never used it again. Nor did any
of his successors. The message could have been this: despite
his primacy, the pope is first and foremost a bishop among
bishops. Whatever the reason, Paul VI kept his own counsel
on his deepest motivation.

And now the inevitable announcement was made: a fourth—
but guaranteed final—session was to be held the following
autumn.

Apart from its unambiguous antagonism to most of 'our'
texts (dealing with ecumenism, the question of the Jews, and
religious liberty), the Council's small but effective opposition's
attitude was also highly negative to the concept of *collegiality*
(chapter 3 in the *schema* 'On the Church'). On 14th November, when the text was to be voted on, we witnessed the following initiative which shocked many: the secretary general,
'on behalf of a higher authority', had a circular distributed with
the heading, 'Prior explanatory note'. Through this circular,
Ottaviani's Theological Commission took it upon itself to
inform us how a certain number of terms, including *collegium*
and *collegiality,* were to be understood. The words were to be
taken in an analogous sense, and not as having a strictly juridical meaning. Thus, it was stated, no valid episcopal collegial
action could take place without the pope's express consent.

The reaction of a large proportion of the assembly was
dismay. Of that there could be no doubt. Cardinal Lercaro, one
of the four moderators, wrote in this connection to a friend:
'The air in the Council is becoming much more oppressive.
There are hard days ahead.'

And a priest who was also present (Dossetti) wrote to
the pope's theologian, Bishop Colombo: 'We listened with

unspeakable bitterness while this was read out. This morning I witnessed more than one wave of opposition, and I heard all sorts of suggestions about how to resist it, particularly if the "explanatory note" is intended to carry special weight.'

Unfortunately, we were to experience a further 'development' of this type, culminating in the so-called 'black week', which was also the session's last.

This is what happened:

Parallel to the editing of the finer points in the chapter concerning the Jews, our Secretariat had worked on the proposals for amendments concerning religious liberty. We had approved many, discarded still more, but given serious consideration to all. A new—and in our opinion very acceptable—text had been delivered to the General Secretariat and 19th November was set as the date for the final voting—all in accordance with correct procedure.

On the same morning, however, Cardinal Tisserant, 'on behalf of the presidency', announced that the discussion on this chapter (a discussion which had been formally declared to have been concluded several weeks previously) would have to be reopened in the following year. The reason given was that a minority (not difficult to guess its composition) had reacted strongly to the fact that this chapter, of which the text had been dealt out only two days earlier (our manuscript had lain for a whole week waiting to be printed, and we had asked ourselves why the process had dragged on for so long), now appeared so altered that it would have to be regarded as a new text. The group had not only demanded more time in order to be able to study it adequately, but—backed by the regulations of the Council—had demanded a completely new discussion with a subsequent fresh ballot as to whether this 'new' text could be accepted as a basis for further discussion: all this *before* the final voting (if any) could take place. Nothing like this had so far happened to any conciliar text.

Saint Peter's all of a sudden echoed with an indignant hum of voices. Cardinal Meyer of Chicago—a member of the presidency—rose ('white as a sheet', said one observer) and contacted the moderators who chaired the daily meetings. It was clear that they too were ignorant of all this. The American bishops and many other prelates and experts now gathered round Meyer in the space behind the altar. After this, the meeting could not continue. Everywhere gesticulating groups took up the discussion. The decibel level rose higher and higher. The secretary general gave up and left his place. Immediately, on the initiative of the Americans, a written protest was drafted and signed by 431 experts and bishops. It was handed to His Holiness the same day by the Cardinals Meyer, Ritter (Saint Louis), and Léger (Montreal). Paul VI— so it was reported—was friendly and polite, but held firm. What the three cardinals did not know was that the Council's tribunal, under its president Cardinal Roberti, had assembled twice on the previous day to assess these protests and had concluded that the reaons given, in accordance with the Council's regulations, would justify such a postponement. It would be difficult even for the pope to set aside this decision.

Next morning Cardinal Tisserant had to make a new statement—now on behalf of the pope himself: the postponement was legitimate according to the regulations of the Council. Many of us were tempted—though wrongly—to assume that the pope had simply allowed himself to be outmanoeuvred by the conservative minority who, as we all knew, were making every effort to have the chapter on religious freedom removed, or at any rate to let the discussion about it drag on so long that it could never be finished.

But things were to become even worse.

The printed *schema* 'On Ecumenism'—again only comprising its original three chapters—was now due to come up for voting. At this juncture, however, the secretary general began to read out no fewer than nineteen amendments to the text, amendments which were simultaneously distributed in stencilled form, a conciliar innovation. We were assured by word of mouth from Felici that these amendments had been put forward by Cardinal Bea's commission 'in accordance with friendly proposals from authoritative quarters'.

In reality our Secretariat had been taken as much by surprise as the fathers in the aula. On the previous day a list with forty proposals (read demands) for amendments had been delivered to Cardinal Bea 'from the highest quarters'. In this case, however, 'the highest quarters' meant merely the vice-chairman of Ottaviani's commission, the former general of the Dominican Order, Michael Browne. The time was too short for Cardinal Bea to be granted an audience with the pope. (Nor was an audience granted to the leading Protestant theologian, Oscar Cullmann, who was keen to see the text unaltered.) Bea next summoned all available colleagues to go through the new proposals. Twenty-one of them were struck out. The remaining nineteen could be accepted, since they were unable to alter the sense of the text on any important point. The list was forthwith laid before the pope, who declared himself satisfied.

Although these 'improvements' were more superficial than fundamental, we in the Secretariat were worried lest this manoeuvre *'in extremis'* might have negative consequences for the Church's relations to our non-Catholic friends, above all to the observers who of course had ringside seats to all this. But I remember that a Lutheran observer reassured me by saying that he thought it a good thing to experience the Catholic Church as it was and not as it was considered (or wished to be considered) to be. Probably it was this very circumstance which 'induced' a still uncertain grey-zone group to vote in favour, for the final ballot saw the text safely into harbour with an overwhelming majority: 2,137 votes against 11.

Finally, on the very last day of the session, the assembly was presented with our enlarged text on the Jews, which had now become an independent conciliar document entitled 'On the Relation of the Church to Non-Christian Religions'— a text finalized at high pressure. It was decided it should be presented for voting (despite all delaying tactics) although we were only at the second-last stage in the long process leading to promulgation. With relief we could note that a total of 1,651 fathers, without reservation, were in favour of the text;

272   A Hand on My Shoulder

242 voted 'yes' with certain reservations (which meant that proposals for amendments must be attached), while only 99 rejected it entirely (including a number of orientals who were to live with the declaration).

In our Secretariat we could give a sigh of relief, but only to gain breath for the next round—for had we not two *schemata* (that on the Jews and that on religious liberty) to present at the next session and some challenging Roman meetings between the rounds to look forward to?

Fortunately other more positive things happened during this period. Of prime importance was that the fundamental theological constitution 'On The Church' had reached harbour safely with all flags flying, approved with only five votes against. The decree 'On the Catholic Churches of the Eastern Rite' was finally confirmed, albeit with more opposition. (The main responsibility for the fact that the text received as many as 39 negative votes may have lain with the orientals themselves.)

During the closing ceremony on 21st November a noticeably fatigued Pope Paul VI promulgated the present session's three completed documents, *On the Church, On Ecumenism,* and *On the Catholic Churches of the Eastern Rite,* but only after in each case having obtained the assembly's consent, which was accorded by our standing up.

In his speech the pope took up the thread both from the first (but truncated) Vatican Council and from his own farewell sermon the preceding year: respectively the Church and the episcopate. He praised the Council fathers' endurance—two months of toil—and stressed the value of our tireless analyses of the Church's character, fundamental elements, and mystical dimension. It was particularly important and memorable, he declared, that the Council fathers' insight into the unique origins and sacred powers of the episcopate had been enriched and become manifest as a result of the bishops' exhaustive studies and deliberations.

Twenty-Three

FOURTH AND FINAL SESSION

THE YEAR IS 1965, the month September. For the final session I have brought with me to Rome a private theologian, the Dominican Father Albert Raulin. We are to lodge, according to my wont, at the Cistercian generalate next to the venerable abbey of Tre Fontane founded by Bernard of Clairvaux. Realizing that this session will be tough work for all concerned, I am glad to have a theologian at my elbow.

There was now a tense, not to say strained, atmosphere in the Church. Would the Council emerge as a newly arisen phoenix or disintegrate in the ashes of unresolved issues? True, much had been gained by the promulgation of the principal document *On the Church*, but the future was still uncertain for the bulk of the remainder. 'On the Church in the Modern World', though not one of the Council's original subjects, had been thoroughly reworked and was now to treat a series of new, complex questions, making it the longest and most complicated document of all. 'On the Ministry and Life of Priests', originally a brief *schema,* was moving to centre stage as a matter of general concern, in the same way as 'On the Mission Activity of the Church'.

No fewer than five 'texts in hand' were still listed. As well as the *schema* on the priests, those up for debate were 'On the

Pastoral Office of Bishops in the Church', 'On Priestly Training', 'On Christian Education', and 'On the Adaptation and
Renewal of Religious Life'. Some of these had required, and
would continue to require, much more intensive reworking
than originally envisaged. The atmosphere in our Secretariat
was consequently somewhat strained, even though the main
text, *On Ecumenism* (the revamped 'On the Catholic Church
and Christian Unity'), had made the grade. The *schema* 'On
the Relation of the Church to Non-Christian Religions' was
still bitterly opposed, from within and without, while 'On
Religious Freedom' had reached a deadlock. Fortunately the
world press kept attention constantly focused on their fate.

At all events it was encouraging to feel that we had the
pope on 'our' side. Indirect evidence to that effect came during the consistory in February when a number of cardinals'
appointments strengthened the Council's progressive wing.
Thus no fewer than four members of our Secretariat received
the red hat: Heenan (Westminster), Jäger (Paderborn), Martin
(Rouen), and Shehan (Baltimore).

With the pope's blessing, Cardinal Bea left in February
for the headquarters of the World Council of Churches in
Geneva. One of the far-reaching ecumenical consequences of
this visit was the establishment of a permanent body for consultation between the WCC and the Secretariat for Christian
Unity.

Paul VI next sent Bea to the patriarch of Constantinople, Athenagoras, in Istanbul, in return for the latter's gesture in sending two metropolitans (Meliton of Heliopolis and
Krysostomos of Myra) on an official goodwill visit to Rome
the previous February.

In the spring of 1965 Paul VI, who in 1964 had founded the
Secretariat for Non-Christian Religions, instituted the Secretariat for Non-Believers under Cardinal König (Vienna). This
was seen as a definite indication of the pope's positive attitude
towards the Council's growing acceptance of an extended idea
of dialogue to include also the non-religious world. (To my
surprise I found my own name among the list of members.)

Moreover, it gradually became clear that the pope was now giving increasing attention to the problems of the conciliar commissions. In fact, the fruitful outcome of the Council became more and more dependent on the ceaseless industry of these bodies, both during and between the sessions. It transpired that Paul VI intended to be even more personally involved in this final stage.

That this fourth period of the Council was to be beyond all question the last was indicated not only by the early start (14th September), but by the fact that no closing date was stated. Those at the top were hopeful that the end could be reached sometime before Christmas, otherwise . . .

To everybody's surprise, just two weeks before the opening date, Paul VI issued a new encyclical. As though he hadn't enough to do! It was entitled *Mysterium fidei* and was concerned in its entirety with the Sacrament of the Altar. It proved to be a profound document which, far from describing Holy Communion and the real presence of Christ in ritualistic or formalistic terms, dwelt on the sacrament as a *mystery*. It was generally well received, although there were certain objections, paricularly from Protestant quarters. Some considered it an unnecessary and unecumenic initiative, coming at the least fortunate juncture. However, subsequent clarification and a more careful perusal of the encyclical's central message disposed of most of the criticism. Christ instituted this sacrament, wrote the pope, primarily as a source of grace, to nourish man's spiritual needs along the way towards his eternal destiny.

The solemn opening takes place on the feast of the Exaltation of the Cross. The pope concelebrates the Mass with fourteen prelates, all from the Council's leading bodies.

Much has been said, written, and surmised about the proposed 'senate' of bishops from all over the world who are to assist the pope in governing the Church. A sense of excitement prevails: Will Paul VI actually dare to launch a novel body of

this type? Since nothing concrete has leaked out on the subject, no one expects him to make any move of the kind just
yet. The astonishment is palpable therefore when he declares
in his opening speech: 'We are pleased to announce the inau-
guration of a Synod of Bishops in accordance with the wishes
of the Council. This assembly will be chiefly composed of
participants chosen by the Episcopal Conferences with Our
approval. It will be summoned by the pope, in accordance
with the needs of the Church, to put forward its views and
offer its assistance.' The sense of astonishment gives way to one
of happiness. Here and now the pope is opening the door to
a new and democratic development from which there can be
no turning back.

Already next day, when he attends our first working meeting, the pope has the complete, newly promulgated rules of
procedure for the coming Bishops' Synod read aloud. Strictly
speaking it is to be a consultative body, but if the pope so
wishes the Synod fathers may have the power of decision in
certain matters, always subject to the pope's final approval. The
Synod's mandate is to inform, to advise, and to coordinate.[1]

Almost in the same breath Paul VI announces that during this session he will visit New York to deliver a message
of peace to the General Assembly of the United Nations,
speaking not only for himself but also, he hopes, on behalf of
the Council as a whole. The warm applause guarantees the
wholehearted approbation of all present.

A telegram from Patriarch Athenagoras of Constantinople
to Paul VI is read out: 'We send You our best wishes for a
successful and worthy conclusion to the work now under way
for the good of the entire Church of Our Lord Jesus Christ.'

In record time the assembly's wavering, indecisive mood
switches to fresh optimism and courage, both of which will
doubtless be needed.

The good news about the Synod (which after all is not the
direct concern of the ongoing Council) has hardly been absorbed before we turn eagerly to the schedule just distributed.
Will the pope allow 'On Religious Freedom', withdrawn due

to pressure from the minority at the tail-end of last year's session, to be entered as the first item on the agenda?

And yes: there it is. During the interim all the proposed amendments had been analysed systematically in Bea's Secretariat. The resultant totally revised text can now be laid before an alert assembly. Bishop De Smedt, the 'guardian' of the text, presents the *schema*. It is couched in neutral, sober phrases completely free of its previous somewhat lofty tone of language.

In the 1963 version, the right to religious liberty was based on a Bible-in-hand theological argument, as a self-evident consequence of the act of faith itself and of man's duty to follow his conscience even when its promptings are based on misapprehension. In session after session the text had been rewrought, simplified, and improved. The opposition to it had thus served a useful, perhaps even necessary, purpose.

The declaration, contends De Smedt, rests on one single argument: The free exercise of religion is a human right, and should be recognized and upheld as such by the international community.

No one is to be subjected to force in matters of religion. The foundation of this liberty lies in the worth of the individual, on which the whole structure of society rests. De Smedt admits that no biblical text asserts that people must be exempt from all coercion. This means that the modern idea of religious liberty cannot be said to be a juridical consequence of evangelical freedom. De Smedt has thus renounced his long-held argument that freedom is based on the primacy of conscience.

It would have been difficult for him and for Bea's collaborators to have gone any further towards meeting the opposition. Some Council fathers ask whether the text does not now include even the atheists! However that may be, certain assertions in Pope John XXIII's encyclical *Pacem in terris* composed several years earlier were in fact more advanced in this respect than our present text. Even so, despite its conciliatory tone, the whole thing yet again led to a violent debate.

And there was still a long queue of speakers, myself included. As a Secretariat member I had wanted to do my bit in defending our achievements so far. Father Raulin had been asked to prepare the draft, then we had worked on the text until we could honestly say we were satisfied with the outcome.

It is beyond the scope of the present work to give an account of the many viewpoints, ranging from Monsignor Lefebvre's 'Only the Church has the right to freedom. This is the Catholic dogma in a nutshell!' all the way to Cardinal Shehan's comment: 'True enough, freedom and heresy cannot *per se* claim the same right . . . , but correctly understood these rights are vested in *people* and not in abstractions'. For one particularly impressive speech, however, I make an exception.

Refusing to sink to the level of endless hair-splitting, Cardinal Beran rose to the defence of the text as it stood.

Beran was one of the authentic martyrs of political dissent, having suffered for decades under the yoke of dictatorship, from Dachau under Hitler to 'detention' under the communist regime in Prague. Shortly before the present session, this Czech primate had been released and sent to Rome—minus his passport. Yet there was no hint of bitterness in him.

I speak from experience. . . . When freedom of conscience was subject to limitations in my homeland, I witnessed what grave temptations many Catholics were exposed to. Even among the priests I could observe not only the great risk for their faith, but also the incitement to mendacity, hypocrisy, and similar vices that abound among people deprived of true freedom of conscience. . . . Everywhere and at all times, attacks on the freedom of conscience will engender hypocrisy in the ordinary man. Indeed, there is no doubt that hypocrisy for the sake of faith represents a greater risk to the Church than the hypocrisy resorted to in order to keep faith concealed. . . . Thus in my homeland of Bohemia today the Church seems to be atoning for the faults and sins which have been committed in the name of the Church in former times against liberty, as was the case in the fifteenth century when John Huss was burnt at the stake and in the seventeenth century when the Catholic faith was forcibly reintroduced among large sections of the population in accordance with the slogan of the time, *cujus regio ejus religio* [the religion of the ruler shall be the religion of the people].

The Church's recourse at that time to the civil authorities, who thought themselves—or claimed to be—well-disposed towards the Catholic Church, has in fact left deep scars in the popular soul. This trauma has been an obstacle to genuine religious progress, and has put—as it still puts—trump cards in the hands of the enemies of the Church. History clearly shows us that it is this Council's duty to proclaim—without dissimulation and without restrictions inspired by opportunistic motives—the principle of freedom of religion and of conscience. . . . I beg you earnestly, reverend fathers: do not water down this text in any way! Rather add the following sentence or some similar wording: 'The Catholic Church demands that all governments in the world grant their citizens—not excepting those who believe in God—freedom to follow their own conscience. Furthermore the Church demands that governments cease to deprive people of freedom, and that they forthwith release all clergy and laypeople who have been sentenced for religious activities.'

By chance my turn came later the same day as Cardinal Beran. I too based my arguments partly on the situation at home, but in reverse. (I have included my paper here as an appendix.)

'You have brought a new tone into the Council', De Smedt said to me afterwards with a smile.

Speech after speech continued to oppose the *schema*. But our consolation lay in knowing that the negative-minded minority normally made up the larger proportion of the speakers. Regardless of the opposition, it was noticeable how significantly the Council had matured. Despite the fact that we were under greater pressure than ever, it was obvious that, spiritually speaking, the assembly had at last found its true form and altogether functioned much more professionally.

A week after the opening we had made so much progress that the following question was addressed to us by the secretary general: 'Do the fathers approve this *schema* as the basic text of the final declaration that is to be perfected in acccordance with the Catholic doctrine on the true religion, and with those improvements proposed by the fathers, which can be accepted in accordance with the Council's working rules?' Not everyone understood such intricate formulations, and some may thus have protested by voting against. At all events 90 per cent voted in favour, with only 224 against.

More than pleased, Bishop De Smedt thanked all the speakers and promised that the *schema,* thanks to this help (and hopefully with subsequent support from the assembly), would be returned for the final voting in a 're-re-re-improved' version.

Intensely aware of the fact that this was our final and crucial session, everyone aspired to reaching a conclusion that would amount to a genuine, vital step forward for the Church. We knew, or at any rate thought we had reason to believe, that the pope identified himself more and more closely with the doings of the Council. The reason for his original reticence had presumably been that the First Vatican Council (1870) strictly followed the medieval rules under which the pope never participated in the working meetings, being represented instead by a presidency. The same practice was also adopted by the present Council. An empty throne-chair on a raised dais behind the presidential table was intended to symbolize the pontiff's presence. During the Council's third session (1964), however, this chair was moved down to the centre of the table, and Paul VI would now and then be present. During the fourth period this was even more frequently the case. Everyone realized that, taking over as pope only after the

Council had begun, he could not be expected to have an immediate grasp of such a vast and intricate apparatus. The Council matured—with him.

The knowledge that no time limit had been set kept us bowed to the task. This was essential, moreover, for the Council's most demanding document was next on the list. 'The Church in the Modern World' (*schema XIII*) was, into the bargain, a subject never addressed by any previous Council. It had now become one of the four great constitutions. While *De ecclesia* dealt with the Church's internal structure and evangelical mission (largely in the eternal dimension), *schema XIII* examined the relation of the Church to the realities of the contemporary human condition. The constitution aims to be the Church's charter for global dialogue. She does not (any longer) wish to instruct the world, but makes a low-key statement: 'Just as it is in the world's interest to acknowledge the Church as an historical reality and to recognize her good influence, so the Church herself knows how richly she has profited by the history and development of humanity. . . . The Church herself admits that she has greatly profited and still profits from the antagonism of those who oppose or who persecute her.' The Church likewise admits and acknowledges her former guilt: 'We cannot but deplore certain habits of mind which are sometimes found too among Christians, which do not sufficiently attend to the rightful independence of science and which, from the arguments and controversies they spark, lead many minds to conclude that faith and science are mutually opposed'.[2]

We had gone into the original draft in such detail the previous year that a totally new text was now put forward, redrafted by a new author. The first had been German (Häring), the new one was French (Haubtmann). We were, however, given only the first—the theoretical—part. The second part, on the practical aspects, was to come later (in other words, it was not yet ready).

Pope John XXIII's earnest wish had been that the broadest possible base be formulated for the dialogue between the Catholic Church and contemporary society, including non-believers. But first the Church would need to acquire in-depth knowledge and insight about modern society, in order to have a more coherent view of the very world she should herself communicate with and serve. The *schema* lays great weight on the extraordinary difference between the world of yesterday and that of today. Advances in science and technology have transformed the static society into one that is ever more dynamic. The tempo of de-Christianization has been accelerating over the centuries. Christianity is no longer the sociological phenomenon and all-pervading reality that it was in medieval times.

The world is being restructured increasingly in accordance with laws outside the jurisdiction of the Church. Even domains where she had a type of compassionate monopoly—hospitals, education, social work, and similar fields—are gradually being taken over by public authorities. The Council theologian Dominican P. Chenu focused on the problem more or less in these terms: 'It is essential to make it clear that the great historical events and important social developments are part of the realization of the Kingdom of God; what counts is interpreting the signs of the times *theologically*.' This led to a debate lasting for two whole weeks. As in the previous year, the critical voices were many and at times overpowering. Some held that between the lines the text (and implying, no doubt, Chenu himself) almost equated scientific or technological progress with the realization of God's plan of salvation and must be rejected.

Some found it difficult to accept the phraseology, maintaining that even if the Church, laudably enough, is ready to speak to the world in a new way—radically different from the authoritarian tone of earlier Councils, which was often partial or prejudiced—the Church must not, in any conciliar text, place herself on a purely secular level as here. Others thought the *schema*'s choice of words and expressions was far from adequate, often inappropriately juxtaposing theological and everyday usage, or again that too much space was allotted to arguments belonging to the fields of philosophy or phenomenology.

Bishop Amici (Modena), who spoke on behalf of his province's episcopacy, would have preferred arguments justified on solid Bible-based views instead of on the philosophical or scientific grounds now much in evidence in the text. Only in that way, he said, can the Church take part in a dialogue on her own terms. A scripture-based analysis of the human condition and problems would serve to reveal the relevant evangelical principles, without pointless comments. And only then would it make sense to supplement the text with analyses of experience and rational arguments. The bishop advocated a return to a spiritual perspective and a religious language rooted in a simple revival of the gospel message.

The Maronite Patriarch Meouchi (Lebanon) sorely missed the theology of the Resurrection, a theme so vital to the oriental mentality. It would have provided a cosmic and universal vision of the history of God's people and of mankind as a whole. Nor, he thought, had the Holy Spirit been given the proper place in this text, a text which was moreover sadly lacking in references to both Holy Scripture and the Fathers of the Church. In addition, he concluded, what was entirely missing was the predeliction of the orientals for the other-worldly and for withdrawal from the world, thus obscuring the eschatological perspective.

It was felt by many that it would be rash to try to improvise a substantial body of doctrines in record time on subjects neglected by the Church for centuries. There was nothing for it but to acknowledge that an unbridgeable gap existed between, on the one hand, the assembly's praiseworthy desire to arrive at new formulations and, on the other, the long process of maturation this would inevitably entail. But such scepticism did not prevent the moderators from continuing the debate, and by late September we had come so far that the newly distributed practical part of the *schema* could be taken up.

I limit myself to just a few reference samples from this wide-ranging debate, which tackled everything from women's liberation to the role of sport, from agricultural problems to economic policy, from psychoanalysis to family planning, from politics to the rebuilding of the international community, from sexual education to conscientious objectors.

A subject of special interest was the field of *culture*. Michele Pellegrino, newly installed as archbishop of Turin, was on home ground here. Briefly put, his point of view was as follows: Historical research must focus more on the individual as such, on his nature, habits, hopes, aspirations—and weaknesses; on everything in fact inherent in human beings, no matter how alike or unalike. This historical-humanistic dimension is of particular relevance to the sphere of religion and must therefore be accorded a privileged position in the study of theology, with regard to both methodology and content. Theology as such is duty-bound to take into account, for example, advances made in biblical research, patristics, archaeology, and in fact everything coming to light in the realm of church history. Those involved in this type of research must be guaranteed total and absolute freedom, for without freedom the obnoxious evils of mendacity and hypocrisy are virtually unavoidable.

As may be seen, this paper too concerned itself with the question of liberty. 'Only in freedom can man direct himself towards goodness. . . . Hence, man's dignity demands that he act according to a knowing and free choice that is personally motivated and prompted from within, not under blind internal impulse nor by mere external pressure.'[3]

Archbishop Wojtyla of Krakow—later John Paul II—aptly made a welcome point here: 'It is as impossible to compel a man to believe as to compel him not to believe.'

An outright condemnation of communism expressed in incendiary terms in the original *schema* had to be deleted because of many objections, or rather it was toned down and instead became an addendum to the Church's view on militant atheism: 'In her loyal devotion to both God and man, the Church has already repudiated and cannot cease repudiating . . . those poisonous doctrines and actions which contradict reason and the common experience of humanity and dethrone a man from his native excellence.' A discreet footnote refers to the condemnation of atheistic communism by former popes.[4]

In particular the concept of *the just war* was hotly debated due to the atom bomb's enormous potential in regard to the murder of civilians. Christopher Butler, the English Benedictine bishop, believed that even the *intention* of using nuclear arms 'as a defence against nuclear attack' was profoundly immoral, adding: 'The end does not justify the means!' Other speakers were more inclined to the view that it must be permissible to react to a nuclear attack by employing corresponding means. In this spirit Cardinal Spellman (New York) collected the signatures of a number of Council fathers on a statement urging that the stockpiling of 'scientific weapons' (the euphemism for nuclear weapons) had in itself safeguarded the liberty of a considerable number of the world's nations. Cardinal Liénart (Lille) contended that a distinction between a just and an unjust war was a thing of the past, while Cardinal Léger (Montreal) found it practically unthinkable to see modern war as a permissible means of restoring a nation's abrogated rights. Several voices agreed with his criticism of short-sighted and anachronistic unilateral policies of national independence. We heard reiterated arguments in favour of supporting 'the international authority' (the United Nations). As might be expected, attention was very much focused on the question of conscientious objection to military service. On this subject the text before us had the following comments: 'No one has the right either to issue or to obey orders which undeniably contradict the law of God; but if one does not know with certainty that such orders do so, one must assume that the responsible authority here is in the right.' This pronouncement was met with much disapproval (among others from Bishop John Taylor of Stockholm), for had not the Nazis in the postwar period justified their atrocities on these very grounds? Once again Cardinal Spellman took up the cudgel in the name of tradition: 'Personal conscience has nothing to do with the mandatory duty of military service. This is something to be decided by the State.'

On 5th October, when the debate has reached boiling point, Paul VI returns from his visit to the United Nations' General

Assembly. His entry into Saint Peter's is staged with a truly Italian sense of drama. Towards the close of the morning meeting we are—appropriately enough—in the middle of a debate on peace. The final speeches are cut short and suddenly the whole interior of the church is lit by a multitude of lamps. A gasp runs through the assembly.

For once I have a ringside seat (being one of the younger guard placed low down in the nave). A few dull thuds are heard against the central one of the three colossal bronze doors which now opens slowly for the pope. He has arrived straight from the airport and enters ahead of a group of attendant, panting cardinals, who are tired after the thirty-six-hour journey and have trouble keeping up with him. The pope strides briskly up the main aisle to a storm of standing applause from over 2,000 Council fathers. Even the 101 observers rise to clap. After a short address of greeting on behalf of the presidency by Cardinal Liénart, the pontiff bids the assembly be seated, but himself remains standing—itself a unique occurrence.

Pope Paul recounts that in his speech to the General Assembly he has laid before the nations 'the message of peace and salvation' as the Council had entrusted him to do. He then briefly touches on the Church's duty to serve the cause of peace, and thus the cause of justice, throughout the world, above all among those living under the most difficult circumstances. He concludes by emphasizing that our faith must be devoted to serving the spirit of compassion, both in our ecumenical endeavours and in all cooperation with men of goodwill, irrespective of religion and race.

Seldom, if ever, can Paul VI's star have stood higher.

Next day we received the decree 'On the Pastoral Office of Bishops in the Church' for the final ballot. We were keyed up about its fate, for in several respects it had been vigorously contested. The result was therefore all the more remarkable: 2,167 votes in favour and 14 against. The process of maturing with time—which I have already mentioned—had developed most convincingly.

The discussion concerning 'On the Church in the Modern World' continued unabated. The many speeches and not least the huge number of proposed amendments—actually several boxloads—led to a round-the-clock marathon for the responsible commission.

The two short *schemata* which had been expanded to proper decrees—'On the Mission Activity of the Church' and 'On the Ministry and Life of Priests'—were the last to come up for debate.

The 'Mission *schema*' had gained appreciably in theological weight. Cardinal Agagianian was the driving force here. He was head of both the congregation (Propaganda Fide) with all the missions under its jurisdiction (at the time still including the Nordic countries) and of the relevant text commission; added to which he was just then the Council's moderator. This latter responsibility possibly helped to put a polite brake on the arguments, since one sensitive area was the fate of precisely Agagianian's own congregation. During the previous year's debate there had been blunt demands for its reform. Cardinal Léger (Montreal) had held that it was absolutely necessary for a nucleus of responsible leaders from all the mission countries in the world to have a place in this forum. Now this wish was to be fulfilled—or so it seemed. The text stated promisingly: 'The Congregation shall in future be constituted by all those cooperating in the missionary activities: bishops from the whole world, as well as responsible leaders representing the religious orders and the specialized papal instances. The advisory body composed in this way will exercise the highest missionary authority under the authority of the pope.' Disappointment was therefore rife when we learned that exactly this text had been radically toned down in an addendum. Now it merely stated that 'bishops and members of orders—selected for the task—will cooperate in connection with missionary activities when the Congregation invites them to participate in the exercise of the highest authority which by right is its concern'.

Strong reactions followed, not least from the mission bishops. Several attempts at solutions were put forward, only to be almost immediately withdrawn, until Bishop Martin of Burundi met with acceptance for his carefully phrased proposal: 'Bishops and members of orders from the whole world will be present in the congregation, not only as advisers but as members as stipulated in the text *On the Pastoral Office of Bishops in the Church.*'

Paragraph 10 in Martin's text specifies: 'Since these [papal] congregations are set up for the benefit of the whole Church, it is furthermore desired that their members, both constituted and advisory, . . . to a greater degree be taken from different areas in the Church, so that the central instances or organs of the Catholic Church demonstrate true universality. It is also desirable that some bishops, who in their capacity as diocesan ordinaries can inform the pope more fully about the views, wishes and needs of all [local] churches, be chosen as members of the congregation.'

When the *schema* was voted on in early November, it was a considerably improved and expanded text that went down well until the voting arrived at the vexed question of the mission bishops' voice in the Propaganda Congregation. Then some 712 *modi* (additional proposals formulated by the Council fathers) necessitated its return for re-re-emendation. When it finally came back for the vote on 2nd December, the new text carried the day against only 18 votes.

Chapter 5, no. 29 now had this to say about the Congregation of the Propagation of the Faith:

> In the direction of this office, an active rôle with a deliberative vote should be had by selected representatives of all those who cooperate in missionary work: that is, the bishops of the whole world (the episcopal conferences should be heard from in this regard), as well as the moderators of the pontifical institutes and works, in ways and under conditions to be fixed by the Roman Pontiff. All these, being called together at stated times, will excercise supreme control of all missionary work under the authority of the supreme Pontiff.

The Council's final debate was on the *schema* concerning the priests. It turned out to be rather less intense and dramatic than expected. We knew that several of the fathers were looking forward to a serious discussion on the question of celibacy. Some wished to see a genuine relaxation of this rule; thus it was a burning issue.

For a long time now, the shortage of priests had made itself felt. It was especially acute in Latin America. Some people thought that celibacy, which had been obligatory in the western part of the Church since the Middle Ages, must bear a large share of the blame for the steady decline in the numbers of candidates for the secular priesthood (since it still went without saying that religious had to live in sexual abstinence).

Many of the fathers dreaded an open discussion on such a delicate subject. (Only the journalists seemed to relish the thought of what was ahead.) Furthermore, a longish debate just now would give rise to a real problem time-wise. We were already conscious of the onset of fatigue, and the good members of the relevant commission had worked themselves to the bone to have the text ready in time.

Some cardinals were said to have drawn the pope's attention to the dilemma. Thus, two days before the *schema* was due to be discussed, the secretary general read out the following announcement on behalf of Paul VI:

> A number of Council fathers are thinking of taking up for debate in the aula the complex problems related to the rule of celibacy applicable to priests in the Latin part of the Church. Without wishing to restrict the fathers' freedom to express their honest opinions, We consider it unfitting to discuss a subject of this nature in public. Our own intention at all events is to retain in unaltered form the obligatory rule of celibacy, even to the extent of reinforcing its observance by reminding the priests in the Latin Church of the reasoning behind this law which is so well suited to today's world and which enables the priests to dedicate all their love to Christ and to the care of souls.

If, however, any father wishes to take up this subject, he stands free to deliver a written paper to the Council presidency which will in turn place it before Us for further perusal.

The reading of the pope's message was greeted with massive applause indicating not only the widespread uneasiness and anxiety attaching to this whole question but also the relief felt by the greater majority that public debate on the subject would now be avoided.

Even so, some bishops allowed their prepared drafts to circulate in secret. The one with perhaps the most serious fundament came from the Belgian Bishop Koop of Lins (Brazil), which amazingly enough could be read in the French newspaper *Le Monde* only the day after the above information had been given to us! Among other things the bishop wrote:

> I suggest the following paragraph be added to the *schema:* 'Since the number of priests in wide areas of the Church is totally insufficient and moreover shows a clear tendency to being proportionately reduced on account of the increase in population, the Council decrees that, in the best interest of the great number of souls and in accordance with the divine injunction, it shall rest with the local hierarchy as a whole—with the pope's approval— to determine how far and where, in the best interest of these souls, it shall be possible to ordain priests mature men who have lived in matrimony for at least five years, according to the norms laid down by the apostle Paul in his epistles to Titus and Timothy.'

Otherwise the actual drafting of 'On the Ministry and Life of Priests' ran smoothly without any drama. The commission had done a splendid job, thanks to the excellent leadership of the archbishop of Reims (Marty), aided by some of the Church's most outstanding theologians (among them Yves Congar).

The final speaker was the aforementioned archbishop of Turin, Pellegrino, an acknowledged specialist on the earliest Christian literature. On behalf of 158 fathers from the five continents, he began by strongly criticizing the regrettably low intellectual level of education too often found among priests. (Perhaps with Italy particularly in mind?) After that he took up the matter of the expected development of what might be called post-conciliar factions:

> We can easily forecast two dangers here: Some people will be tempted to weaken the form and content of all Council norms designed to alter our traditional customs, while on the opposing wing we shall find all those who, convinced that whatever is old is out-of-date, will warmly welcome anything new simply because it is novel. To counteract the risk of these two extremes, the priests must not content themselves merely with being meek and loyal . . . nor merely with being inwardly inspired by their faith; they must equally strive to acquire a real grasp both of the true nature of the problems at hand and of the realities of the historical framework within which the problems must be set and solved.[5]

On the same day Cardinal Lercaro (Bologna) wrote that the 'sincere and authoritative voice' of Archbishop Pellegrino had here brought to a dignified close the endless round of speeches begun four years earlier.

When the text on the priests came to its first vote, the result was unexpectedly positive: 2,243 for and 11 against (3 invalid). On 7th December, it did even better: 2,390 for, 4 against (5 invalid).

The concluding phase of the Council was a period of hard work for everybody in the commissions still busy on the revision of texts, for example our Secretariat, which held meetings at high pressure in order to have 'On Religious Freedom' finished in time.

Other fathers were left with almost nothing to do. It was scarcely a surprise when a whole week's break was announced in the middle of October. For many it was a chance to 'visit' their respective dioceses, although the majority (particularly the mission bishops for whom this would have entailed long and expensive journeys) chose to unwind locally. At all events, a holiday feeling filled the air, as well as an undoubted sense of relief as we approached harbour.

What did the programme for after the vacation week have in store?

Ballots and promulgations.

No decision is valid before it has been promulgated by the pope, even if it has been signed by all the Council fathers.

Voting is carried out in writing. A two-thirds majority is required for acceptance. In the first instance the texts are voted on in portions dealing with the same subject, paragraph by paragraph. Additions and/or substantial alterations made since the last ballot are voted on separately. Moreover, the *modi,* which, on the *recommendation of the relevant commission,* have been worked into the new proposed text in italics, will be voted on one by one. (The name of the proposer is always given—now and again it is the pope himself.)

There was special excitement about the voting (25th and 26th October) on Bishop De Smedt's 're-re-revised' *schema* 'On Religious Freedom'.

As we have seen, the text had been subjected to an unusual barrage of sometimes angry criticism, if not sabotage. Fortunately we were reassuringly informed that the pope was firmly behind it. Our new text was divided into eleven portions, all of which now received positive voting results. But on this occasion too a great mass of *modi* came in—about 1,600. I limit myself to reporting the voting on the complete text: 1,954 fathers were in favour, 249 were against—with 13 invalid votes, unusually many. In the Secretariat we were only moderately satisfied, nevertheless relieved, because now the text was saved, even if it might have to be put to yet another vote on any approved *modi* that materialized.

On 28th October—the seventh anniversary of John XXIII's election as pope—there was a promulgating round for five texts: 'On the Pastoral Office of Bishops in the Church', 'On the Adaptation and Renewal of Religious Life', 'On Priestly Training', 'On Christian Education', and 'On the Relation of the Church to Non-Christian Religions'. Paul VI, who appreciated such symbolic actions, concelebrated Mass with twenty-four bishops from countries that were either at war or under the yoke of dictatorship.

The written round of voting took time. But it was only in connection with 'On the Relation of the Church to Non-Christian Religions' that there was excitement in the air, for on this subject there was still massive opposition from a certain sector of the assembly and from certain countries. Again the result was reassuring: only 88 voted opposed.

The next day too was important. The *schema* 'On Divine Revelation' (formerly entitled 'On the Sources of Revelation') had reached the point of its final ballot after a long and difficult passage through the debating stage. One after another, the seven paragraphs were approved, even with a solid majority, and the final count showed only 27 votes of *non placet* (thumbs down), while at the first ballot in 1962 the *schema* had been rejected by 1,368 fathers.

Later on, in November, we received the long-awaited message: The Council's last working day is scheduled for 7th December and the ceremonial conclusion for the day after (the feast of the Immaculate Conception). So we could all be home in good time for Christmas.

The *schemata* to be voted on followed in quick succession. 'On the Apostolate of the Laity' was the text that came best out of the voting apparatus, with only two negative votes. For once there were no invalid votes—possibly a sign of fatigue? But no. This is the point at which 'On the Mission Activity of the Church' received its 712 setbacks in the form of *modi*. Clearly there were more missionaries than lay people in the assembly.

With reason, the real excitement concerned 'On the Church in the Modern World', of which the much-revised version was to come up for voting in the middle of November. The improved text ran to over 150 pages. When I received my copy in the aula it was quite warm—as if straight from a baker's oven. Our admiration for the staff of the Vatican press grew all the time. Their willingness to labour on night shifts was a lay apostolate in itself.

Fortunately there were to be no more speeches. From now on only the figures would count. Personally I see the aula fathers' will and ability to finalize the complicated and highly untraditional *'schema XIII'* as perhaps the Council's most miraculous achievement. For the opposition to it was still rampant. The ultra-conservative Cardinal Siri (Genoa; chairman of the Italian Episcopal Conference) had written to the pope opposing both this *schema* and 'On Religious Freedom'. He expressed his 'gravest anxiety' concerning the positive attitude of these documents to freedom of conscience and the correlated negative attitude towards the rights of the civil authorities in the domain of religion.

At almost the same time the pope sent in four personal *modi* to the chapter on birth control. He stressed the clear-cut doctrines of his predecessors (Pius XI and Pius XII) on the subject. In the present text Paul VI thought it possible to detect a relaxation of the Church's permanent moral doctrine on matrimony, and he wished to avoid any backsliding. When the commission (which was partly composed of lay *auditores*—including a married couple) next convened, a debate of unwonted liveliness ensued. It ended with acceptance, though only in part, of the pope's proposed amendments— which they slightly recouched in a less rigid style 'to make them easier to incorporate in the whole'.

The whole, yes. *Schema XIII* was now so wide-ranging that once again no global vote could be taken. It was deemed sufficiently reassuring that all thirty-three sub-votings had won through successfully. When the *schema* came back for the last and decisive time (4th–6th December) as many as 56 of the several hundred new *modi* had been accepted and worked into the text, which could now only be approved or rejected. First the chapters were voted on separately. All passed, some more easily than others. For example, the chapter on world peace and the United Nations received a total of 483 votes against (happily not enough for it to be rejected). It was interesting therefore that the result of the formal voting on its promulgation in Saint Peter's square on 8th December was almost an apotheosis: 2,309 for, 75 against (7 invalid).

A thought which had struck me and never left me was that the Council texts ought to be translated into Norwegian—and the sooner the better. The constitution *On the Sacred Liturgy,* the first to be promulgated (1963), was published by our own Sankt Olav Forlag during the course of this 1965 session. (The translation was done by Father Thomas Patfoort, OP, our best—if not indeed only—liturgical specialist.) It was encouraging to find that the publication filled a need which led to its large re-issue. But would it be possible to deal with sixteen Council texts, some of considerable length? Had we the necessary expertise to do justice to such a demanding task?

Another idea provided the solution. How about Denmark? The country's new bishop, the Jesuit Hans L. Martensen, was immediately fired by the proposal to publish the Council's *opera omnia*, divided between our two closely related languages, with identical format and so on. In this way we could manage to produce the texts without delay.

The series was completed before the end of 1966, a year after the Council closed. The theologian Father Raulin, who had come with me to Rome, became a formidable ally in accomplishing the Norwegian part of this project, including the publication of the four main pillars, the constitutions *On the Church*, *On the Church in the Modern World*, *On Divine Revelation*, and *On the Sacred Liturgy*.

At the very tail end of the Council a great deal happened. On 4th December, for example, the secretary general read out a letter to the Council fathers from the observers. They expressed their deepfelt gratitude to us and said that in their eyes the Council's declared wish to initiate a dialogue had not been a mere empty or meaningless phrase, and that the representatives for the different non-Catholic religions had followed the fathers' endeavours—which they furthermore planned to comment on separately—with a feeling of genuine collegiality. They enthusiastically pointed out that the churches, despite their separation, had remained 'united in the name of Christ' and that 'the friendship already previously established' had been strengthened. Very true words, for had we not become used to associating with the observers as though they were part of our assembly?

And things continued along the same lines. Later that day the Council fathers and the observers were invited to an ecumenical service to be held on 6th December in the vast basilica of San Paolo fuori le Mura. It was here that Pope John XXIII had proclaimed to the world his intention of summoning an ecumenic council.

From the printed programme we learned that it was to be a *Sacra celebratio ad Christianam unitatem fovendam* (in other words, 'the celebration of a service for the promotion of Christian unity'). The ceremony took place at floor-level in the nave. Face to face with us Council fathers, the pope sat on a chair amid a wide circle of conciliar observers. A new constellation to be sure!

After sundry prayers and readings from Holy Scripture, Paul VI gave an address in a movingly simple manner, thanking the observers for the friendship that had now arisen. He underlined as the Council's 'ripened fruit' the recognition of the importance of this whole set of problems. He himself was convinced that he had been dealing throughout with 'Christian communities, people who are living, praying and active in the name of Christ . . . worthy in terms of both their doctrine and their convictions'. And he expressed his hope that, 'slowly, step by step, with loyalty and generosity', the differences of confession would eventually be resolved.

Suddenly a loud, indignant, American episcopal voice rang out behind me: 'But the pope can't do this!' Clearly, the ecumenical spirit had not yet entered into everybody's heart, even after four years in the aula. Indeed in the days that followed, the pope's initiative was the target of an unreasonable amount of criticism which was doubtless hurtful. The ecumenical form of service he adopted here, however, soon became the model for the entire Christian world.

That same afternoon, still 6th December, another welcome piece of news reached us: the reform of the Holy Office (Cardinal Ottaviani's 'sacred fortress'). From now on its name is to be the Congregation of the Faith, and it shall no longer be called—or be—the 'supreme congregation'. (This rank was later accorded to the Secretariat of State.) The reform of the Holy Office had been under way for at least two years and was the direct result of the Council. Cardinals Lefevbre and Mayer, and later Shehan (the latter two USA) had been appointed by the pope to be members of the working committee. The announcement came in the form of a papal *motu proprio, Integrae servandae.*

In his written announcement of this reform, Paul VI pointed out that the faith can be better preserved by an institution whose mandate is to promote the teaching of the faith. If the Congregation still intends to condemn or apply sanctions to written works dealing with questions of faith or morals, it shall no longer do so without first having obtained the views of the author. But first and foremost, the theologian's own bishop must be consulted.

An important task of the Congregation shall be to promote positive studies of 'new problems and points of view', in particular through organizing seminars and congresses. Advisers from every nation are henceforth to be attached to this institution, which hitherto has only availed itself of theologians resident in Rome. From now on the two functions of the former Holy Office, the administrative and the legal, are to be kept strictly apart. (The brunt of the general criticism had concerned the way in which administrative sanctions had been applied to unsuspecting people who had never been contacted, let alone sentenced.)

That evening we had a great deal to celebrate and talk about.

The next day, during the Council's last working session we witness yet another ecumenical sensation, this time too at the highest level. The pope is present in the aula, because several texts (the majority of which I have already mentioned) are to be promulgated. A magnificently robed oriental prelate, unknown to most of us, has been installed at a short distance from Paul VI. Archbishop Willebrands, the second-in-command of our Secretariat, goes up close to the altar to read—in French—a moving joint declaration in which the Roman Catholic Church and the Greek Orthodox Patriarchate of Constantinople together undertake to regret most deeply, and to wipe out completely from the memory and body of the Churches the excommunications they had inflicted on each other in 1054. Then Cardinal Bea mounts the podium and reads out the actual document of formalization by which the Church of Rome's excommunication of the Patriarch of Constantinople is declared null and void. The document, signed by the pope himself, is now handed over by him to the oriental dignitary who proves to be the patriarch's personal emissary, Metropolitan Meliton of Heliopolis, just arrived from Istanbul. (In fact there were two emissaries, but the other was detained by the Turkish police as they were about to board their aircraft.)

The story is not complete without recounting that Athenagoras in his patriarchal church Fanar in Istanbul at this same moment is delivering a corresponding document to the pope's *ad hoc* emissary Cardinal Shehan (Baltimore). It seems the Council has become almost demonstratively ecumenic.

That same morning, when we were about to take a break for lunch, we were requested to remain seated: Paul VI wished to give the bishops a personal souvenir to express his thanks for their cooperation. The gift, acknowledged by a signature from each of us, was a bishop's ring in gold. It was not inlaid with any gemstone as was usual for prelates' rings. Instead it was engraved with Christ bearing the crown of thorns, flanked by the apostles Peter and Paul. This was undoubtledly a signal from the Holy Father to the bishops to cut down on signs of outward show. Since then it has been easy to identify a fellow bishop from the Council. Indeed, without thinking about it, we had become something of an 'apostolic clan'.

Finally the day we have all been waiting for, the Council's last. It is December, and everything is to take place in the open. The weather is sunny and not cold. When I reach Saint Peter's Square it is already packed with people, a couple of hundred thousand, local Catholics, clergy and nuns, pilgrims who have come for this event, tourists, spectators, all eagerly expectant. The Council fathers, about 2,300 of us, are in full robes upstairs in the Vatican or else wander around in the waiting time to say our goodbyes—so many friends! We have gained a worldwide net of contacts, each right hand bearing the same ring.

In a long file, four abreast, we go down the long, impressive internal staircase and out of the great bronze door into the sunshine. A large but simply furnished altar has been erected in front of the basilica's façade. We take our places up there, at each side, facing the altar. Both papal and civil bands are playing. The singing of the Sistine Chapel choir comes over shrill, badly adjusted microphones. But the sound improves as time goes on and in the end the music matches the scene.

For the occasion the pontiff has taken the traditional place on his *sedes gestatoria*, a necessity when everyone is eager to see him. Even the once obligatory silver trumpets play the long-neglected 'Entrance of the Pope', tempting us to join in by humming the typically Italian folk-music melody. In the festive atmosphere the whole of Saint Peter's Square shouts '*Viva il Papa!*' Roman folklore.

The pope celebrates Mass, movingly simplified to match the spirit of the Council. The liturgical reform having captured their imagination, the elated crowd participates actively. After the Gospel reading, Paul VI speaks briefly in Italian: 'My greeting is for all of you . . . and goes beyond you out into the whole world. Indeed how can it be otherwise now that the Church has designated itself as *ecumenic*, that is to say universal? My greeting goes both to those who are willing to receive it, and to those who are not, and no less to those who oppose us, possibly on grounds of deep conviction. . . . In the eyes of the Catholic Church no one is a stranger, no one is excluded, no one is an outsider. Our greeting is sincere, peaceful, and modest, and it is no less full of hope and—believe me—full of respect and love.' Here he was interrupted by a tremendous burst of applause.

During the offertory we witness the reverse of the traditional offering of gifts by the congregation to the altar. Cardinal Tisserant announces that, on behalf of the Church, gifts of 90,000 dollars will go to each of the five chosen bishops—the money to be directed by them to charitable objectives around the world: for the completion of the hospital in Bethlehem, for the further development of 'The Little Brothers of Jesus' in Argentina, and for an educational project in South India, as well as for Caritas Pakistan and Caritas Cambodia.

A few symbolic acts are still to be carried out: The pope offers Holy Communion to six children from the five continents (America both North and South) and shortly afterwards he blesses the foundation stone for a Marian church to be erected outside Rome commemorating the title 'Mother of the Church' with which he has recently honoured her, with the backing of the Council fathers.

Right at the end, very much in the spirit of *schema XIII*, a series of 'messages to mankind' are read out. They concern various categories of people such as political leaders, women, workers, intellectuals, artists, the poor, the sick, and the young. The messages are read out in French by cardinals appointed for the task, while a representative for the relevant category is brought forward to the pope to be presented by him with a document carrying the matching message, for example:

To women: 'The time is approaching, indeed it is already here, when the vocation of women will be fully realized, with an influence, a charisma, and an authority in our societies such as they have never before enjoyed. Therefore it is at this moment of time when mankind is undergoing such profound changes that women, pervaded by the spirit of the Gospel, can do so much to arrest the downward course of humanity.'

To artists: 'The Church has long stood side by side with you artists. You have erected and ornamented our churches. You have helped to translate Holy Scripture by giving it its final form. Do not let such a unique and fruitful alliance founder.'

To intellectuals: 'Continue to seek the truth, undeterred, without ever losing hope! Happy are those who both know the truth and continue to seek it . . .'

As the last official act, Cardinal Felici reads out the decree announcing the conclusion of the Council. The age-old conciliar acclamations follow: 'This is the faith that Peter and the apostles professed; this is the faith of the fathers. This is what we believe, what we think. May the reign of Christ arrive!'

The pope's moving final words are: 'The hour of farewell has come. In a short while you will leave the Council and go out to meet people everywhere and share with them the good news of the gospel of Christ and of his Church's renewal, on which we have worked together for the four full years we have shared.'

After having given his blessing, the Holy Father cries out: *'In nomine Domini Nostri Iesu Christi, ite in pace!'* (In the name of Our Lord Jesus Christ, go in peace.)

Paul VI's final words are still with us as we leave the Eternal City.

And so, home! Home to our own *aggiornamento!*

EPILOGUE

WHEN I WAS CONFIRMED in the crypt of Saint Peter's as a young convert to Christianity, I wrote that I suddenly perceived my life, which had hitherto seemed so meandering and haphazard, as the road God had intended for me—everything having harmoniously fallen into place.

Something very similar was the case regarding the two decennia following my episcopal ordination. When I took over the diocese in 1964, I was somehow persuaded that this too was what the good Lord had steered me into, though admittedly much against my inclination.

The apparently casual remark made at Caldey by Father Shanahan, my quondam novice master, to the effect that God sometimes seemed to send people to the monastic life in order to inculcate in them the discipline they would need for the task in store for them, now appeared to be much to the point. The mental and moral stamina that had been wanting in my early life had been instilled into me by the thirteen years of Cistercian formation. But also the Roman administrative years had providentially re-accustomed me to functioning in a wider context, easing the transit to the necessary demeanour and the multifarious duties of a diocesan Ordinary. Not least I considered the eighteen-month period spent in Oslo prior to my entering Caldey to have been providential, for this had given me the chance to get to know and appreciate most of the clergy and the leading lay people of the time. So now I really did come home, not only to my mother country, but also to my own church.

Nevertheless, the ways of God seemed as mysterious as ever, for I found it incomprehensible that He should have chosen for the post someone who lacked all professional qualifications. However, there it was.

According to the practice instigated by Vatican II, this overwhelming challenge was to have lasted until my seventy-fifth year, possibly longer—at any rate more than three decades. Yet, by the end of 1982, as my twentieth year in office approached, I felt myself overcome by a sense of tiredness sometimes bordering on exhaustion. Occasionally I gave way to the temptation to make things easier for my myself, for example by rehashing earlier sermons and talks.

On the positive side, it seemed clear that the principal concerns of the Council had now in general been accepted locally, and they were adopted without serious difficulty or countermoves; something for which I have remained grateful to this day.

Feeling increasingly convinced that a new broom in the shape of a younger man was called for, I set about engineering my retirement. Having requested and, against the odds, obtained an assistant bishop with the right of succession, the final step of handing over the reins proved less insuperable than forecast by my colleagues—even vehemently so by Bishop Suhr.

Did I want to return to the monastic life? I have sometimes been asked that question, and indeed asked it myself. The answer must be *not really*. The Cistercian formation needs a long time to penetrate, until it permeates your entire being and sinks in deeper as you go on. The preceding Roman years undoubtedly had a negative effect in this respect. But even more so, the ensuing twenty years in Oslo continued this process of 'de-formation'. An example of this could easily be the case of my friend Bishop Suhr who, after twenty-five years in office, did not feel up to returning to the cloistered life.

To be formed—then 'de-formed'—and again 're-formed' would be a taxing process of personal and spiritual structurization beyond the powers of an ageing prelate.

In my case, no new irresistible call to the cloister made itself felt. I continued for some years as the president of the Scandinavian Episcopal Conference and, subsequently, as its assistant secretary general.

Finally, I yielded to the urge to return to the south, settling on a remote spot on the coast of Corsica to recuperate and think things over in peace—and, perhaps, to learn something from the life I had so strangely been granted.

And here a standing invitation to publish my memoirs proved a welcome challenge. In what I have written here, I have tried to discern the underlying pattern of a destiny very different from the one I had envisaged.

But there it is and, God willing, may it there remain.

Appendix 1

THE COUNCIL DOCUMENTS

English title	Latin title	Initial words	Date of promulgation
Constitution on the Sacred Liturgy	*Constitutio de sacra liturgia*	*Sacrosanctum concilium*	4.XII.1963
Decree on the Media of Social Communication	*Decretum de instrumentis commu- nicationis socialis*	*Inter mirifica*	4.XII.1963
Dogmatic Constitution on the Church	*Constitutio dogmatica de ecclesia*	*Lumen Gentium*	21.XI.1964
Decree on the Catholic Churches of the Eastern Rite	*Decretum de ecclesiis orientalibus catholicis*	*Orientalium ecclesiarum*	21.XI.1964
Decree on Ecumenism	*Decretum de oecumenismo*	*Unitatis redintegratio*	21.XI.1964

continued

English title	Latin title	Initial words	Date of promulgation
Decree on the Pastoral Office of Bishops in the Church	*Decretum de pastorali episcoporum munere in ecclesia*	*Christus Dominus*	28.X.1965
Decree on the Adaptation and Renewal of Religious Life	*Decretum de accommodata renovatione vitae religiosae*	*Perfectae caritatis*	28.X.1965
Decree on Priestly Training	*Decretum de institutione sacerdotali*	*Optatam totius*	28.X.1965
Declaration on Christian Education	*Declaratio de educatione christiana*	*Gravissimum educationis*	28.X.1965
Declaration on the Relation of the Church to Non-Christian Religions	*Declaratio de ecclesiae habitudine ad religiones non-christianas*	*Nostra aetate*	28.X.1965
Dogmatic Constitution on Divine Revelation	*Constitutio dogmatica de divina revelatione*	*Dei verbum*	18.XI.1965
Decree on the Apostolate of the Laity	*Decretum de apostolatu laicorum*	*Apostolicam actuositatem*	18.XI.1965
Declaration on Religious Freedom	*Declaratio de libertate religiosa*	*Dignitatis humanae*	7.XII.1965

English title	Latin title	Initial words	Date of promulgation
Decree on the Mission Activity of the Church	*Decretum de activitate missionali ecclesiae*	*Ad gentes*	7.XII.1965
Decree on the Ministry and Life of Priests	*Decretum de presbyterorum ministerio et vita*	*Presbyterorum ordinis*	7.XII.1965
Pastoral Constitution on the Church in the Modern World	*Constitutio pastoralis de ecclesia in mundo huius temporis*	*Gaudium et spes*	7.XII.1965

Appendix 2

ADDRESS TO THE COUNCIL

R EVEREND FATHERS,

The draft for the Council's declaration on religious liberty is short, but of vital significance. Here we have, as it were, a testing ground for our own uprightness and that of the Catholic Church in its encounter with the family of mankind in our time.

The work which has already been put into the document, as well as the revisions of the text which have been carried out, show that the subject bristles with difficulties. The position of liberty in relation to religion is ambivalent and open to many interpretations.

In its present form, as put forward for voting, this declaration has my full and unreserved support.

Because its one and only object is to consider the right of the individual vis-à-vis society to act in his public and private life in accordance with his conscience, within the accepted limits, it is clear that there is no contradiction between the religious liberty discussed here and the basic principles of the Christian religion. This liberty, therefore, represents no threat to the Church's missionary aims, neither does it encourage dogmatic indifference, nor cast doubt on the duty of every individual to seek and serve the truth. It does not justify lies or errors by granting them the right to exist. After all, only the individual or society itself can possess rights. This right to liberty is accorded to all members of the human family in that they are called by God to turn freely to Him, if they so wish.

The declaration provides a useful corrective to the absolute formulas of the past, which were a response to the specific problems of their time. Today it seems clear that advances in people's thinking, together with the spirit of the New Testament, make such a corrective necessary. Yet some of the opponents of the declaration have proposed the omission of the entire paragraph referring to the acts of Christ and the apostles, as if wishing to avoid any comparison between their own theory and the example of Christ and the apostles.

I support the declaration in its present form, first and foremost because it exactly answers what we are often asked by people of goodwill, namely: Is the Catholic Church willing to safeguard and defend our right to freedom in questions of religion and matters of conscience?

Sad to state, we note that the view to the contrary still has its advocates. In their opinion the Catholic Church can rightfully

1) deny to other religious communities and people in good faith the right to liberty which it claims for itself, and

2) yet at the same time, join forces with these communities, when this course serves its purpose under certain circumstances.

This smacks of opportunism. The time has come to denounce such ambiguity, which has already caused much harm. Certainly only a minority accepts this line of thought, which is probably also abhorrent to most Catholics.

As a member of the Scandinavian episcopate it is my duty, reverend fathers, to make you aware that feelings would run high in our Northern countries if the Council should fail to tackle this question openly and straightforwardly. We live widely dispersed among a non-Catholic population. We are a very small flock. Nonetheless, we enjoy a great measure of freedom. Every day we experience how the authorities in our non-Catholic countries ensure our religious liberty, not because they agree with us on every point but out of respect for our human dignity. Shall not we do unto others as we desire they shall do unto us? (Matthew 7:12)

Our daily experience teaches us that all liberties are interdependent. In today's society it is of fundamental importance that we aim to further an authentic *freedom of lifestyle*. Anyone who attempts to gain the benefits of liberty for himself, without defending the claims of others to liberty, undermines the idea of social solidarity and weakens the links that join people together. The correct relationship of Catholics to this mode of living is decisive for the Church's own sense of freedom.

I therefore believe that the declaration ought to attach even more importance to this 'mode of living in freedom'. In many countries religious liberty is acknowledged by the constitution although not respected in practice. The equality of citizens before the law is abused on religious grounds, not blatantly but underhandedly on false premises.

For that reason I consider it desirable to amend the text of the declaration on page 10 (line 21) by adding the words *whether openly or covertly*, so that the passage would then read: *It must be ensured that the equality of citizens before the law . . . is never violated on religious grounds, whether openly or covertly.* [The proposed amendment was approved and added to the text (No. 6).]

The Catholic Church, which has often been exposed to such injustice, cannot rally an effective defence unless it genuinely becomes the champion of such a mode of living in freedom.

Experience shows that the deepfelt and open wish of many non-Catholics is to come to know us better. But their legitimate counter-demand is that we Catholics ourselves demonstrate a determination to abstain from coercion, and that we concede to others the right to seek the truth freely without any interference on the part of the civil authorities. In the absence of a give-and-take of this nature no real dialogue is possible.

There is no doubt that the large majority of the Council supports religious liberty, and that the text will therefore be adopted without reservations, in particular the second paragraph which summarizes the declaration in a few sentences intended for consumption by the modern world. However, this is not enough: In this assembly the declaration should not face opposition of a kind that might seem to signalize a lukewarm attitude in a matter of such far-reaching significance where the recognition of human values is concerned.

The principles should now be clear, and the necessary discussions have taken place. What is now required for the honour of both the Church and the Council is unanimous support for religious liberty as at present formulated. The Catholic Church is otherwise hardly likely to be regarded as a potential partner in a dialogue with other religions.

It is naturally open to us to propose amendments for the improvement of the declaration in order to enable the Secretariat for

Christian Unity to arrive at an even clearer formulation of the principles already set out. And the text can doubtless be still further improved upon. But let us not contest the right of the human individual and of the various churches to freedom in matters of religion. The time has come to face the ultimate consequence of the Church's doctrine that adherence to the faith is voluntary, *free* adherence.

Appendix 3

DEFINITIONS OF TERMS

Gk, Greek.
L, Latin.

aggiornamento: Bringing up to date, updating.

auditor (L, *audire,* to hear): Listener.

concelebration (L, *con,* with; *celebratio,* celebration): Mass celebrated by several priests together, speaking in unison the words of consecration that transform the bread and wine on the altar into the body and blood of Our Lord.

congregation (L, *grex,* flock): Several meanings; here, a 'department' in the papal curia.

curia (L): Historically, each of the thirty groups into which the Roman people were divided; here, the papal central administration.

delegate (L, *delegatus,* one who is delegated): An *apostolic delegate* is a titular archbishop, trained as a diplomat, who represents the Holy See vis-à-vis the local Catholic hierarchy and vice versa. Normally his area is one country, but it may consist of several, as is the case in Scandinavia because individually the local churches are small. If diplomatic relations are established between the country in question and the Holy See, the delegate is also *apostolic nuncio* in that country—a purely diplomatic function.

encyclical (Gk, *enkuklos,* circular): Formal letter from a pope to the bishops, and the Church at large. Its title is taken from the opening words.

eschatology (Gk, *eschatos,* final; *logos,* teaching): Teaching on the final, last things; life after death.

generalate: Administrative headquarters of a religious order. All the larger orders have such an institution, with varying designations.

Lauds (L, *laudare,* to praise): The liturgical prayer, the first office of the day, lasting about twenty minutes, intended to be at sunrise. Lauds and Vespers, the evening office, are the main pillars in the round-the-clock series of liturgical prayers, also called the canonical hours.

maronites (derived from Saint Maron monastery south of Antioch): Christians belonging to the Maronite Church which declared its loyalty to the papacy in the twelfth century. Based in Lebanon where, under its patriarch, it plays a significant role.

melchites (Syriac, *makka,* king): The Christians in Syria and Egypt who accepted the decrees issued by the Council of Chalcedon (451). After the great East-West schism in 1054, some went back to Rome in the eighteenth century.

metropolitan (Gk, *metropolis,* principal city): Head of an Eastern church province, ranking between patriarch and archbishop.

monsignor (Old French, 'my lord'): Honorary title given to princes or other persons of high rank. In church usage, a non-episcopal (honorary) prelate.

motu proprio (L, of one's own accord): a document written by the pope of his own accord, rather than in response to a particular occasion or the requests of others, such as his curia.

officium/ufficium (L, *officium,* service): A word with several meanings; here, office.

patristics (L, *pater,* father): History of Christian teaching at the time of the Fathers of the Church.

Propaganda congregation or *Propaganda Fide* (L, *propagare,* to spread, for instance information): Here, the pontifical missionary congregation (see *congregation*).

schema (L, *schema,* representation of concept): In the conciliar context, a draft for discussion which, if accepted as a basis for further revision, will result in a document ready for promulgation.

sedes gestatoria (L, *sedes,* chair; *gestare,* to carry): Chair on which the pope is borne in certain ceremonies so that he is clearly visible and can impart blessings all around.

soteriology (Gk, *soteria,* salvation; *logos,* teaching): Teaching on salvation through Jesus Christ.

synod (Gk, *synodos,* assembly): Here, leaders of the Church called together by the pope to give their view on a given set of problems.

tiara: Originally a cone-shaped turban worn as a symbol of power by the Assyrian and Persian kings. In church usage (now obsolete): a papal crown made of superimposed, narrowing rings of precious metals, set with gemstones.

uniate (Russian, *unyia,* union): The usual term for churches of Eastern (oriental) rite, the so-called uniate churches, which have retained or restored formal relations with the papacy. Can also mean a person belonging to such a church.

NOTES

CHAPTER THIRTEEN

1. As translated (1970) by Dom Bernard Basil Bolton OSB, monk of Ealing Abbey. In the present book various other translations into English are also quoted in short extracts from the Rule.

2. In antiquity, without our mechanical system of time based on the clock, the twenty-four-hour period was divided in two: the day, between dawn and dusk, and the night. The day was divided into twelve equal hours (much shorter in midwinter than at midsummer), while the night was divided into three watches of four 'hours' each. The canonical hours of the night were intended to sanctify each of these watches. Lauds was to be sung at sunrise and Vespers at sunset. (In certain regions, such as the North with its summer 'white nights', it was necessary to resort to artificial arrangements for the monks to get enough sleep.) Except for Compline, which was recited before bedtime, the other liturgical prayers were said, as designated (Prime, Terce, Sext, and None), at the first, third, sixth, and ninth hour of the day. The invention of the clock has modified the system. Benedict also laid down that the three night-watches should be taken as one; otherwise the monks would have to rise for prayers at least twice each night.

3. Saint Benedict of Nursia—'the first Benedictine monk' —in c. 530 drew up the Rule for Monks that provided an

315

operative code for Western monasticism for the next thousand-plus years.

4. At that time (1950s), a coarse cotton smock with a hood was worn for work. This was later replaced by hooded overalls, which were less likely to catch in any machines.

5. The two brothers Jerry (Jeremiah) and Richard Cummins had come from Ireland after the First World War. Jerry, who was the elder, never married. Richard arrived after discharge from the Forces. His marriage resulted in three girls and three boys, all of whom felt themselves firmly bound to Caldey.

CHAPTER FOURTEEN

1. There had been other rules, not only in Egypt and in the Near East, but also in the West, in particular those of Saint Augustine and the Irish Saint Columban. Benedict's guidelines and regulations, however, were clearer and more concrete in their challenges than earlier rules. In addition, they were fortunately so free of the former tendency to go to extremes that they could be practised almost everywhere and by ordinary people of perhaps less robust character than the heroic ascetics of former days. Here was a practicable set of rules which came to be adopted further and further afield. Behind Benedict's precepts one glimpses a man of magnanimity, wisdom, and moderation, who consciously eschews anything tainted by exaggeration or exhibitionism. From the sixth to the twelfth century practically no other form of monastic life was known in the West than that based on Benedict's Rule, like Basil the Great's in the case of the Eastern church.

2. In one of Egypt's desert monasteries, as early as c. 320, the father of monachism, Pachomius (282–346), had drawn up regulations for the first groups of solitaries to become communities of cenobites, that is, monks living in common, instead of as isolated hermits. He laid down the principle of obedience to the monastery's superior who was entitled

Abbas (from *abba*, the Aramaic for 'father'), though without equating this with obedience to Christ himself.

3. Cîteaux (Latin *Cistercium* from *cisterna*, water tank, cistern) acquired its name from the swampy terrain where the founders settled.

4. The reform from La Trappe, however, eventually came to split the Order into the Cistercians of the Common Observance and the Cistercians of the Strict Observance (or the Reformed Cistercians). The division was not formalized by the Holy See until 1892. A parallel development was the division in the Carmelites following the reforms initiated by Saint John of the Cross and Saint Teresa of Avila in the sixteenth century. Both splits resulted in two independent orders with the same standing and rights.

5. It was the duty of the prior to take the decision regarding profession, together with his council. Benedict, who leaves little to chance, states: 'Whenever anything of importance is to happen in the monastery, the Abbot [in our case the prior] shall call in and consult the entire community. For less weighty decisions, it is enough to ask the elders for advice.'

CHAPTER FIFTEEN

1. The liturgical prayer is the prayer of the *Church*, not of the individual. Its fundamental purpose is praise. The so-called Psalms of David (the Book of Psalms) in the Old Testament were taken by the early Church to become the mainstay of its sung liturgy. As soon as persecution of the Christians ceased, the Roman Church institutionalized the use of the psalms as the basis for the canonical hours. Saint Benedict adopted the practice and laid down that all 150 psalms should be recited or sung in the course of each week.

2. Later on the Rule fixes the seniority from the date of receiving the novice's habit.

3. At a signal from the superior all make the sign of the cross and recite or sing (from the 70th Psalm): 'O God, come

to my aid. O Lord, make haste to help me. Glory be to the Father, and to the Son and to the Holy Spirit; as it was in the beginning, is now and ever shall be; world without end. Amen'. Then one side starts with the first verse of a hymn written in the Middle Ages. The second verse is taken up by the opposite side, and so on alternately. The last verse is always a doxology. The hymn is sung standing, the doxology reverently bowed. Only now begins the real alternating prayer consisting of a selection from the 150 Psalms of David in accordance with a set plan laid down by Benedict. Each psalm concludes with the doxology 'Glory be. . . .'

After the antiphonal chants the week's liturgist recites a short reading—often from Saint Paul. One or two verses from a suitable psalm follow, and a prayer is said aloud while all again stand with bowed head. The superior brings the service to a close: 'May the help of the Almighty be with us always', and all respond: 'And with our absent brethren'.

The night office—Matins—is almost as long as the others taken together. (A curiosity worth mentioning is that, because it was the Church's intention that liturgical prayers should never be lacking at any moment of time, it was early on stipulated that the various monasteries and the communities of canons-regular were to begin their night office at different hours: the Carthusians at midnight, the Cistercians at two, the Benedictines at four, and so on.)

Matins is divided into three nocturns, the historical origin being the three watches into which the night was divided in antiquity. Each section contains three of the Psalms of David and three lessons from, respectively, the Bible and the Fathers of the Church. On the principal feastdays we chant all this, which prolongs the service by about one hour. This can mean four hours in continuous liturgical prayer, since Lauds (whatever the position of the sun) always follows immediately.

4. Father Thomas Litt later published a treatise of over four hundred pages on the subject in the series Philosophes Médiévaux (vol. 7): *Les corps célestes dans l'univers de saint Thomas d'Aquin* (Nauwelaerts: Louvain, 1963).

5. In a recent survey (1998) of European beers, Scourmont's was classified among the top five beers for quality and flavour.

6. Fifty letters from Father Daniélou to Gunnel Vallquist were published later in the *Bulletin des Amis du Cardinal Daniélou.*

7. The General Chapters, meetings of the superiors of all the monasteries, were traditionally opened in the mother abbey of Cîteaux every year on 14th September (the Exaltation of the Cross).

8. Father Boylan's works include *Difficulties in Mental Prayer* and *This Tremendous Lover,* among others. We heard that Princess Margaret (of England) was so entranced by his books that she contacted our monastery to find out how she might meet the author.

CHAPTER SIXTEEN

1. Adolf von Harnack (1851–1930) was a leading German Lutheran theologian with an enormous literary output. His main work, considered very radical for its time, *Das Wesen des Christentums,* provoked violent and prolonged controversy in many quarters.

2. Bishop Johannes Olav Smit was a Dutch priest who was appointed vicar apostolic for Norway in 1922. He had to retire in 1928 and had since then been a canon of Saint Peter's.

3. Over the centuries the subdiaconate had remained an unclarified stage of ordination to Holy Orders. Was it a sacrament or not? Vatican II finally decided the matter by declaring that only the diaconate was part of the sacrament of ordination. The subdiaconate was thus (in principle) abolished.

4. The bishop, John Petit, administered the diocese of Menevia which covered all southwest Wales, with its seat in Swansea.

5. Edwin Scott-Davies was actually a barrister, but had for long been a legal adviser to the British tax authority.

6. The *Index Librorum Prohibitorum* was an official list of

books Roman Catholics were forbidden to read without special permission, as contrary to Christian faith or morals (or which were to be read only in expurgated editions). First issued in 1557, it was revised at intervals and abolished in 1966.

CHAPTER SEVENTEEN

1. *The Seven-Storey Mountain* (New York: Harcourt, Brace and Co., 1948). In Great Britain, *Elected Silence* (London: Hollis and Carter, 1949).

2. 'DUKW' is not an acronym. The letters are specifications from the army equipment code: 'D' for 1942, 'U' for utility (amphibian), 'K' for front-wheel drive, and 'W' for its two rear-driving axles. DUKWs, incidentally, are still being maintained and used—as commercial tour vehicles in the US.

3. A congregation of English Dominican sisters had permission to spend summer holidays on Caldey. Their mother general, Mother Ansgar, had fallen for Norway and was working to found a daughter house in Bodø, not far from the Arctic Circle. To arouse interest in things Norwegian, as she said, she and the sisters organized an annual Norwegian Festival in the Westminster Cathedral Hall. My talk had been included in the programme that year (1958).

4. It was not unknown in diplomatic circles that the Holy See's choice of Roncalli for Paris had been regarded as an insult by the French government—which indeed perhaps it was, for relations between them were almost at zero level. However, during his time there, Roncalli succeeded in skilfully preventing the dismissal of a number of French bishops from their posts by the French authorities on the grounds of alleged collaboration with the power of occupation during World War II.

CHAPTER EIGHTEEN

1. In reality the events were somewhat more complex. Peter Hebblethwaite, in his admirable *John XXIII, Pope of the*

Council (London: Geoffrey Chapman, 1984), devotes an entire chapter to the genesis of the pope's decision to launch the Council.

Only two days after his election, the pope mentioned his idea of convening an ecumenical council to his secretary, Monsignor Loris Capovilla, and two days later, to Cardinal Ernesto Ruffini (archbishop of Palermo)—in both instances some three weeks prior to his famous retreat.

In the weeks following the retreat he spoke of his idea to some close friends: his successor as patriarch of Venice, G. Urbani; the bishop of Padua, G. Bortignon; Don Giovanni Rossi of the Pro Civitate Christiana institute in Assisi; and even to Italy's prime minister, Giulio Andreotti. The idea was always communicated as top secret, the pope being extremely wary lest it reach the ears of his own curia—and rightly so, as it turned out.

Only on 20th November 1958, after definitely having made up his mind, did he break the news to his ('all-powerful') secretary of state, Cardinal Domenico Tardini, still *'sub secreto'*. Finally, on 25th January 1959, he came out in the open to a gathering of seventeen curia cardinals during a kind of minor consistory held in the Benedictine monastery of Saint Paul outside the Walls (San Paolo fuori le Mura). Surprisingly, there was no apparent reaction. The cardinals seemed stunned at the idea.

2. In 'The Value of the Western Text of the Acts according to Recent Authors' I give an account of the research results concerning the Greek early parchment codex, *Codex Bezae* or *Cantabrigiensis,* in which particularly the Acts of the Apostles shows interesting variations.

CHAPTER NINETEEN

1. One example is typical. My predecessor had bought sugar in suitable small amounts for 175 lire per kilogram. Now we had one and a half tons delivered direct for 154.50 lire per kilogram, agreed to under mild protest from the producer.

CHAPTER TWENTY

1. Of course, there have been exceptions. About the turn of the century the archbishop of Reims, Cardinal Langenieux, badly needed an auxiliary, while the French state—which was anticlerical, indeed anti-church—proved deaf to such entreaties. Even the Holy See was powerless. The decision the government had taken was to the effect that not a single new prelate could be appointed. The archbishop, who had an astute legal mind, knew just how to handle this: an abbot, according to canon law, is a *prelate of the first class*. In his archdiocese the Cistercian abbey of Igny had survived, despite all opposition. The archbishop won the day by arguing that the abbot, Dom Augustin Marre, could be his auxiliary—he was *already* a prelate! In 1900 Marre was appointed auxiliary to the archbishop of Reims by the pope (although he held the position for only a few years, after which he was elected general of the Order and *ipso facto* abbot of Cîteaux).

About fifty years previous to that, two other episcopal nominations had honoured the Cistercians of the Strict Observance. The superior of New Melleray (USA), Dom Clement Smyth, was appointed bishop of Dubuque. What's more, his immediate successor as head of that monastery, Dom James O'Gorman, subsequently became the first vicar apostolic of Nebraska. (See Dr Dominicus Willi, 'Cistercienser Päpste, Kardinäle, und Bischöfe', in *Cistercienser Chronik,* 1911 and 1912.)

2. The conservatives wanted to keep the two sources—Holy Scripture and Tradition—distinctly separated (in accordance with the Council of Trent). The progressives wished to return to the earlier patristic doctrine which taught that faith has only one source: *Christ,* who has spoken to us partly in his own words through Scripture, and partly through the Church that he founded to carry on his teaching. The Bible and the tradition of the Church are, according to them, not two independent, separate sources but rather two streams running side by side from the same source, or—as some put it—as two

currents in the same river. The New Testament has its roots in the Church and has grown out of the life of the Church. It was, moreover, the tradition of the Church that decided which books should be regarded as Holy Scripture—the living word of God in the Church.

(About Cardinal Ottaviani see chapter 21, 'An Apprentice Again', note 5.)

3. Just as the Jesuit general is jokingly called the 'black pope', so the prefect of Propaganda Fide, always a cardinal, is referred to as the 'red pope', because in practice a large part of the world is under his ecclesiastical jurisdiction.

4. Hallvard Trætteberg was senior archivist at the National Archives and at the time Norway's only official expert in heraldry.

5. The Council, which went into the theology of ordination in depth, defined the relationship between the consecration of respectively deacons, priests, and bishops thus: the ordination is basically the same, but it consists of three stages, whereby only the bishops receive the sacrament of ordination in its plenary form. The priests are united with the bishops in the priestly dignity while they are dependent upon them in the exercise of their pastoral duties. The deacons are ordained to Holy Orders for serving in specific, more limited, roles in the Church.

CHAPTER TWENTY-ONE

1. Gunnel Vallquist, Swedish literary critic, author, and translator (of, among others, Proust), has been since 1982 one of the eighteen members of the Swedish Academy, which awards the Nobel Prize for literature. See also chapter 15, 'The Hold Tightens', at note 6.

2. Taizé was—and is—a monastic brotherhood founded in the south of France by two laymen belonging to the Presbyterian church, Roger Schutz and Max Thurian. The latter later became a Catholic and was ordained a priest. Their

main concern was ecumenism. In later times the community has exercised an increasingly magnetic attraction on Europe's young Christians who come to Taizé in the thousands.

3. Before the Council got started, the Central Committee had plans to cover about seventy subjects with as many texts for drafting. These were systematically cut down, reshuffled, and compressed under sixteen titles: On the Church, On Divine Revelation (originally On the Sources of Revelation), On the Sacred Liturgy, On the Church in the Modern World, On the Media of Social Communication, On Ecumenism, On the Catholic Churches of the Eastern Rite, On the Pastoral Office of Bishops in the Church, On the Adaptation and Renewal of Religious Life, On the Ministry and Life of Priests, On Priestly Training, On the Apostolate of the Laity, On the Mission Activity of the Church, On Christian Education, On the Relation of the Church to Non-Christian Religions, and On Religious Freedom. (See appendix 1 for more details on the titles of the Council documents as finally promulgated.)

4. The following are examples of pioneer spirits with constructive views: the Cardinals Alfrink (Utrecht), Döpfner (Munich and Freising), Frings (Cologne), Léger (Montreal), Liénart (Lille), and Suenens (Brussels and Malines), as well as—not least—Augustin Bea (Pontifical Secretariat for Christian Unity), and the Bishops Butler (England) and De Smedt (Bruges). Fortunately there were also a fair number from the other continents.

5. Cardinal Alfredo Ottaviani was vice prefect of the (until then) highest-ranking of all the pontifical congregations: The Holy Office, whose mandate was to ensure that the Catholic faith was upheld both in scope and purity. The prefect was traditionally the pope himself. Cardinal Ottaviani was a dominating personality who also headed the Council's Commission for Questions of Faith, which was responsible for the *schema* 'On the Sources of Revelation' (withdrawn by John XXIII for radical re-drafting) as also for the defeated draft 'On the

Church'. It became all too clear that it was beyond the powers of the ageing Ottaviani to differentiate between the two areas of responsibility, yet he considered it his duty to protect the traditional doctrine of the faith against the swelling majority of Council fathers in favour of updating in several areas not concerned with the essential truths of the faith.

6. Gunnel Vallquist, *Dagbok från Rom* (Skellefted, Sweden: Artos Bokförlag, 1999), part 2, pp. 209–10. This edition is a reprint in one volume of the four volumes published by Bonniers, Stockholm, 1963–1966.

7. In his *motu propio* titled *Finis concilio,* just after the end of the Council, Pope Paul VI laid down that the Secretariat for Promoting Christian Unity was to consist of the same members that belonged to it during the Council. Episcopal members of such bodies are traditionally appointed for four years if they do not mean to live in Rome and work full time; thus I remained a member of the Secretariat until 1970.

8. Apart from the fact that some of the Council's most forward-looking prelates were members here, a number of the Church's topmost theologians were appointed as experts and advisers; for example, Gregory Baum, Yves Congar, Jean Daniélou, Jérôme Hamer, Bernard Häring, Hans Küng, Bernard Lonergan, Henri de Lubac, Pierre Michalon, Charles Moeller, John Courtney Murray, G. Philips, Karl Rahner, O. Semmelroth, G. Tavard, M. Taverne, and J. M. Oesterreicher.

CHAPTER TWENTY-TWO

1. Mariaholm was able to open in 1968 (free of debt) and has been in use ever since, not only for the younger generation but also as a seminar centre for many different groups and organizations, both Catholic and non-Catholic.

2. New York was home for Gregory Baum, but he was originally a convert Jew from Berlin. He and I had become

friends during the Council, and he agreed to lead our week-long seminar, provided it could be held close up to the third session.

3. *On the Relation of the Church to Non-Christian Religions,* 4. Numbers in references to Council documents refer to numbered sections in the published texts.

4. A brief resumé of the debate might be given as follows:

Religious freedom must be clearly proclaimed; if not, it will be impossible for ecumenism to become a reality.

Also Protestantism has a rôle to play in South America where the Catholic Church alone is unable to prevent dechristianization.

If this text is not accepted, the world will not have confidence in anything else the Council may come to say or do.

To allow people's liberties and rights to rest on the assumption that they already possess the truth would be to deny their right to think independently and to ask questions, which in turn would mean denying them freedom of thought and expression.

People are not free *because* they possess the truth, but in order to be able to *seek* it.

There is no doubt objective truth exists. But no one can be *compelled* to receive this objective truth. Every individual must follow the dictates of his or her own conscience where faith is concerned. It must even be clearly stated that also unbelievers are entitled to their unbelief. [Murmuring.]

We must demand religious freedom in all countries. Naturally there is a certain risk involved in permitting the free expression of all possible and impossible doctrines, but freedom outweighs such considerations. Indeed, experience proves that state intervention in matters of religion is invariably detrimental.

Proselytism is an evil, because rather than endeavouring to unite people with Christ, it attempts to entice them into the proselytizer's own flock.

After this Council no doubt must remain as to the Church's honesty in its relations to non-Catholics in those countries where it is itself in the majority.

CHAPTER TWENTY-THREE

1. The majority of the participants of the Bishop's Synod are to be elected on a worldwide basis by and from among the actual members of the Episcopal Conferences (over one hundred participants will thus be elected, with one each from the smallest conferences, and up to four each from the largest). In addition, ten are to be designated by the Roman union of heads of religious orders. Members 'by birth' are the uniate patriarchs, together with those metropolitans and major bishops whose functions are permanently outside their respective patriarchates. Also any bishops, representatives of religious orders, or experts whom the pope adjudges appropriate to balance the whole, provided these do not exceed 15 per cent of the total. The curia cardinals shall be entitled to be present at the meetings. Altogether this ruling means that roughly 80 per cent of the participants during a main assembly will be freely elected.

It is the pontiff's prerogative to summon the Synod whenever its assistance is deemed opportune. He himself will appoint both the permanent secretary general and the *ad hoc* secretaries who will serve as the pontiff's representatives at meetings.

The Synod shall be permanent in character. Apart from the main assembly (every third year) the pope may summon an extraordinary Synod meeting consisting of the chairmen of all the Episcopal Conferences. The curia cardinals may likewise attend these meetings. A final category is the Special Synod on a geographical basis, such as a country or a continent. Several such were held under John Paul II.

2. *The Church in the Modern World,* 44 and 36.

3. *Ibid.,* 17.

4. *Ibid.,* 21.

5. See Gunnel Vallquist, *Dagbok från Rom* (Stockholm: Bonniers, 1963–1966), vol. 4, pp. 92–93. This work, originally published in four volumes, one following each session of the Council, was later printed in one volume by Artos Bokförlag, Skellefted, Sweden.